An Anthology of CONTEMPORARY BUSINESS TRENDS

A Research Compilation

Edited By

Dr. Tahir Ahmad Wani

Dr. Sumaira Jan

Dr. Nufazil Altaf Ahangar

Dr. Mohammad Rafiq Teli

Dr. Rahul Mirchandani

2022

PARTRIDGE

Copyright © 2022 by Dr. Tahir Ahmad Wani, Dr. Sumaira Jan, Dr. Nufazil Altaf Ahangar, Dr. Mohammad Rafiq Teli & Dr. Rahul Mirchandani.

ISBN: Softcover   978-1-5437-0875-2
       eBook   978-1-5437-0874-5

All rights reserved. No part of this book may be used or reproduced by any means, graphic, electronic, or mechanical, including photocopying, recording, taping or by any information storage retrieval system without the written permission of the author except in the case of brief quotations embodied in critical articles and reviews.

Because of the dynamic nature of the Internet, any web addresses or links contained in this book may have changed since publication and may no longer be valid. The views expressed in this work are solely those of the author and do not necessarily reflect the views of the publisher, and the publisher hereby disclaims any responsibility for them.

Print information available on the last page.

To order additional copies of this book, contact
Partridge India
000 800 919 0634 (Call Free)
+91 000 80091 90634 (Outside India)
orders.india@partridgepublishing.com

www.partridgepublishing.com/india

Foreword

The World of Work is rebooting. Businesses are re-imagining and re-engineering themselves. Challenging established norms and rebuilding livelihoods are essential imperatives. In the era of intelligence and changing global landscape, the approach of doing business has been transformed significantly, which has provided scope for different trends and paradigms in the field of business management. These changes are being experienced in cultural, social, political, and technological spheres as well. The COVID related pandemic has also elevated business practices and allied disciplines. This has revolutionized the working styles of business entities which opens the doors for researchers to think and ponder upon the contemporary business trends. The impact of the COVID-19 is being felt by all businesses across the globe. Leaders are navigating a broad range of interrelated issues that span from keeping their employees and customers safe, shoring-up cash and liquidity, reorienting operations and navigating complicated government support programs. The world of work is being profoundly affected by the pandemic. In addition to the threat to public health, the economic and social disruption threatens the long-term livelihoods and wellbeing of millions. The pandemic is heavily affecting labour markets, economies and enterprises, including global supply chains, leading to widespread business disruptions.

In light of this, the prime focus of this book is to identify multiple ways to manage these changes across the globe. The book aims to enable to reflect, deliberate, and suggest necessary and desired measures in the present challenging business scenario in fields of marketing, human resources management, financial management, technology management, sustainability etc.

The book will highlight on the different challenges which are presently being faced by the global and Indian business environment and suggest measures, trends for shaping and reshaping future business opportunities and possibilities. Moreover, it will bring an exploratory insight on the best business practices in the era of innovation and novelty.

I am sure that the book will be useful in terms of bridging the gap between existing literature and future research requirements with respect to contemporary business trends in the Post COVID scenario. This book shall provide an interdisciplinary platform for stakeholders to present and deliberate the most recent innovations, trends, and concerns as well as emerging challenges encountered and solutions adopted in their respective disciplines during the post COVID scenario.

Prof. Rakesh Sehgal
Director
National Institute of Technology Srinagar

Preface

The business environment in contemporary times operate at the intersection of AI and public policy, which has led to creation of new frontiers in relation to sustainable development. While the COVID pandemic brought new challenges for policy makers as well as for businesses, it also provided an opportunity for businesses to reintegrate their processes so as to widen the spectrum of economic wellbeing. That the global supply chain disruption has dominated the economic discourse and communities are feeling the heat of inflation did not stop the businesses from coming up with innovative changes in spheres ranging from leadership to financial literacy and blockchain to banking interventions. The sudden surge in work from home, which is now becoming the norm, is a universal phenomenon which goes on to show universal alignment of business processes. The economic policies and financial intervention programs undertaken by government bears the imprint that government is eagerly trying to reimagine the public private participation in order to create a balanced consumption-production cycle.

To the extent of how businesses have changed course and its metastasizing effect on society, this book "Contemporary Business Trends" serves a repertoire of these trends and documents the patterns which will be of immense help to policy makers as much as to academics and practitioners. This book is an attempt to re-imagine the ways of doing business and optimization of constraints on a path to sustainable development and prosperous future. This book is a result of an international conference which was a unique meeting of minds that brought various stakeholders like academics and practitioners on one platform and threadbare deliberated on issues which impact our economic well-being. The book has been thematically structured and organized for the readers in a manner that they will take joy in reading the scholarly papers on various issues, in whatever order they want to read it. That the book not only draws readers towards pressing issues of our times but also provide plausible frameworks to navigate them successfully. The 18 papers, written by erudite scholars and academics on themes *"Contemporary issues in Human Resources Management, Financial Management, Technology Management, Entrepreneurship and Sustainability and Challenges brought by Covid pandemic"* have been written in a lucid manner so that readers can get the most out of this book. Every paper has engaged in the critical analysis of the issues and almost all the contours of respective themes have been covered. Besides, this book is an invitation to intellectual engagement to re-imagine the pedagogy of the most significant economic concerns of contemporary times

Dr. Tahir Wani
Dept. of Humanities, Social Sciences and Management
NIT Srinagar

Introduction

In a world slowly coming to terms with post-Pandemic life and radically changed business environments, new megatrends have emerged in various sectors, creating unique imperatives in the world of work.

The 2nd edition of the Conference on Contemporary Business Trends (ICCBT) was hosted by NIT Srinagar, in partnership with Confederation of Indian Industry's Young Indians (CII-Yi) as a platform to present a blend of rigorously researched papers and live discussions with industry experts, focussed on emerging issues in the world of business.

Over 100 well researched papers spread across **nine tracks** were presented. The broad themes covered by the researchers included, but were not limited to, the following:

• *Changed Marketing Models • New products and services emerging during the Pandemic • Renewed efficiency in operations • Dealing with supply chain disruptions • Reverse urbanisation trends • Stress in Cash flow and working capital management • Digitisation and Information Technology • Occupational Health and Safety • Ethics and Economics • The Great Resignation and the churn of Human resources • Women at Work • Fostering Workplace Inclusivity • Building Corporate Culture in Remote Work environments • Agricultural Practices and Climate Change • New Habits and Consumer Behaviour trends • Reskilling to stay employable • The Metaverse and Privacy • Using Sport for Development and Peace • The Pace and Platforms of Human Interactions • New Media for targeted Information Delivery • The New Indian Food Plate and its implications*

In addition, text based dialogue using the abstracts of the papers and curated classic and contemporary literature were also used as anchors for moderated huddles where all participants shared their thoughts in discussion groups and breakout rooms on issues ranging from **Skills, Empathy, Agility & Resilience, Justice and Fairness, The Responsibility of Heroism, Leading in a Crisis, Re-energizing legacy businesses, Cryptocurrency & New global payment systems.**

Thus, a wide range of megatrends were researched and deliberated and a curated set of interesting papers have been put together in this anthology on contemporary business trends to preserve some of the key learnings for a wider audience.

Many thanks are due to the ICCBT 2022 organising team, CII and Young Indians' leadership from across India, Academic Partner Institutions, Researchers, Faculty and Scholars who provided stellar inputs during the conference and helped organise a world class event, hosted at the NIT Srinagar campus. Sincere appreciation to Dr Shama Zaidi, Aries Agro Limited, for her timely assistance and attention to detail while getting this book ready for publication.

We do hope that this Anthology will serve as a timely and informative reference guide to researchers and practitioners who are navigating through our fast changing world.

Dr Rahul Mirchandani
ICCBT 2022 Conference Chairman
& National Chairman (2009-10), CII Young Indians

Acknowledgements

This Research Compilation would have been impossible without the support, efforts and co-operation of the following Institutions and Individuals.

Organiser of the International Conference on Contemporary Business Trends 2022

About National Institute of Technology, Srinagar: www.nitsri.net

National Institute of Technology Srinagar is the only Technical Institute of National Importance in the UT of Jammu & Kashmir and is one of the premier technical institute of India. The Institute was one of the first eight Regional Engineering Colleges, established in 1960, by the Government of India. In 2003, the institute was converted to the National Institute of Technology by the Ministry of Human Resource Development, Government of India, as an institute of National Importance. NIT Srinagar has been imparting quality education since its inception by focusing on technical advancements and research. The institute offers B. Tech courses in eight different disciplines. Besides B. Tech courses, the institute offers various M. Tech, MSc programmes and Ph.D programmes in all departments.

About the Department of Humanaties, Social Sciences and Management of NIT, Srinagar:

The Department of Humanities, Social Sciences and Management is one of the oldest departments of NIT Srinagar. The department offers a very rigorous syllabus to familiarize engineering students with modern concepts of Management, Social Sciences, Communication Skills and English language. The department has started an MBA programme from the academic year 2020 keeping in view the contemporary management curriculum offered by top B-Schools. HSS&M department has also started an MTIEM programme in collaboration with the IIED Centre of NIT Srinagar to boost the culture of innovations and entrepreneurship in the region. The department of HSS&M also offers Ph.D. programmes in various areas of Management and English.

Chief Patron	Prof. Rakesh Sehgal, Director NIT Srinagar
Patron	Prof. M.F Wani, Dean R&C, NIT Srinagar
Chairman	Prof. Abdul Liman, Head, Dept. of HSS&M, NIT Srinagar
Organising Secretaries	Dr Tahir Ahmad Wani
	Dr Sumaira Jan
	Dr Nufazil Altaf
	Dr Mohd Rafiq Teli
Coordinators	Dr Jaya Shrivastava
	Dr Nasir Faried Butt
Organising Team	Dr Fouzia Jan
	Dr Shahid Lone
Technical Partner	IEEE Student Branch, NIT Srinagar

IN PARTNERSHIP WITH

www.cii.in   www.youngindians.net

About Yi (Young Indians): www.youngindians.net

Young Indians (Yi) is a movement for Indian Youth to converge, lead, co-create and influence India's future. As an integral part of the Confederation of Indian Industry (CII), a non-government, not-for profit, industry led and industry managed organisation playing a proactive role in India's development process. Formed in the year 2002, Yi has created a platform for young Indians to work towards realizing a dream of a developed nation. It has a growing, inclusive membership across all geographies and demographics with over 4600 + direct members in 57 chapters, and 29500 students YUVA members from colleges. The Yi membership includes young progressive Indians between the age group of 21-45 years and comprises of entrepreneurs, professionals and achievers from different walks of life.

About Confederation of Indian Industry (CII): www.cii.in

The Confederation of Indian Industry (CII) works to createand sustain an environment conducive to the development of India, partnering Industry, Government and civil society, through advisory and consultative processes. CII is a non-government, not-for-profit, industry-led and industry-managed organization, with over 9000 members from the private as well as public sectors, including SMEs and MNCs, and an indirect membership of over 300,000 enterprises from 294 national and regional sectoral industry bodies. For more than 125 years, CII has been engaged in shaping India's development journey and works proactively on transforming Indian Industry's engagement in national development. CII charts change by working closely with Government on policy issues, interfacing with thought leaders, and enhancing efficiency, competitiveness and business opportunities for industry through a range of specialized services and strategic global linkages.

CII's Young Indians ICCBT 2022 Organising Team

ICCBT 2022 Conference Chairman		Dr Rahul Mirchandani	
Yi National	Mr Raunak Goyal	Mr Anuj Kothari	Mr Kartik Shah
	Mr Jacob Joy	Mr Dilip Krishna	
Yi Srinagar	Mr Iqram Shafiee	Mr Iqbal Bakshi	Mr Sardar Nasir Ali Khan
CII J&K	Mr Khurshid Dar	Mr Shobhit Vaid	
Yi Delhi	Mr Varun Jain	Mr Sreevats Gopalakrishnan	Ms Yashodhara Bajoria
Yi Kolkata	Ms Alifiya Calcuttawala	Mr Mohan Agarwal	
Yi Mumbai	Mr Vivin Mathew	Mr Akshay Mirchandani	
Syngrity	Mr Vikram Badhwar	Dr Keya Bardalai	Mr Blessin Varkey
WTFares.com	Mr Vedant Sarda		
Aries Agro Limited	Dr Shama Zaidi	Mr Armaan Mirchandani	Ms Karishma Talekar

KNOWLEDGE PARTNERS

www.ariesagro.com

www.syngrity.com

www.cultinno.in

PARTNER INSTITUTIONS

www.ariesagro.com

Centre for Family Business & Entrepreneurship
www.spjimr.org

www.itm.edu

www.rapodar.ac.in

www.dschoolofbusiness.com

www.ruiacollege.edu

Contents

CHAPTER 1   CONTEMPORARY ISSUES IN HUMAN RESOURCE MANAGEMENT 1

1.1 Rashi Kulkarni — Women at Work- A Boon to Society 2

1.2 Zubair Ahmad Khan & Dr. Mohd Rafiq Teli — Impact of Leadership Styles of School Heads/Principals on Outcomes of Leadership in Public Schools using Full Range Leadership Model (FRLM): Evidence from Select Educational Institutions of the Kashmir Division of J & K State 15

1.3 Nadiya Nazeer & Dr. Farzana Gulzar — Exploring the Relationship Between Women Empowerment and Higher Education: A Review 35

CHAPTER 2   CONTEMPORARY ISSUES IN FINANCIAL MANAGEMENT 49

2.1 Tulsi Jayakumar — Professionalization and Managerialization of Family Firms: Influence of Induction of the Next-Generation 50

2.2 Syed Javed Iqbal Kamili & Prof. (Dr.) Mohi Ud Din Sangmi — Self Help Groups and youth empowerment: A Study of Union Territory of Jammu and Kashmir 67

| 2.3 | Sana Bala & Prof. Farooq Ahmad Shah | Assessment of Financial Literacy across various Demographic Groups in India .... 82 |

CHAPTER 3   CONTEMPORARY ISSUES IN TECHNOLOGY MANAGEMENT 115

3.1	Rachana Jaiswal	Blockchain Technology in the Financial Sector: A Bibliometric Analysis of the Dimensions AI Database 116
3.2	Anil Vaidya	Cryptocurrency market in pandemic exhibited unusual behaviour 137
3.3	Mohd Iqbal Dar, Irfan Ahmad Sheikh & Dr. Sugandha Chhibber	Role of ICT in Promoting Financial Inclusion Among Rural Households: Empirical Evidence from Kashmir Valley, India – A Case Study 150
3.4	Karishma Khadiwala	Mental Health Apps: Using technology to accelerate the curve on acceptability amongst college students 158

CHAPTER 4   CHALLENGES BROUGHT UP BY COVID-19 PANDEMIC 169

| 4.1 | Ms. Sunita A. Panja & Nikita M. Tanksali | Effect of lockdown on Consumer behavior with reference to usage of Fitness apps in Mumbai District .... 170 |
| 4.2 | Pallavi Anant Gurav, Shreya Ravi Agrawal, Priyanka Dinanath Koli & Aditi Umesh Patwardhan | MASK: A Protective Measure or A Potential Hazard? .... 191 |

4.3 Ishrat Shaheen	Maintaining Corporate Culture with Special Reference to Remote Working in Covid-19 Crisis: Issues and Challenges	214
4.4 Dr Rahul Mirchandani	Leading through the Crisis of 2020	237
4.5 Dr. Mehraj Ud Din Shah	Re-engineering of Hybrid Workplace System for Management Education: An Empirical Analysis	253

CHAPTER 5   ENTREPRENEURSHIP AND SUSTAINABILITY 283

5.1 Dr. Amruta Krishna Patil	New Indian food plate and its implications on agriculture and human health	284
5.2 Dr. Shabana Ali	Entrepreneurs in Jammu and Kashmir— A Case Study of Women Entrepreneurs	294
5.3 Saba Reshi & Mohd Rafiq Teli	Does gender play a role in Sustainability orientations? A Study on Sustainable entrepreneurship	301

Author Details 319
Editor Information 325

Editorial Disclaimer

The views, opinions, positions or strategies expressed by the authors and those providing comments are theirs alone, and do not necessarily reflect the views, opinions, positions or strategies of the editorial team, NIT Srinagar, Confederation of Indian Industry, Young Indians and employees/members thereof. The editorial team and partner institutions make no representations as to accuracy, completeness, correctness, suitability, or validity of any information presented by the authors and will not be liable for any errors, omissions, legal or copyright infringements in the research papers included in this publication.

Chapter 1
Contemporary Issues in Human Resource Management

1.1 Women at Work- A Boon to Society

Rashi Kulkarni

ABSTRACT

Purpose: Women help build an inspiring work culture as the research will clearly document. Having women in the workforce is extremely beneficial and its advantages are innumerable. The main purpose of the paper is to show exactly why and how a women's presence at work is extremely important not just to the organisation but to the world at large.

Methodology used: A quantitative study was conducted wherein an online questionnaire was sent to women of different age groups to get real-life inputs. Articles on similar topics were also referred to.

Major findings: A report from the World Bank mentioned that India ranks very low in the female labour force participation rates in the world. Low female LFPR has a huge impact on the GDP and proves to be a hindrance to the countries overall growth. Countries like USA have 56% women working and in China the rate is over 64% which is the highest in the world. Countries like Nepal and Bangladesh outperform India. A huge proportion of women in India usually drop out of work after marriage and or after having children. This study has revealed various experiences of women employees and their views on the organizational culture and atmosphere.

Discussion: Firms must take steps to stop the inequality between providing job opportunities to men and women. Other than offering 6 months paid maternity leave, firms should give other benefits to new moms which can be en- cashed upon later. Secondly, allowing women half-days and work from the comfort of their home until they are ready to come back to the workplace will help. Most women in our country have the responsibility of handling households and that should be taken into consideration and women should be allowed flexible working hours so that they can balance both home and work. Thirdly, firms should intentionally hire competent women who have taken work breaks to support and empower women.

Implications: Women help in building an inspiring work culture and create healthy competition, foster teamwork, bonding and help a company grow to its full potential. Women help build an inspiring work culture and add their much needed values to the organisation.

Key words: Challenges, discrimination, Women, workplace

INTRODUCTION

Before the First World War, a woman's life was guided by domestic responsibilities. Nowadays more women are speaking out for change, but it wasn't until the global outbreak of war that there was a shift in the gender dynamics. World War 1 allowed women to work; it was on them to keep the home running.

Millions of women joined the workforce between 1914-1918, helping to fill the gap left by a generation of military men. Women worked as drivers, postal workers and police. Despite the opportunities the conditions were poor. They were earning more than they had but were paid less than men for doing the same jobs. This has been going on till date.

This clearly shows how women in the workforce perform diverse roles and play a vital role in the workforce but despite that would and still do face inequality.

A report from the World Bank mentioned that India ranks very low in the female labour force participation rates in the world. Low female LFPR has a huge impact on the GDP and proves to be a hindrance to the countries overall growth. Countries like USA have 56% women working and in China the rate is over 64% which is the highest in the world. Countries like Nepal and Bangladesh outperform India.

The percentage of women in the workforce is below 47%. While with men, its 72%. That's a difference of 25%, while some regions face a gap of 50%.

"Women are less likely to work in India than they are in any country in the G2O, except Saudi Arabia" a Deloitte report mentioned.

"While disparities in basic rights; in schooling, credit, and jobs; or in the ability to participate in public life take their most direct toll on women and girls, the full costs of gender inequality ultimately harm everyone... ignoring gender disparities comes at a great cost—to people's well-being and to countries' abilities to grow sustainably, to govern effectively, and thus reduce poverty".

When a woman is involved in the economy everyone is better off. A lady's economic involvement increases the GDP which is the basic standard for higher living.

Despite progress, the gaps in the participation of men and women in the workforce remain large. No economy has reduced the gender gap below 7 percent.

There are enumerable advantages of having women as a part of the workforce. On a smaller level, working women become financially independent and will have greater control over their own lives. This encourages women to stand against physical and emotional abuse, enabling them to handle social issues and pressures on their own. At the macro level, greater female force at work is good for the overall economy and will help raise the countries standards. Women are as important as men to not just the organisation but the economy as a whole and these are some of the few benefits of having more women in the workforce:

- A boost to growth: women bring new skills to the workplace, the productivity and growth gains from adding women to the labour force (by reducing barriers to women's participation in the labour

force) are larger than previously thought. Indeed, our calibration exercise suggests that, for the bottom half of the countries in our sample in terms of gender inequality, closing the gender gap could increase GDP by an average of 35 percent. Four fifths of these gains come from adding workers to the labour force, but fully one fifth of the gains are due to the gender diversity effect on productivity.
- Greater productivity: The contribution to growth from improved efficiency is overstated. A portion of the gain attributed to productivity is actually due to the increased participation of women over time.

The study discusses the reason why there are less women in the workforce, why the drop out of the work force and to show exactly why and how a women's presence at work is extremely important not just to the organisation but to the world at large

REVIEW OF LITERATURE

Researcher's researching about women at work have taken multiple different approaches. Most studies focus on the difference between men and women in the workplace with one study recording how organisations benefit from gender-diversity. (Women at work: how organisational features impact career development-Naomi Ellemers) They found out that there is "a consistent gender difference in career development and payment and women who feel undervalued at work will re-evaluate their priorities and are tempted to opt-out. The study helped to show what organisations could do to reap the benefits of gender diversity". Another research showed how despite significant promotion of diversity in companies, as well as legislation for equal opportunities for women and men, it must be noted that women still remain largely in the minority in decision-making positions. This observation reflects the phenomenon of the glass ceiling that constitutes vertical discrimination within companies against women. (The Glass Ceiling for Women Managers: Antecedents and Consequences for Work-Family Interface and Well-Being at Work-Audrey Babic and Isabelle Hansez). Both these research studies provide a good basis for the research. The research proposed aims on the prior existing research but explore topics that have not been dealt with and focuses on the reasons why there are less women in the workplace, why they are dropping out of the workforce, how having more women can help grow the economy and how can the problem of having less women in the workforce be solved.

AIM:

To identify the need and the importance of having more women in the workforce and how having more women be a part of the workforce will help grow the economy and create higher sales and profits in an organisation v/s the one simply dominated by men.

STEPS TO ACHIEVE THE AIM:

Firms must take steps to stop the inequality between providing job opportunities to men and women. Other than offering 6 months paid maternity leave, firms should give other benefits to new moms which can be en- cashed upon later. Secondly, allowing women half-days and work from the comfort of their home until they are ready to come back to the workplace will help. Most women in our country have the responsibility of handling households and that should be taken into consideration and women should be allowed flexible working hours so that they can balance both home and work. Thirdly, firms should intentionally hire competent women who have taken work breaks to support and empower women.

METHODOLOGY

The present study is an empirical research which is done with the help of data collection by collecting the survey. The survey was conducted with help a well-structured questionnaire which was prepared with the help of the objectives. The sample size of the data collection recorded was about 80 respondents who belong to various organizations. The present study is based on both the primary and secondary sources of data which included many research articles, newspapers, blogs and books. The questionnaire contained questions regarding the respondent's age, educational qualification as well as their per annum income. Questions regarding the level of satisfaction women have with their current job, whether their organisation pays attention towards women's needs and their problems, whether their organisation provides high security was also asked. They were questioned about the reason why they started working, for how long have they been working, if they have stepped down from work and if yes, the reasons behind doing so. Questions like whether they think there is disparity between men and women in the workforce, if men are preferred over women for better positions in their organisation, whether there are equal number of women and men in their workplace and on what basis promotions are given in their organisation was asked. They were finally questioned if they think we as a country will be able to achieve getting more women in the workforce in the coming years.

ANALYSIS AND INTERPRETATION

1. Out of the 80 respondent's a majority of 40.7% belonged to the age group of below 25 years and 33.3% belonged to the age group of above 41 and the rest 25.9% belonged to the age group of below 30.

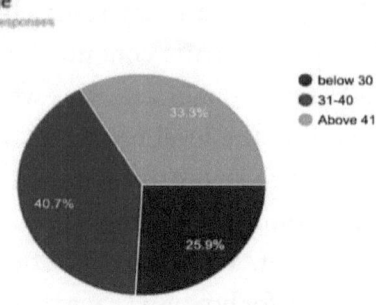

2. The respondent's educational qualification was recorded and a majority of 74.1% respondents were post-graduates and the remaining 25.9% were undergraduates.

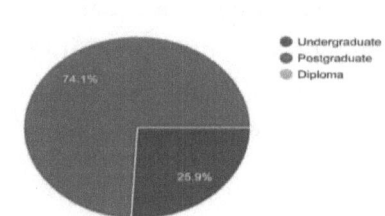

3. The respondents were asked regarding their yearly income and a majority of 74.1% of the respondents earned above 4 lakhs per annum, 22.2 % earned between 1-4 lakh and the remaining 3.7% earned less than a lakh per annum.

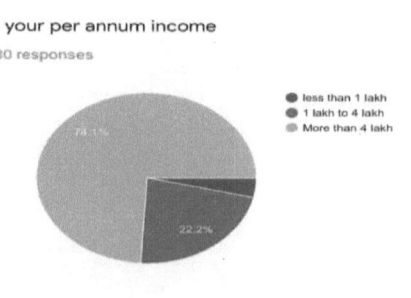

4. When asked about their level of satisfaction with their current job about 51.9% said that they were satisfied and 25.9% said that they were very satisfied whereas 14.8 % of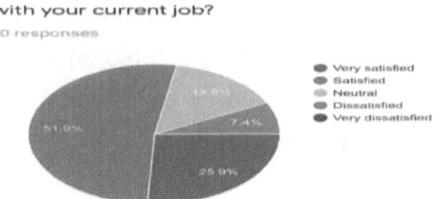
the respondents were neutral in their opinion and the remaining 7.4% said that they were dissatisfied.

5. Most of the respondents which included 70.4% said that they started working for personal fulfilment while 11.1% said that it was either mandatory or they needed money for personal expenses and the remaining 7.4% started working because it was mandatory.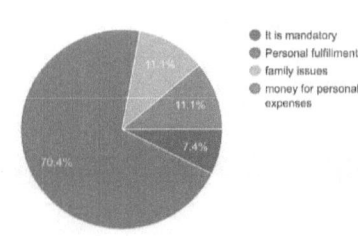

6. When asked for how long they have been working 77.8% of them have been working for more than 5 years while 11.1% have been working for less and more than a year respectively.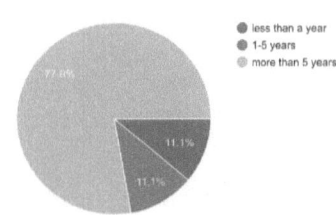

7. Around 70.4% of the respondents had stepped down from work and the remaining 29.6% had not.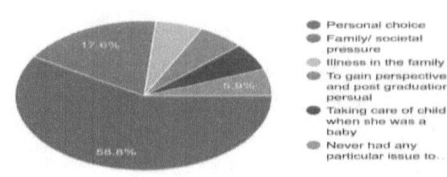

8. Out of the ones that did leave their job 58.8% did it as a personal choice and 17.6% of them did it because of Family/Societal pressure.

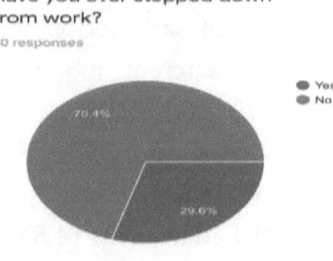

9. When asked if their organisation pays attention to women's needs 81.5% said yes while 18.5% strongly disagreed.

10. When asked if their organisation provides for a sufficient maternity leave period 81.5% of the respondents and the remaining 18.5% said no.

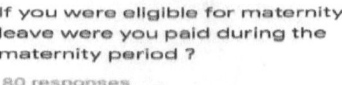

11. 37% of the respondents were eligible for the maternity leave and 11.1% were not.

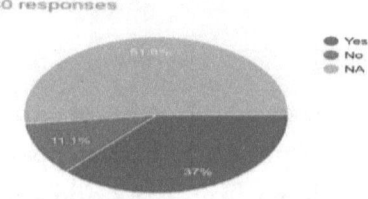

12. When asked if there is disparity between men and women in their workplace 66.7% said no while 33.3% said no.

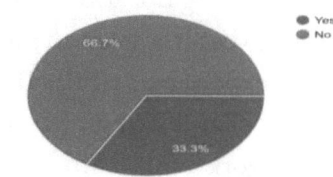

13. 88.9% of the respondents said that their organisation did provide high security while 11.1% said theirs didn't.

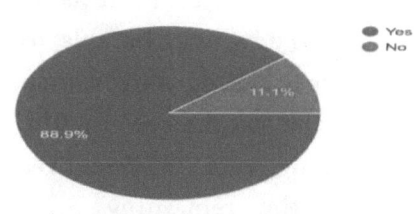

14. 63% of the respondents said that their organisation did not prefer men over women for better job positions while 37% said that their organisation did.

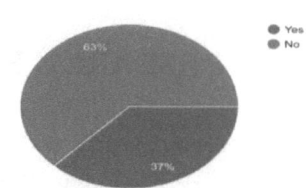

15. 66.7% respondents claimed that their organisation had almost equal male and female staff while 33.3% said it did not.

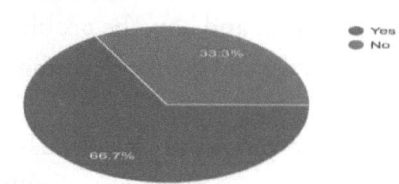

16. When asked on what basis promotions were given in their organisation 51.9% said that it was on the basis of experience while 18.5% said that it was on the basis of work ethic while 14.8% said that it was due to familiarity with the person and 11.1% claimed it was on the basis of team handling skills.

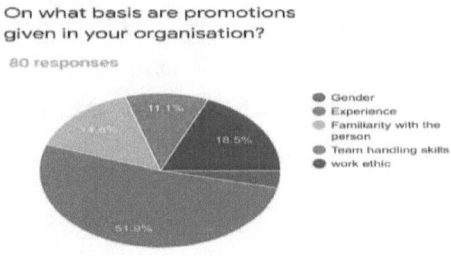

17. Lastly when asked if as a country we will be able to achieve getting more women in the workforce in the coming years 96.3% said yes and the remaining 3.7% said no.

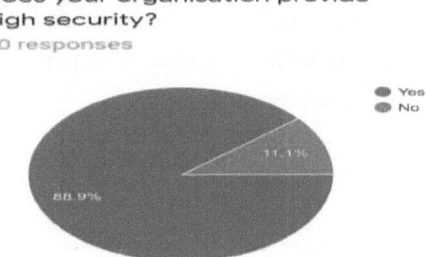

RESEARCH FINDINGS AND DISCUSSIONS

The present study states that women employees face many issues at their workplace as well as their reasons for remaining absent from the work front. It discusses in detail why there is disparity between men and women in the workplace, how having more women can not just grow the economy but add more value to an organisation. The study shows the various opinions and experiences of women employees at their organisation and how the problems of women at workplace can be solved and how we can get more women to the work front.

There are various points discussed in this study such as the respondent's atmosphere, environment and culture at their workplace and what they think about disparity at work, equal pay, the future of women in the workplace.

By certain findings we can say that some of the reasons for fewer women in the workforce are:

1) Patriarchal value systems: A negative symbol is attached to women working in patriarchal societies as women are considered to be reserve labour force used only at the time of distress.
2) Higher education is more important than secondary education: Women who are college-educated or have a graduate degree are more likely to join the workforce and only a small fraction of Indian women have attained higher education.
3) Women workers have also had a difficult time moving out of the rapidly shrinking agricultural sector and obtaining other non-agricultural jobs.
4) Major sections of India's female workforce usually drop out of work after marriage and or after having children.

CONCLUSION

Hence the present study concludes that there are many issues faced by the women at their workplace. The study reveals various experiences of women employees and their views on the organizational culture and atmosphere. Hence this study concludes that there are many problems face by the women employees at their workplace but still the women employees are breaking these obstacles and emerging successful in their respective field. However, we as a country need to as mentioned take steps to reduce disparity between men and women and bring more women to the workforce. Women are unique and they help build an inspiring work culture by bringing in healthy competition, fostering teamwork, bonding and thereby helping the company grow to its full potential. Our lives would be extremely bland without women adding their much-needed uniqueness and flavour not only in workplaces but also in our daily lives. Women help build an inspiring work culture and add their much needed values to the organisation.

REFERENCES

Aláez-Aller, R., Longás-García, J. C., & Ullibarri-Arce, M. (2011). Visualising gender wage differences in the European Union. Gender, Work & Organization, 18, e49-e87. doi: 10.1111/ j.1468-0432.2009. 00469.x

Cailin S Stamarski and Leann S Son Hing, (2015). Gender Inequalities In The Workplace.Fjfst.Vol.10. Issue.2. Pp.1-15.

Manuela Tomei, (2006). Gender Inequalities at Work. Iloj. Vol.10. Issue.2. Pp.2-28.

Shweta Hotwani, (2017). Work Life Balance of Women at Workplace. Ijetmas.Vol.5. Issue.7. Pp.702-711.

1.2 Impact of Leadership Styles of School Heads/ Principals on Outcomes of Leadership in Public Schools using Full Range Leadership Model (FRLM): Evidence from Select Educational Institutions of the Kashmir Division of J & K State

Zubair Ahmad Khan and Dr. Mohd Rafiq Teli

ABSTRACT

The present briefly explores the leadership styles in public high schools in the Kashmir division of the state of J & K. The study further determines the impact of these leadership styles on the outcomes of leadership using Full Range Leadership Model (FRLM). By using simple random sampling, a survey of around 225 respondents (teachers) throughout the state has been carried out. For the purpose of collecting data, Multifactor Leadership Questionnaire (MLQ-5X) Rater Form has been used and to analyze the data, descriptive statistics and multiple linear regression analysis has been conducted. The findings of the study confirm that Transformational and Transactional Leadership positively influence the Outcomes of Leadership, while Passive Avoidant Leadership negatively influences the Outcomes of Leadership.

Keywords: Leadership, MLQ (Multifactor Leadership Questionnaire), FRLM (Full Range Leadership Model), Primary Education, Principals, Covid-19 Pandemic

INTRODUCTION

The present study briefly explores the leadership styles of Principals/ School Heads in public schools in the Kashmir division of the state of Jammu and Kashmir and also determines the impact of these leadership styles on the outcomes of leadership using Full Range Leadership

Model (FRLM). The study considers three dimensions of Leadership Styles (Full Range Leadership Model); Transformational Leadership, Transactional Leadership and Passive Avoidant Behavior. Further it considers three dimensions of Outcomes of Leadership; Extra Effort, Effectiveness and Satisfaction with the Leader (Bass & Avolio, 2004). The research instrument used for the study is MLQ-5X (Multifactor Leadership Questionnaire) which comes in two forms i.e. Leader Form and the Rater Form, but the present study uses only MLQ-5X Rater form. This means that the School Principals/Heads will not rate themselves but the teachers will rate their respective Principals through the MLQ-5X rater form. This has been done in order to avoid any respondent bias.

Full Range Leadership Model (FRLM) and Multifactor Leadership Questionnaire (MLQ)

The Full Range Leadership Model (FRLM) (Avolio and Bass, 1991) has been developed to expand the variety of leadership styles. The Full Range Multifactor Leadership model comprises of Transformational Leadership, Transactional Leadership and the Passive Avoidant Leadership. Bass and Avolio (1985) articulated what is considered as one of the most comprehensive leadership theory so far. Extending the work of Burns (1978), Bass proposes that leadership is composed of three domains: Transformational, Transactional and Laissez-faire. Subsequently this led to the development of the Multifactor Leadership Questionnaire (MLQ). The MLQ (Multifactor Leadership Questionnaire) has evolved over a period of 25 years, based on a lot of research about leaders in private and public organizations. The key constructs of leadership of the model shape a new paradigm for understanding the impact of leadership styles. This model is built on previous models of leadership - like those of democratic versus autocratic leadership, participative versus directive leadership, and task- versus relationship oriented leadership—which have been dominant in the past in theory as well as practice.

REVIEW OF LITERATURE

Andrej N. (2022), has studied the impact of leadership style and knowledge management on organizational performance with moderation effects via PLS-SEM. With a sample size of 135 respondents, the study has implemented Gold's validated questionnaire and Multifactor Leadership Questionnaire (5X). Further, Partial Least Squares Structural Equation Modeling has been used for the purpose of analyzing data. The study establishes that leadership style has a positive impact on the knowledge management. While the study found that transformational leadership enhances organizational performance, it did not find that transactional leadership had the same effect.

Mohamad A., Mouazen and Lara A.B.H. (2022), have conducted a 16-year bibliometric review to capture the evolution and the quality of transactional and transformation leadership research using 1059 articles. The systematic review through bibliometric and descriptive techniques confirmed that among other developed countries, the United States has the most contributions and citations, followed by the United Kingdom, China, Germany, and Canada. Furthermore, the number of publications in Asian nations has grown in the previous three years. The publication result from the United States is anticipated, given that leadership research originated there. In light of the worldwide influence of the fast changing economic and political circumstances, the study proposes that additional research on transactional and transformational leaders be performed in Asian and Middle Eastern nations.

Belias D. et. al. (2021), have studied the impact of leadership styles on job satisfaction. The study has adopted Job Satisfaction Survey Questionnaire and Multifactor Leadership Questionnaire (5X) and used descriptive statistics and spearman correlation for analyzing the data. The study argues that the supervisor's leadership style has a considerable influence on how employees feel about their work. The outcomes of the study back up the hypothesis that leadership, specifically transformational leadership, may fulfill the needs of employees.

Quintana T.A. et. al. (2014), have explored the effects of leadership styles on employees' outcomes in international luxury hotels. Multifactor Leadership Questionnaire (5X) has been used for the purpose of data collection from 191 respondents. Further Descriptive Statistics and Partial Least Square Analysis (PLS) techniques have been used for data analysis. The outcomes of the research establish that 'Idealized attributes' of transformational leadership and 'contingent reward' from transactional leadership are the most vital factors that have a positive impact on extra effort, perceived efficiency as well as satisfaction.

Cerni T., Curtis G. J. & Colmar S. H. (2010), examined the impact of a coaching intervention programme of 10-weeks. The study was based on Epstein's CEST theory on transformational leadership amongst fourteen secondary school principals. With respect to the research design, the study set up as a pre-test, post-test control-group, and it tested whether changes to CEST information-processing systems could bring about changes in leadership style. All school staff in the selected schools at the start of the coaching intervention programme were invited to rate their school principals. The rating instrument used was the Multifactor Leadership Questionnaire (MLQ-5X). The outcomes of the study establish that for the intervention group, there was a considerable difference between pre-test and post-test scores. The control group remained unaffected. The study's qualitative findings reveal that the intervention group's school principals became more introspective about their thinking processes and leadership behaviours. Furthermore, the study provides preliminary evidence that changing rational and constructive thinking can boost coachees' usage of transformational leadership practices.

From the preliminary literature review, it may be concluded that several studies have been conducted to explore different dimensions of the leadership in school education mostly in the western countries. In Indian context, in general, the review of literature reveals dearth of study on leadership in school education, while in the particular context of state of Kashmir there is more scarcity of research. The literature review undertaken for this study does not give sufficient evidence to infer that a significant amount of work has been done in this area. The study therefore aims to investigate the various aspects of leadership in the school education in the State of Kashmir and determine the impact of leadership styles of Principals/institutional heads on outcomes of leadership of these institutions and make a significant contribution to existing literature of leadership in school education.

BACKGROUND AND CONTEXT

The contemporary literature on leadership in general and academic leadership in particular may provide a clearer view of how to improve leadership effectiveness, but needs to be studied in a broader context. It's hard to predict whether or not an institution will face a crisis. We can, however, influence how prepared we are and how we react to it, and we can acquire strategies that will help us defend our students, teachers, and staff, as well as our institutions' image.

The transformation of India's educational system is resulting in significant progress in our society. The national literacy rate is increasing and fascinating everyone, regardless of caste, gender, or social class. Educational institutions are growing in number, accumulating our society's knowledge and intellectual strength. For a long time, government-run schools have been the primary provider of education, but privatization has drastically altered the landscape of existence. Government schools have traditionally been a vital source of education for the children of India's vast poor population, who cannot afford to send their children to private schools. Despite the fact that modernization and privatization are important contributors to education, public schools in the state of J&K are suffering from poor performance, despite the high wages and other advantages paid to instructors in government-run schools. In comparison to private institutes with issues, government finances are always sufficient for any changes in government-run schools (Amin. S. et al, 2014). It is evident that the government's educational system has practically come to a halt. Only in the private sector it seems to be possible to keep the flame of learning alive. In today's world, private institutions, although being self-funded, are a source of offering high-quality education and attracting a large number of students. With a few exceptions, such private institutions consistently outperform public institutions. Burn Hall, Tyndale Biscoe, Delhi Public School, Presentation Convent, Mallinson, Iqbal Memorial Institute, and others are just a handful of the many private schools in Jammu and Kashmir that routinely provide exceptional results. On the other hand, government institutes' outcomes are steadily declining, and they are falling well behind their private-sector counterparts. With some exceptions, government schools are mostly populated by children from low-income families, and parents are rarely willing to send their children to a government school. The magnitude of the problem is such that even government school instructors prefer to send their own children to private institutions. (Amin. S. et. al. 2014).

The recent results (Session 2021) declared by the J & K Board of School Education (BOSE) have again provided an evidence of the miserable performance of public schools which produced 67.25 % pass percentage compared to 91.18 % by the private schools in the Valley. The disparity in results is significant and humongous. In 2020, the public schools' pass percentage was 62.76 % while that of the private schools was 89.82 %. In 2019, the pass percentage of the government schools was 62.96 % while that of private schools was 86.26 %. In 2018, the government schools stood at 63.71 % and private schools at 85.85% in terms of pass percentage. We can clearly infer form the statistics the dismal performance of public schools in the Kashmir Valley with respect to their private counterparts.

Academic leaders may exercise substantial impact on their schools' success (Harris et al., 2007 and Day et al., 2009). School leaders must accept responsibility for their institutions' adaptation to the dynamic environment. As per Lynch (2012), leadership is closely linked to tangible outcomes such as improved student performance, work ethics, and staff motivation (Schuh, Zhang, & Tian; 2013Aydn, Sarer, & Uysal, 2013 and others).

The present study shall aid in better preparing for and responding to crises, as well as lead to procedures and practices that will reduce the likelihood of repeat occurrences and instill confidence in long-term success, resilience and survival of the government educational institutions within the leadership context. Studies like this should be conducted in order to provide critical information about proactive training and planning so that public educational institutions can implement effective leadership practices and crisis management systems prior to a catastrophic event.

In context of the literature review and theoretical background for leadership in school education we have proposed the research problem, research objectives, hypothesis and conceptual framework as follows:

RESEARCH PROBLEM

To investigate whether Leadership Styles have a significant impact on the Outcomes of Leadership.

OBJECTIVES OF THE PRESENT STUDY

1. To analyze three leadership concepts (i.e., Transformational, Transactional, and Passive-Avoidant Behavior or Non-Leadership) with respect to the public schools in the State of Kashmir.
2. To determine the impact of Transformational Leadership, Transactional Leadership and Passive / Avoidant Behavior on Outcomes of Leadership (i.e., Extra Effort, Effectiveness, and Satisfaction) in the public schools of the State of Kashmir.

HYPOTHESIS OF THE PRESENT STUDY

Following directional hypotheses have been proposed for the study:

H1: Transformational Leadership has a significant positive impact on the Outcomes of Leadership.

H2: Transactional Leadership has a significant positive impact on the Outcomes of Leadership.

H3: Passive avoidant behavior has a significant negative impact on the Outcomes of Leadership.

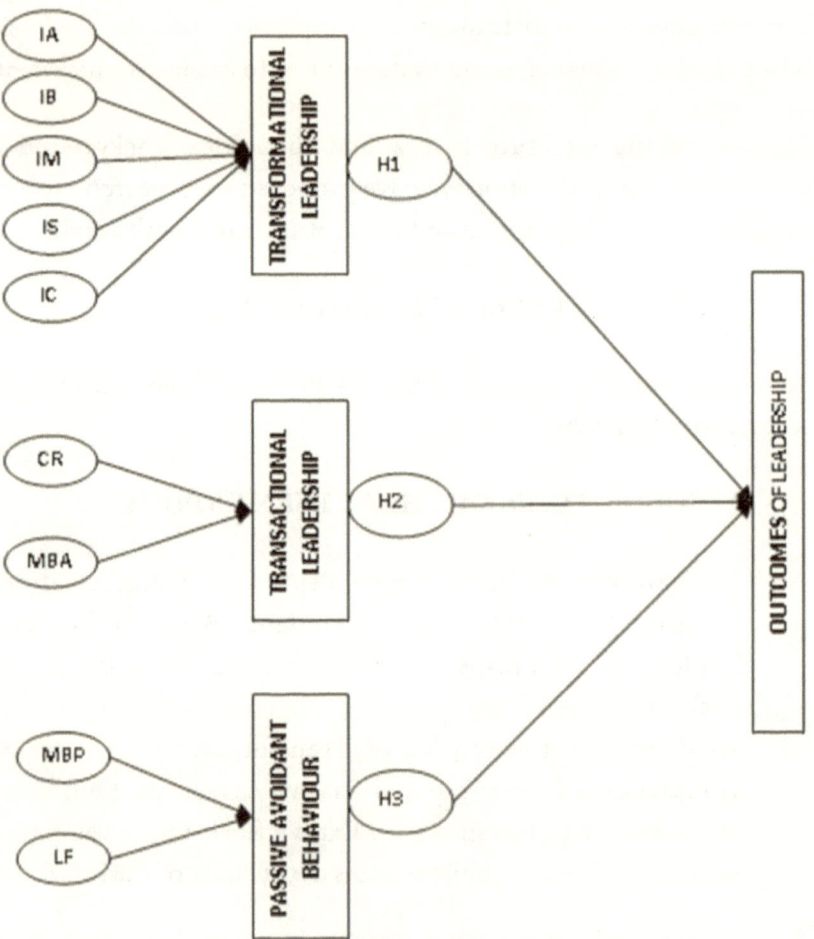

Figure 1: Conceptual Framework of the Study

RESEARCH METHODOLOGY

The present study has adopted a descriptive research design to analyze transformational leadership style, transactional leadership style and passive avoidant behavior and to determine the impact of these leadership styles on the outcomes of leadership. The targeted sample for the study was around 225, but ultimately after actual responses and preliminary data screening only 167 responses were complete and fit for analysis and were hence incorporated in the study. With respect to the sampling technique, simple random sampling has been used to avoid any element of bias in sampling process. The sampling frame for the study comprises of teacher of government/public high schools of Kashmir Division of the state of Jammu and Kashmir. The present study has adopted Multifactor Leadership Questionnaire (MLQ-5X Rater Form) as the research instrument. Another self-rating instrument of MLQ i.e. MLQ-5X Leader Form has not been incorporated in the study due to a high possibility of respondent bias. For the purpose of analyzing data Descriptive Statistics and Linear Regression techniques have been implemented. Mainly IBM-SPSS and MS Excel software have been used for analyzing the data.

PRE ANALYSIS DATA SCREENING

In order to ensure that the data collected from respondents is fit for analysis, the data has been screened for normality, reliability and other issues using standard test

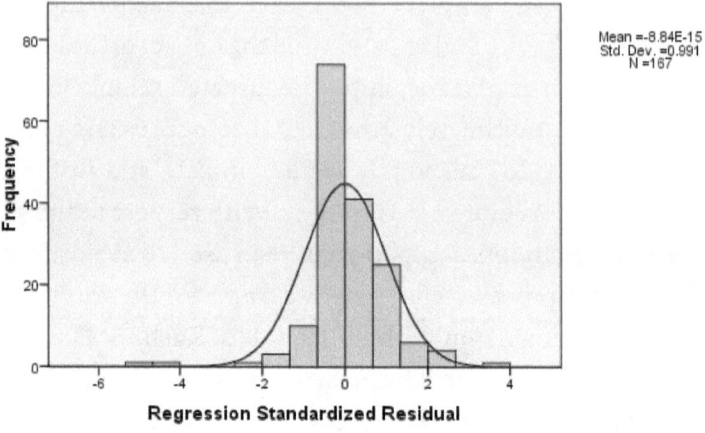

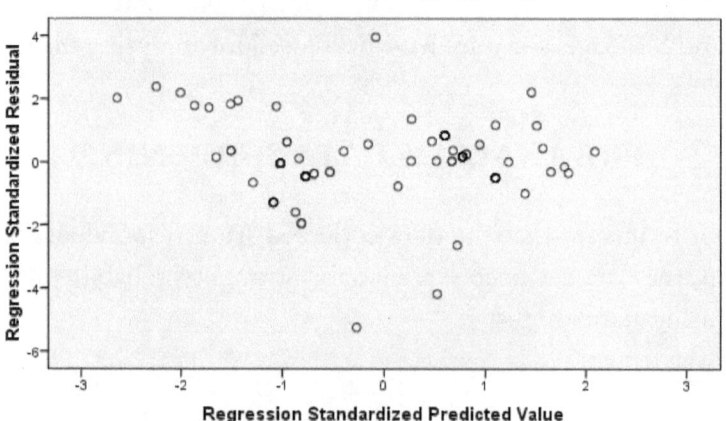

Figure 2 and Figure 3: Tests for normality

The above outputs (Histogram and Scatter plot) generated from the data by IBM SPSS software confirm that the data may be considered as roughly normal given the smaller sample size of the study.

Table 1. Test for Reliability

Cronbach's Alpha	N of Items
.739	28

The value of Cronbach's Alpha test for reliability is 0.739 as produced by the IBM-SPSS software output. As per the Nunnally (1978), who offered a rule of thumb of 0.7 for Cronbach's Alpha, the reliability of the present study is within the standard of acceptance. Hence there are no issues of reliability in the present study.

DATA ANALYSIS

Descriptive statistics

The data analysis performed through IBM SPSS produced the following descriptive statistics output construct-wise and variable-wise:

Table 2. Descriptive Statistics Construct Wise

Descriptive Statistics					
	N	Minimum	Maximum	Mean	Std. Deviation
IB_MEAN	167	.33	4.00	2.4651	.68641
IC_MEAN	167	.00	4.00	1.7066	1.32770
TRANSF_MEAN	167	.67	4.00	2.4167	.64621
CR_MEAN	167	.50	4.00	2.6407	.84826
MBEA_MEAN	167	.00	4.00	2.4132	.73012
TRANSAC_MEAN	167	.50	3.75	2.5269	.62937
MBEP_MEAN	167	.00	3.25	.9237	.70802
LF_MEAN	167	.00	2.75	.7814	.62826
PASSIV_AVOID_MEAN	167	.00	2.25	.8525	.61088

Table 3. Descriptive Statistics on the basis of Leadership Styles

DESCRIPTIVE STATISTICS			
Mean	Mean	Std. Deviation	N
TRANSF_MEAN	2.4167	.64621	167
TRANSAC_MEAN	2.5269	.62937	167
PASSIV_AVOID_MEAN	0.8525	.61088	167

According to the descriptive statistics report, overall in the public schools Transactional Leadership is prevalent, immediately followed by Transformational Leadership, while Passive Avoidant Leadership is marginally present. With a mean of 2.465, Idealized Behavior is the most dominant construct in Transformational Leadership. In Transactional Leadership, Contingent Reward is the dominant construct with a mean of 2.64, while in the Passive Avoidant Behavior, the dimension of Management by Exceptions Passive has highest mean of 0.923

Table 4. Significance of the Model (ANOVA-Test)

ANOVA[b]						
	Model	Sum of Squares	Df	Mean Square	F	Sig.
1	Regression	51.758	3	17.253	109.761	.000a
	Residual	25.621	163	.157		
	Total	77.379	166			

a. Predictors: (Constant), PASSIV_AVOID_MEAN, TRANSAC_MEAN, TRANSF_MEAN

b. Dependent Variable: OUTCOMES_OF_LEAD_MEAN

In order to check whether the model is regressible or whether the model is fit or significant, ANOVA test has been conducted. The results of this test through SPSS software generated a P value of .000 which is less than the critical value of 0.05 which proves that the model is statistically significant or regressible. Hence we may state that the Independent Variables i.e. Transformational Leadership, Transactional Leadership and Passive Avoidant Leadership are good predictors of the Dependent Variable i.e. Outcomes of Leadership with respect to the model adopted.

Table 5. Correlation Matrix displaying the correlation coefficients

		CORRELATIONS			
		OUTCOMES_ OF_LEAD_ MEAN	TRANSF_ MEAN	TRANSAC_ MEAN	PASSIV_ AVOID_ MEAN
Pearson Correlation	OUTCOMES_OF_ LEAD_MEAN	1.000			
	TRANSF_MEAN	.706	1.000		
	TRANSAC_MEAN	.538	.328	1.000	
	PASSIV_AVOID_ MEAN	-.394	-.200	-.068	1.000

Table 6. Standardized Matrix with Collinearity Statistics

	Standardized Coefficients	t	Sig.	Collinearity Statistics	
	Beta			Tolerance	VIF
TRANSF_MEAN	.541	11.139	.000	.861	1.162
TRANSAC_MEAN	.342	7.167	.000	.892	1.121
PASSIV_AVOID_MEAN	-.262	-5.694	.000	.960	1.042

In order to check the issue of Multi-collinearity issues (i.e. the inter-correlation among the variables), the correlation matrix displays Tolerance and VIF values. Since all the Tolerance values are more than critical value 0.1, hence Multi-collinearity does not exist in the model. Further all VIF values are less than the critical value 3, hence confirming the absence of Multi-collinearity issues in the data.

From the Coefficient Matrix, it can be observed that Transformational Leadership significantly predicts the Outcomes of Leadership, Transactional Leadership significantly predicts Outcomes of Leadership and Passive Avoidant Leadership also significantly predicts the Outcomes of the Leadership. Now, with respect to the direction of relationship, it can be observed from the Correlation Matrix Standardized Coefficients that Transformational and Transactional Leadership positively influence the Outcomes of Leadership, while Passive Avoidant Leadership negatively influences the Outcomes of Leadership. Further with respect to the magnitude of relationship, Transformational Leadership is strongly correlated to Outcomes of Leadership, while Transactional Leadership has a lesser influence on the same. Finally, Passive Avoidant Leadership has a lesser magnitude of correlation with the Outcomes of Leadership. The findings of the study confirm with the results of N. Berber et al. (2019), Author (2018), Amirul S.A. et al. (2012) and others.

THE PROBLEM

To investigate whether Leadership Styles have a significant impact on the Outcomes of Leadership.

Table 7. Hypotheses

Hypotheses	Regression Weights	Beta Coefficient	p-value	R2	F	Hypotheses Supported
H1	TFL→OL	.541	.000			YES
H2	TNL→OL	.342	.000	0.67	109.761	YES
H3	PAB→OL	-.262	.000			YES

Table 8. Model Summary

Model	R	R Square	Adjusted R Square	Std. Error of the Estimate	Durbin-Watson
1	.818a	.67	.663	.39646	1.874

Predictors: (Constant), PASSIV_AVOID_MEAN, TRANSAC_MEAN, TRANSF_MEAN
Dependent Variable: OUTCOMES_OF_LEAD_MEAN

To determine the degree of predictability of the model, R-square value from the regression output has been determined from the SPSS software and displayed in the Model Summary. The R-square value of about 0.67 indicates a strong predictability power of the model. As per the value, about 67% variability in the Dependent Variable (Outcomes of Leadership) can be explained by the Independent Variables (Transformational Leadership, Transactional Leadership and Passive Avoidant Behavior).

CONCLUSION

The investigation of the leadership styles in the present study discloses the average leadership behavior prevalent in our public school education system. This might be a strong reason behind the dismal performance of public schools in our valley. The contemporary literature is witness to the fact that leaders can have a favorable influence on students' educational performance. We are more aware than ever before of the leader's impact on culture and teacher performance, both of which have a direct impact on students. Further the results of the study highlight the positive influence of Transformational Leadership on Outcomes of Leadership and negative influence of Passive Avoidant Behavior on the Outcomes of Leadership. This simply reflects that a positive and active school leader will positively influence the followers/teachers and ultimately the students and student outcomes. While a negative or passive leader will negatively influence the teachers, students as well as student and institutional outcomes.

LIMITATIONS OF THE STUDY

The findings of this study may be subject to inevitable constraints due to a lack of human and material resources, as well as the researcher's limited time. Furthermore, the range of the findings may be restricted to the topic chosen, the instruments used, the technique used, the design used, and finally the strategy used for data analysis and interpretation. The perspectives and experiences of the sampled group of instructors may restrict the findings of this study. It focuses solely on Transactional, Transformational, and Laissez-faire leadership styles, as well as just three Leadership Outcomes: Satisfaction, Extra Effort, and Effectiveness.

REFERENCES

Alonderienė, R., Müller, R., Pilkienė, M., Šimkonis, S., & Chmieliauskas, A. (2020). Transitions in balanced leadership in projects: The case of horizontal leaders. *IEEE Transactions on Engineering Management.*

Amin, S., Singh, S., Chauhan, R., & Shafi, R. (2014). GOVERNMENT SCHOOLS IN JAMMU AND KASHMIR: SCENARIO AND STRATEGIES. *International Journal of Logistics & Supply Chain Management Perspectives,* 3(1), 846.

Amirul, S. R., & Daud, H. N. (2012). A study on the relationship between leadership styles and leadership effectiveness in Malaysian GLCs. *European journal of business and management,* 4(8), 193-201.

Ancona, D., Malone, T. W., Orlikowski, W. J., & Senge, P. M. (2007). *In praise of the incomplete leader.* Harvard Business Review. Retrieved from https://hbr.org/2007/02/in-praise-of-the-incomplete-leader.

Andrej, N., Breznik, K., & Natek, S. (2022). Managing knowledge to improve performance: The impact of leadership style and knowledge management on organizational performance with moderation effects via PLS-SEM. *Journal of the Knowledge Economy*, 1-30.

Avolio, B. J., & Bass, B. M. (2004). Multifactor leadership questionnaire (MLQ). *Mind Garden*, 29, 481-498.

Avolio, B. J., Yammarino, F. J., & Bass, B. M. (1991). Identifying common methods variance with data collected from a single source: An unresolved sticky issue. *Journal of management*, 17(3), 571-587.

Bass, B. M. (1985). Leadership and performance beyond expectations. *New York: Free Press.*

Belias, D., Rossidis, I., Papademetriou, C., & Mantas, C. (2022). Job satisfaction as affected by types of leadership: A case study of Greek tourism sector. *Journal of Quality Assurance in Hospitality & Tourism*, 23(2), 299-317.

Berber, N., Slavić, A., Miletić, S., Simonović, Z., & Aleksić, M. (2019). A survey on relationship between leadership styles and leadership outcomes in the banking sector in Serbia. *Acta Polytechnica Hungarica*, 16(7), 167-184.

Brauckmann, S., Pashiardis, P., & Ärlestig, H. (2020). Bringing context and educational leadership together: Fostering the professional development of school principals. *Professional Development in Education*, 1-12.

Burns, J. M. (1978). Leadership. *New York: Harper & Row.*

Caminiti, S. (2020). How the Coronavirus Crisis Has Elevated the Role of HR Chiefs in the C-suite. *CNBC*, April 22. https://www.cnbc.com/2020/04/22/the-coronavirus-is-elevating-the-role-ofhr-chiefs-in-the-c-suite.html.

Cerni, T., Curtis, G. J., & Colmar, S. H. (2010). Executive coaching can enhance transformational leadership. *International Coaching Psychology Review,* 5(1), 81-85.

Day, C., Sammons, P., Hopkins, D., Harris, A., Leithwood, K., Gu, Q., ... & Kington, A. (2009). The impact of school leadership on pupil outcomes. *Final report.*

Dirani, K. M., Abadi, M., Alizadeh, A., Barhate, B., Garza, R. C., Gunasekara, N., ... & Majzun, Z. (2020). Leadership competencies and the essential role of human resource development in times of crisis: a response to Covid-19 pandemic. *Human Resource Development International,* 23(4), 380-394.

Echevarria, I. M., Patterson, B. J., & Krouse, A. (2017). Predictors of transformational leadership of nurse managers. *Journal of nursing management,* 25(3), 167-175.

Ertem, H. Y. (2021). Relationship of School Leadership with School Outcomes: A Meta-Analysis Study. *International Education Studies,* 14(5), 31-41.

Fernandez, A. A., & Shaw, G. P. (2020). Academic leadership in a time of crisis: The Coronavirus and Covid-19. *Journal of Leadership Studies,* 14(1), 39–45. https://doi.org/10.1002/jls.21684

Hallinger, P., & Heck, R. H. (2011). Exploring the journey of school improvement: Classifying and analyzing patterns of change in school improvement processes and learning outcomes. *School Effectiveness and School Improvement,* 22(1), 1-27.

Harris, A., & Jones, M. (2020). COVID 19 – school leadership in disruptive times. *School Leadership & Management,* 40(4), 243–247. https://doi.org/10.1080/13632434.2020.1811479

Harris, A., Leithwood, K., Day, C., Sammons, P., & Hopkins, D. (2007). Distributed leadership and organizational change: Reviewing the evidence. *Journal of educational change, 8*(4), 337-**347.**

Lalani, K., Crawford, J., & Butler-Henderson, K. (2021). Academic leadership during COVID-19 in higher education: technology adoption and adaptation for online learning during a pandemic. *International Journal of Leadership in Education,* 1-17.

Legood, A., van der Werff, L., Lee, A., & Den Hartog, D. (2021). A meta-analysis of the role of trust in the leadership-performance relationship. *European Journal of Work and Organizational Psychology, 30*(1), 1-22.

Lynch, M. (2012). *A guide to effective school leadership theories.* Routledge.

Morris, J. E., Lummis, G. W., Lock, G., Ferguson, C., Hill, S., & Nykiel, A. (2020). The role of leadership in establishing a positive staff culture in a secondary school. *Educational Management Administration & Leadership, 48*(5), 802-820.

Mouazen, A. M., & Hernández-Lara, A. B. (2022). Visualising the quality and the evolution of transactional and transformation leadership research: a 16-year bibliometric review. *Total Quality Management & Business Excellence,* 1-35.

Nunnally, J. C. (1978). Psychometric Theory 2nd edition (New York: McGraw).

Quintana, T. A., Park, S., & Cabrera, Y. A. (2015). Assessing the effects of leadership styles on employees' outcomes in international luxury hotels. *Journal of Business ethics, 129*(2), 469-489.

Waterman, H. (2011). Principles of 'servant leadership' and how they can enhance practice. *Nurs. Manag.* 17, 24–26. doi: 10.7748/nm2011.02.17.9.24.c8299

Witziers, B., Bosker, R. J., & Krüger, M. L. (2003). Educational leadership and student achievement: The elusive search for an association. *Educational administration quarterly, 39*(3), 398-425.

Zhao, Y. (2020). COVID-19 as a catalyst for educational change. *PROSPECTS, 49*(1–2), 29–33. https://doi.org/10.1007/s11125-020-09477-y

1.3 Exploring the Relationship Between Women Empowerment and Higher Education: A Review

Nadiya Nazeer and Dr. Farzana Gulzar

ABSTRACT

Patriarchal structures since long have been known for unequal power distribution and gender inequality. This has often led to violence and discrimination against women which has increasingly made them submissive and given rise to a sense of inferiority being developed. Gender inequality has been recognized as a key obstacle to achieve the objective of women empowerment and societal growth. Education can therefore rightly be considered a solution for a majority of these societal issues as it develops a progressive outlook. Illiterate parents were more likely found to be against education. Poverty was also identified as one of the most significant factors which acts as a barrier between women and their educational attainment. It was seen that higher levels of income in a household led to higher levels of education. This paper aims to explore the relation between higher education and women's overall empowerment. The review of literature predominantly suggested that merely attaining higher education cannot lead to empowerment. It was found that education arouses the need for self-esteem which contributes to empowerment especially among women as they are the most underprivileged. Highly educated women were found more passionate about their careers and wanted a personal income of their own. They did not like dependence on the male members in their family as it seemed to lower their self-esteem.

Keywords: Women Empowerment, Higher Education, Society, Gender Equality, Self-esteem, Decision Making.

INTRODUCTION

Women's education can broadly be classified as literary, non-literary, academic or vocational. All the forms of health information provided to women is also encompassed in the idea of female education. In fact education is considered as a key to social and economic development of any nation given the benefits it brings along. Education as a concept is equally important for both the genders but women are often subjected to discrimination owing to societal constraints and hence are not given equal opportunities to pursue higher education let alone the careers of their choice. Women are never given equal opportunities as their male counterparts. Throughout their lives they suffer in silence as they don't have the confidence to decide for themselves. Educating women has never been a priority for a society like this. Education facilitates the development of skills and abilities, information, ethics, routines, views and ideas, as well as providing infinite learning possibilities (Yousuf, 2019). The basic aim of education is to reform the society for good and thus, females with higher levels of education were perceived to have greater awareness of polity and their role in its development (Naz et al., 2020).

The concept of empowerment has been widely established in literature with greater relevance particularly to women. Empowerment as a process of change can be defined as being at a modified state of empowerment from a state of not being empowered. But the condition here is that change must come from within, it should not be forced from the top. This is what (Narayan et al., 2000i and 2000ii; Oxaal & Baden, 1997; Rowlands, 1995) define as a bottom up approach to development. This state of empowerment should come from the grass root level and must not be a top down approach. Also Kabeer (1994) argues that empowerment must be self-generated as it cannot be forced by external factors. In another study Kabeer (2001) explains empowerment through the process of disempowerment and rightly addresses the idea of power as being able to choose and make decisions. Also she doesn't consider powerful people who can take their decisions as empowered because of the fact that they have always been able to negotiate for themselves. Therefore, empowerment can rightly be addressed as a state of mind (psychological). There has also been a clear distinction between the two forms of empowerment i.e. intrinsic empowerment and the extrinsic empowerment (Ahmed & Rizk, 2020), while intrinsic empowerment boosts women's self-esteem and efficacy, instrumental empowerment equips them with the necessary skills for their economic independence.

OBJECTIVES

1. To analyse and explore the relationship between educational attainment and the empowerment of women.
2. To identify various factors that arouse the need for women to be economically empowered.
3. To examine how educated women act as a change agent in society.
4. To build a conceptual model depicting the relationship between the identified variables of the empowerment in this study.

Empowerment and Gender Relations

The available literature has a huge variety of phrases, ideas, theories and statistics that are perhaps appropriate for evaluating the concept of "empowerment"; for e.g., a number of studies have intended to measure women's "autonomy" (Basu & Basu, 1991; Dyson & Moore, 1983), patriarchy (Malhotra et al., 1995), power (Agarwal, 1997), agency, household financial control & status (Mason, 1998), gender discrimination and equality. Kabeer (1999) emphasises on the significance of assessing and classifying empowerment, differentiating between aspects related to resources, women's agency, and accomplishments or outcomes. Stromquist (2002) acknowledged four components of empowerment related to education- the cognitive (critical understanding of reality), psychological (self-esteem), political (awareness of inequalities & capacity to organise), and economic (capacity to generate income).

Gender disparity is generally higher among the poor; both within nations and between the them (Duflo, 2012). When a family is under crisis, disparity in the treatment towards girls becomes much more severe. During droughts in India, the disproportionate death rate of females is higher than that of boys. The welfare of girls is unreasonably compromised when a family cannot afford to feed everyone (Rose, 1999). When there is significant imbalance of power in family, children and also females are not raised to be self-reliant and are instead taught to conform and obey. Women in these cultures learn to accept the unequal allocation of power as they grow up (Hofstede, 2001).

Maintaining a balance between personal and work life is tough for women.; these problems are far greater than those faced by males (Nelson & Burke, 2000). A majority of studies demonstrate a clear separation of duties with men taking responsibility for jobs outside home and women handling the children duties and chores of the household (Baxter, 1993; Berk, 1985; Pleck, 1985; Sharpi, 1984; Sullivan, 1996; Warde & Hetherington, 1993). In addition, women devote two times more time to the household chores as their male counterparts (Berk, 1985 & Sullivan, 1996). Various studies indicate that despite women having significant domestic responsibilities, they are still content with the unequal distribution of work (Benin & Agostinelli, 1988; Blair & Johnson, 1992; DeMaris and Longmore, 1996; Greenstein, 1996; Lennon & Rosenfield, 1994).

These observations raised questions about familial injustice, equality and the approach towards household tasks as well as the possibilities of certain positive reforms. Several theories have been propounded to explain these absurd stereotypes, such as the shortage of resources and authority in marriage which often leaves women with a very few options with respect to these stereotypes. The stereotypical gender ideology forces females to accept the household duties and finally, the belief that they work less in the outside world than their husbands, reinforcing the notion that domestic work is solely the obligation of women (Baxter & Western, 1998).

Agency Development and Economic Independence

In the paradigm of empowerment, the significance of the concept of agency stems from the "bottom up" approach to the development techniques (Narayan et al., 2000i & 2000ii; Oxaal & Baden, 1997; Rowlands, 1995). It highlights the relevance of involvement as well as the "social inclusion" at the institutional and aggregate levels (Chambers, 1997; Friedmann, 1992; Narayan et al., 2000i & 2000ii). On an individual level, it is based on the idea of self-efficacy and the consequence of individual women comprehending that they can be their own agents of change. Educational attainment has improved women's confidence, decision-making, self-esteem, self-reliance and also the understanding of their rights; all of which has improved their career prospects (Heaton et al., 2005; Khan & Awan, 2011; Kishor & Gupta, 2004; Nayak & Mahanta, 2009; Rahman & Naoroze, 2007; Sridevi, 2005). Womenfolk need be able to understand their options and self-interest and believe that they are not just capable but also empowered to make their own decisions (A. Sen, 1999; Chen, 1992; G. Sen, 1993; Kabeer, 2001; Rowlands, 1995).

Studies have also shown that women who get married at a young age usually have children early and are less likely to work and often end up dropping out of the educational institutions (Ambrus & Field, 2008; Duflo et al., 2011; Miller, 2010). They are generally married off to much older men which as a result leads to a substantial reduction in their independence and potential. Also personal income enhances women's negotiating power inside their family which gives them more authority and position to question the patriarchal norms that limit their ability to make decisions (Ashraf et al., 2010; Khan & Awan, 2011; Swain & Wallentin, 2008). Studies have found that females in science and technology receive less support, exposure, and opportunities because instructors and the institute administrators regard it as a "male" discipline in which girls lack the abilities, comprehension and the required potential (Altermatt et al., 1998; He & Freeman, 2010; Huffman et al., 2013; Peterson, 2010). Telling girls that they are not fit for certain careers or just aren't as good as males can have a direct and indirect impact on their potential for entering the job market or even obtaining an additional degree for advancing in their lives. This "stereotype threat," as it's known by psychologists has been proven to be quite potent (Duflo, 2012).

RESEARCH METHODOLOGY

This paper is purely conceptual and is based on the review of literature available on the topic. The study mainly draws on the secondary sources which includes research papers from online sources like journals, magazines and also some reports. The focus of the study is on the already established research as well as some recent developments in the subject matter from years 1984 to 2020. All the papers have been accessed from the top rated journals of national and international repute. These papers have been extensively reviewed and an attempt has been made to propose a conceptual model/ framework in order to add and contribute to the existing body of literature.

Conceptual Model

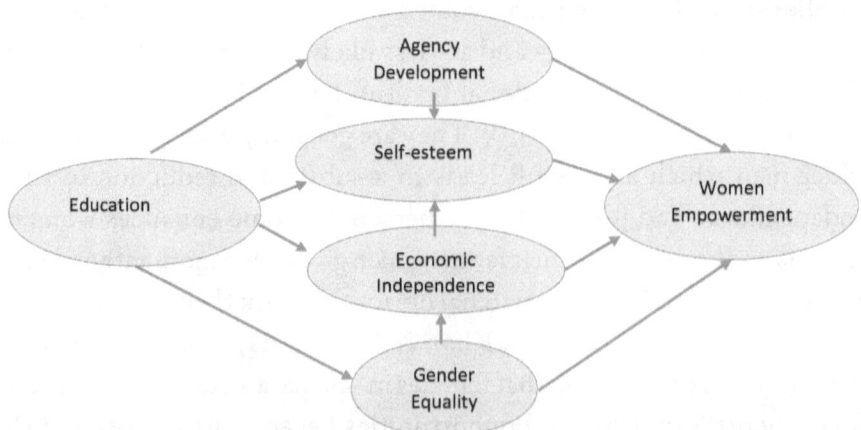

Figure 1: Conceptual model depicting the relationship between education and women empowerment

.Source: Authors

The conceptual model proposed in this study depicts the relationship that the identified variables have with each other. It also shows the dependence of other variables on the independent variable. The variables that have been identified are: attainment of higher education (independent variable), women's overall empowerment (dependent variable) and four other variables that influence the relationship of these dependent and independent variables. These variables are: women's agency development, self-esteem, economic independence and gender equality. It was found that mere attainment of education does not empower women. It empowers them when some other factors also come into light. So, this is where other variables play their part.

The model depicts how attainment of education leads to a sense of agency being developed in women through which their self-efficacy is achieved and further empowers them. This encourages women to negotiate and decide for themselves. Agency development also enhances women's self-esteem which contributes and leads to empowerment.

Economic independence can also be achieved after the accomplishment of higher education which again empowers women and gives their self-esteem a boost. So, self-esteem has a key role to play in the overall empowerment of women.

Another relationship that the model illustrates is the increased awareness of gender relations. Through the tool of higher education women become conscious of the prevalence of gender inequality and therefore, increasingly become advocates of the concept of equality. Gender equality also gives rise to economic independence as there is no discrimination and both the genders get equal opportunities to employment. This relationship also leads to the overall empowerment of women.

CONCLUSION AND RECOMMENDATIONS

This paper attempts to explore the relationship between the overall empowerment of women and their attainment of higher education. Through the review of literature and the conceptual model proposed, it can positively be concluded that education does empower women; if not alone but surely with the arousal of other factors like self-esteem, economic independence and autonomy in decision making. Gender equality is also a significant factor that can be achieved by means of attaining higher education, which further leads to women's overall empowerment. All these factors come into light when women are educated as they feel the need to be economically independent and are confident enough to challenge the patriarchal norms of the society.

Women's empowerment necessitates structural change in various structures, but predominantly in those areas which endorse patriarchal hierarchies (Batliwala, 1994; Bisnath & Elson, 1999; Kabeer, 2001; Sen & Grown, 1987). Women must be able to express their self-interest and choice, and should believe that they are not only capable but also entitled to do so (A. Sen, 1999; Chen, 1992; G. Sen, 1993; Kabeer, 2001; Nussbaum, 2000; Rowlands, 1995). This technique was described by Kabeer (2001) as "thinking outside the system" and "challenging the status quo."

Women must be active members and take part in this dynamic process of transformation (G. Sen, 1993; Mehra, 1997). Higher education's role in the economic and social empowerment was indeed perceived to be influenced by the intersection between education and the external economic setting, job markets, societal structures, and the societal gender construction (Jayaweera 1997).

Despite the fact that the gender inequality has narrowed in recent times in a lot of aspects, the aforementioned research shows that gender discrepancies in education and employment still persist to a considerable extent. It was also seen that irrespective of the same levels of education and capabilities women had, they were still paid less which resulted in a wide spread 'gender wage gap'.

REFERENCES

Agarwal, B. (1997). "Bargaining" and gender relations: Within and beyond the household. *Feminist economics, 3*(1), 1-51.

Ahmed, R., & Hyndman-Rizk, N. (2020). The higher education paradox: Towards improving women's empowerment, agency development and labour force participation in Bangladesh. *Gender and Education, 32*(4), 447-465.

Altermatt, E. R., Jovanovic, J., & Perry, M. (1998). Bias or responsivity? Sex and achievement-level effects on teachers' classroom questioning practices. *Journal of educational psychology, 90*(3), 516.

Ashraf, N., Karlan, D., & Yin, W. (2010). Female empowerment: Impact of a commitment savings product in the Philippines. *World development, 38*(3), 333-344.

Basu, A. M., & Basu, K. (1991). Women's economic roles and child survival: the case of India. *Health Transition Review*, 83-103.

Batliwala, S. (1994). The meaning of women's empowerment: New concepts from action. *Population policies reconsidered: Health, empowerment and rights, 17*.

Baxter, J. (1993). *Work at home: The domestic division of labour.* University of Queensland Press.

Baxter, J., & Western, M. (1998). Satisfaction with housework: Examining the paradox. *Sociology, 32*(1), 101-120.

Benin, M. H., & Agostinelli, J. (1988). Husbands' and wives' satisfaction with the division of labor. *Journal of Marriage and the Family*, 349-361.

Berk, S. (1985). The Gender Factor: The Apportionment of Work in American Households. New York: Plenum Press.

Bisnath, S., & Elson, D. (1999). Women's empowerment revisited. Background paper. *Progress of the world's women 2000*.

Blair, S. L., & Johnson, M. P. (1992). Wives' perceptions of the fairness of the division of household labor: The intersection of housework and ideology. *Journal of Marriage and the Family*, 570-581.

Chambers, R. (1997). *Whose reality counts* (Vol. 25). London: Intermediate technology publications.

Chen, M. (1992). Conceptual Model for women's Empowerment. *International Center for Research on Women*.

DeMaris, A., & Longmore, M. A. (1996). Ideology, power, and equity: Testing competing explanations for the perception of fairness in household labor. *Social Forces*, 74(3), 1043-1071.

Dreze, J., & Sen, A. (1999). India: Economic development and social opportunity. *OUP Catalogue*.

Duflo, E. (2012). Women empowerment and economic development. *Journal of Economic literature*, 50(4), 1051-79.

Duflo, E., Dupas, P., & Kremer, M. (2015). Education, HIV, and early fertility: Experimental evidence from Kenya. *American Economic Review*, 105(9), 2757-97.

Dyson, T., & Moore, M. (1983). On kinship structure, female autonomy, and demographic behavior in India. *Population and development review*, 35-60.

Field, E., & Ambrus, A. (2008). Early marriage, age of menarche, and female schooling attainment in Bangladesh. *Journal of political Economy, 116*(5), 881-930.

Friedmann, J. (1992). *Empowerment: The politics of alternative development.* Blackwell.

Greenstein, T. N. (1996). Gender ideology and perceptions of the fairness of the division of household labor: Effects on marital quality. *Social forces, 74*(3), 1029-1042.

He, J., & Freeman, L. A. (2010). Are men more technology-oriented than women? The role of gender on the development of general computer self-efficacy of college students. *Journal of Information Systems Education, 21*(2), 203-212.

Heaton, T. B., Huntsman, T. J., & Flake, D. F. (2005). The effects of status on women's autonomy in Bolivia, Peru, and Nicaragua. *Population research and policy review, 24*(3), 283-300.

Hofstede, G. (2001). *Culture's consequences: Comparing values, behaviors, institutions and organizations across nations.* Sage publications.

Huffman, A. H., Whetten, J., & Huffman, W. H. (2013). Using technology in higher education: The influence of gender roles on technology self-efficacy. *Computers in Human Behavior, 29*(4), 1779-1786.

Jayaweera, S. (1997). Higher education and the economic and social empowerment of women—the Asian experience. *Compare, 27*(3), 245-261.

Kabeer, N. (1994). Empowerment from below: learning from the grassroots. *Reversed Realities: Gender Hierarchies in Development Thought,* 223-263.

Kabeer, N. (1999). Resources, agency, achievements: Reflections on the measurement of women's empowerment. *Development and change, 30*(3), 435-464.

Kabeer, N. (2001). Reflections on the measurement of women's empowerment.

Khan, S. U., & Awan, R. (2011). Contextual assessment of women empowerment and its determinants: Evidence from Pakistan.

Kishor, S., & Gupta, K. (2004). Women's empowerment in India and its states: evidence from the NFHS. *Economic and Political weekly*, 694-712.

Lennon, M. C., & Rosenfield, S. (1994). Relative fairness and the division of housework: The importance of options. *American journal of Sociology, 100*(2), 506-531.

Malhotra, A., Vanneman, R., & Kishor, S. (1995). Fertility, dimensions of patriarchy, and development in India. *Population and development review*, 281-305.

Mason, Karen. (1998). "Wives' Economic Decision-making Power in the Family: Five Asian Countries." Pp. 105-133 in The Changing Family in Comparative Perspective: Asia and the United States. Karen Oppenheim Mason, ed. Honolulu: East-West Center.

Mehra, R. (1997). Women, empowerment, and economic development. *The Annals of the American Academy of Political and Social Science, 554*(1), 136-149.

Miller, G. (2010). Contraception as development? New evidence from family planning in Colombia. *The Economic Journal, 120*(545), 709-736.

Narayan, D., Chambers, R., Shah, M. K., & Petesch, P. (2000i). *Voices of the Poor: Crying out for Change.* New York: Oxford University Press for the World Bank.

Narayan, D., Chambers, R., Shah, M. K., & Petesch, P. (2000ii). *Crying out for change: Voices of the poor.* The World Bank.

Nayak, P., & Mahanta, B. (2012). Women empowerment in India. *Bulletin of Political Economy, 5*(2), 155-183.

Naz, A., & Ashraf, F. (2020). The Relationship between Higher Education and Women Empowerment in Pakistan. *UMT Education Review, 3*(2), 65-84.

Nelson, D. L., & Burke, R. J. (2000). Women executives: Health, stress, and success. *Academy of Management Perspectives, 14*(2), 107-121.

Nussbaum, M. C. (2001). *Women and human development: The capabilities approach* (Vol. 3). Cambridge University Press.

Oxaal, Z., & Baden, S. (1997). *Gender and empowerment: definitions, approaches and implications for policy* (No. 40). Bridge, Institute of Development Studies.

Peterson, V. S. (2010). Global householding amid global crises. *Politics & Gender, 6*(2), 271-281.

Pleck, J. H. (1985). *Working wives, working husbands.* Published in cooperation with the National Council on Family Relations [by] Sage Publications.

Rahman, M. H., & Naoroze, K. (2007). Women empowerment through participation in aquaculture: Experience of a large-scale technology demonstration project in Bangladesh.

Rose, E. (1999). Consumption smoothing and excess female mortality in rural India. *Review of Economics and statistics, 81*(1), 41-49.

Rowlands, J. (1995). Empowerment examined. *Development in practice, 5*(2), 101-107.

Sen, Amartya. (1999). Development as Freedom. Oxford: Oxford University Press.

Sen, G. (1993). Women's empowerment and human rights: The challenge to policy. *population summit of the world's Scientific Academies, 294*, 1-275.

Sen, G., & Grown, C. (2013). *Development crises and alternative visions: Third world women's perspectives*. Routledge.

Sharpe, S. (1984). *Double identity: The lives of working mothers*. Harmondsworth, Middlesex: Penguin Books.

Sridevi, T. O. (2005). Empowerment of Women-A systematic analysis. *India Development Foundation IDF Discussion Paper*.

Stromquist, N. P. (2002). Education as a means for empowering women. *Rethinking empowerment: Gender and development in a global/local world, 20*, 22-38.

Sullivan, O. (1996). Time co-ordination, the domestic division of labour and affective relations: Time use and the enjoyment of activities within couples. *Sociology, 30*(1), 79-100.

Swain, R. B., & Wallentin, F. Y. (2009). Does microfinance empower women? Evidence from self-help groups in India. *International review of applied economics, 23*(5), 541-556.

Triventi, M. (2011). *The gender wage gap among recent european graduates* (No. 32).

Warde, A., & Hetherington, K. (1993). A changing domestic division of labour? Issues of measurement and interpretation. *Work, Employment and Society, 7*(1), 23-45.

Yousuf, P. (2019). Role of education in women empowerment (A sociological study of the women Professors of Gwalior city MP India). *Research Journal of Social Sciences, 10*(1), 4–8

Chapter 2
Contemporary Issues in Financial Management

2.1 Professionalization and Managerialization of Family Firms: Influence of Induction of the Next-Generation

Tulsi Jayakumar

ABSTRACT

Family firms (FFs) are often seen as enterprises which favour family over non-family human capital, with such biases manifesting in the preponderance of family members in the top management team. As family firms grow, they have much to gain from professionalization and managerialization. However, giving up control to non-family managers has been found to be difficult in the case of FFs, especially when the founder-promoter still continues to lead the FF. Succession and induction of the next-generation may then pose opportunities for FFs to improve their firm performance through adoption of formal controls, systems and practices and/or through hiring professionals This paper seeks to understand the influence of induction of the next-generation into their family businesses on the FF strategies of professionalization and managerialization. It studies whether a generational change can induce a transformation from a family owned-family managed business to a family-owned, professionally-managed business.

The study uses a case-study approach to assess professionalization and managerialization strategies in Indian FFs where the next-generation had been inducted into the business. A judgement sampling method was used to select ten businesses which had exhibited growth in the last few years and which had restructured their businesses in terms of professionalization and adoption of formal management systems, especially after the induction of the next-generation. Depth interviews with scions of these FFs were conducted between July and October 2019.

While the next -gen considers professionalization as critical to scaling up and business longevity, it does not equate hiring of 'professionals' to professionalization. Professionalization is seen as a means of adopting systems and processes and involving a mindset change. Most FFs did not have a formal family board, which could help coordinate the interests of the family members with that of the family business at the corporate board level. The absence of a formal family board could be because most of the FFs were in the second generation. Within managerialization, while control systems are more successful in key areas like finance, it is less visible in areas such as human resources or even governance. While HR practices to recruit, train, evaluate and compensate non-family managers exist, FFs have not been able to overcome the bias between family and non-family human resources.

KeyWords: *Family Firms, India, Induction, Managerialization, Next-generation, Professionalization*

INTRODUCTION

Family firms are often seen as enterprises which favour family over non-family human capital, with such biases manifesting in the preponderance of family members occupying the top management positions within family enterprises. As family firms grow, the role of professionalization, traditionally conceptualised as hiring full-time non-family employees who enjoy managerial authority delegated to them (Dekker et al., 2015; Klein & Bell, 2007; Stewart & Hitt, 2012), becomes critical for firm performance. The benefits of a professionalization strategy involving hiring such 'professionals' have been stated as three-fold: one, mitigation of agency costs as qualified applicants, rather than less qualified family members are selected for various roles; two, talent acquisition which helps family enterprises make sense of the competitive environment and increases strategic decision making quality; and three, reduction in resource appropriation by members of the owning family, through the presence of non-family members acting as agents of oversight (Madison et al., 2018).

REVIEW OF LITERATURE

However, the Collins Dictionary defines the term professional (in its noun form) literally as 'persons who engage in an activity with great competence', while in an adjectival from refers to 'jobs requiring advanced education or training' (https://www.collinsdictionary.com/dictionary/english/professional). We may then define professionalization within family enterprises as 'the introduction of professional competences, acquired by individuals through their educational paths and business experiences' (Petrolo et al., 2019). This definition goes beyond the introduction of non-family members, and refers to the desired competences required to manage formal managerial systems being acquired by either family or non- family members. The emphasis, thus, is on the competences than on the human resources.

Another term relevant in the context of family firm strategy, especially given their informal nature and lack of systems, processes and business practices (Songini, 2006), is that of 'Managerialization'. The latter refers to the process of introducing formal systems, such as strategic management, human resource control systems, accounting and financial control systems, governance systems, marketing, and operation management systems (Petrolo et al., 2019; Songini et al., 2015), as also practices such as selection, compensation and performance evaluation within the human resource domain (Dekker et al., 2015; Gimeno & Parada, 2014).

However, giving up control to non-family managers has been found to be difficult in the case of family firms (Hiebl, 2013), especially when the family firm continues to be led by the founder-promoter. Succession and induction of the next-generation may then pose opportunities for family firms to improve their firm performance through adoption of formal controls, systems and practices and/or through hiring professionals.

Extant literature on the influence of the next-generation on adoption of professionalization and managerialization is sparse (Petrola et al., 2019; Songini et al., 2015). This study addresses a research gap in understanding the influence of a generational change in the adoption of strategies influencing growth and business longevity of family firms. It moves beyond assessing professionalization and studies the under-researched strategy of managerialization in the context of family firms.

The study uses a case-study approach to assess the scope for professionalization and managerialization strategies in Indian family firms in the presence of the next-generation. Drawing on Eisenhardt (1989, p. 545), we use a multiple case research design to help understand patterns. Again, following Eisenhardt (1989), a judgement sampling method was used to select ten businesses which exhibited growth in the last few years and which also restructured their businesses, adopting professionalization and adoption of formal management systems, especially after the induction of the next-generation. We conducted depth interviews with next-gen family members of these family firms.

The study sought to gain a deeper understanding of the strategies of professionalization and managerialization of Indian family firms, with particular emphasis on the 'what', 'why' and 'how' of these strategies, *from the view point of the next-generation.*

The research question considered was: Does induction of the next-generation hold the key to successful professionalization and managerialization of family firms which were largely family owned and family managed? Can such change that accompanies the induction of the next-generation help in the transition towards professionally managed firms?

METHODOLOGY

Between July and October 2019, a qualitative study involving the scions of 10 Indian family firms was conducted. A preliminary questionnaire was followed by interviews to understand the various aspects of professionalization and managerialization in their respective organisations. A second round of interviews was sought wherever further clarification were needed. Interviews were conducted so as to draw out rich material for the cases. Questions were asked to gather views and insights from scions regarding professionalization and managerialization, using a multi-dimensional perspective as drawn from theory. A general inductive approach was followed for analyzing the interviews (Thomas 2006). N-vivo qualitative analysis software was used to store and manage the data. Table 1 *(Refer to Table 1 on Pg. 62)* gives the characteristics of the scions and family firms studied. The scions were mostly in the age group of the thirties, with their ages ranging from 24-38, and had been inducted into the family business.

FINDINGS AND DISCUSSION

Professionalization of Family Firms

Understanding 'Professionalization': The 'What'

The scions of the family enterprises understood the term 'professionalization' and 'professionals' not so much as a noun, in terms of a specific category of non-family members with clear merit-based qualifications. Rather, they viewed the term 'professional' more in an adjectival sense as possession of professional competences, which could ensure that a business was run honestly and profitably in a sustained manner. It was also seen as reliance on systems and processes which were dependent on a management team, rather than individual-led. The presence of professionalization was also equated with the availability of time for the owners and/or founders to concentrate on more strategic activities, beyond the daily operations. The scions of business families also equated professionalization with their being seen as people with trust and following ethical practices. It was also interpreted as methods used to ensure that outcomes were 'predictable', 'documented' and 'transferable'.

These interpretations are not surprising, given that most family firms depend on informal systems, often following questionable means/

shortcuts to achieve outcomes, which even they understand to be unethical. Moreover, they have over-dependence on a single owner-founder for driving key processes. Such an interpretation of professionalization as provided by the family business scions may be seen as representing the aspirational scenario for most family firms.

Professionalization was also seen as decentralization of decision-making. However, the 'pilots' given the task of changing the growth path of the business would need to possess the same commitment levels and passion as the owners. This would require motivation through sharing profits and incentivizing these 'outsiders'. Interestingly, professionalization was also seen as a 'mindset' which would first need to be embraced by the owners, and then could percolate down to the rest of the organization.

Thus, scions of family firms conceptualized professionalization as a mindset, as a process, as a phenomenon, as a perception and as a pathway, and not merely as the presence of non-family members with merit-based qualifications.

The need for professionalization: The 'why'

Scions recognized the need for professionalization as 'integral for business growth', especially after a certain turnover had been achieved, since 'the old style of working is just not sustainable'. The need for professionalization ranges from the short-term, tactical – in order to streamline operations- to the long-term, strategic- as necessary for the scalability and longevity of the business. It was seen as helping the promoters move beyond the operational short-term roles and to participate in organisation building activities. The latter included driving innovations so as to make the organization more customer-centric, while at the same time paying attention to the organizational culture and employee morale and motivation. It also involved building more efficient and accurate systems.

The scions agreed that professionalization had to be undertaken to correspond to the growth phase of the organization's life cycle, when the promoters' style of functioning was no longer in sync with what was expected by the customers and other stakeholders. The persistence of such style, while having its relevance in the entrepreneurial founder stage, could be detrimental to the organization as it enters the growth phase. Another view was that the promoter/owner and family had limited skill sets and as the company grew, they could not be expected to play the multiple roles required of a growing organization. At this stage, the promoter-entrepreneur should restrict himself to his core skill set. The remaining roles could be 'professionalized', with non-family members taking the roles and 'moving ahead'.

The need for professionalization was also seen in pragmatic terms. A family firm, which was interested in short-term money probably did not need to professionalise; however, if an organization wished to survive and operate in the long-run without its founder, the family or the trusted old-time employees holding key positions, it would need to undertake professionalization. This would reduce the key personnel risks as well, and help in making the company 'independent'.

It was felt that professionalization brought in the discipline for the organization to move on the growth path. It was also seen as necessary for achieving the desired competitive advantage in the industry, besides increasing the company's valuation.

The 'need' for professionalization was thus conceptualised more from the viewpoint of need for professional human resources, than the need for professional competences and/or systems. Such professionals could then act as bridging the gaps in the skill sets available among members of the family and help in scalability and longevity of the organization.

The way to professionalise: The 'How'

One of the family firms studied had recently sold off part of its stake to a private equity firm, which in turn had brought in professionals to run the company. The scion of this company viewed professionalization as creating a blend of professionals, who could seek the promoter family's guidance from time to time, but who would be responsible for having a Business Continuity Plan (BCP) in place.

Besides this, most other firms felt that they were still undertaking the journey towards professionalization. One way to professionalise, according to this group, was to create a second line of management, comprising non-family members from multiple functions. The second line of command would participate in the organisational vision and would be the drivers for change, while the family managers would act as the 'catalysts' for such change.

The next-gen members interviewed also felt that the manner in which the organization could be transformed to a professional organisation could be through recruitment of professionals for particular functional roles facilitating organizational growth. These included the roles of a chief financial officer (CFO) and a chief marketing officer (CMO). With this in place, professionalization was also seen as being implemented through a complete delegation of power and authority.

The next-gen saw professionalization as being achieved by using a combination of technology, standardization of offerings, clarifying job roles and creating a knowledge base, with the goal of ensuring professional work driven by systems and processes as the default mode. This view held that employees in family firms tend not to follow systems and processes not because of their inability to do so, but because of the lack of importance accorded to the same, as also the relative difficulty in implementing such processes in the absence of the required culture. Improvement of such processes then held the key.

MANAGERIALIZATION IN FAMILY FIRMS

Managerialization, distinct from professionalization, refers to the adoption of formal management systems, as well as business practices, especially within the human resource domain, involving selection, compensation and performance evaluation. The study tried to assess the adoption of financial and human control systems, as also HR practices in family firms.

Financial Control systems

Financial control systems, in the form of annual budgets, both at the disaggregated and overall organisational level, exist in case of most family firms. Budget evaluations are undertaken at the end of every financial year to see whether the organisation has under-spent or over-spent. The firm's financial performance is monitored every quarter, if not on a monthly basis. The most important metrics are the cash flows, which are monitored closely. Other metrics used are Return on Equity, Operating Profit, Profit Before Tax (PBT), Profit After Tax (PAT), Return on Investment (ROI), Debtors over 90 days, Return on Assets (ROA) and Net Profit per employee. The next-gen noted that where there are multiple divisions within the family business, metrics used may include comparisons of the respective overheads versus the turnover ratio. They may also assess the individual contributions to the bottom line.

The meetings to discuss financial performance are restricted to family members in most cases, with optimization of taxes the chief concern of such financial control, besides strategizing for growth. In the case of larger family firms which have diversified businesses, senior business heads may be involved in the evaluation of financial performance. However, the deciding authority remains vested with family members.

Human Control Systems

All family firms studied had formal recruitment, training and performance evaluation systems for non-family employees and fairly decentralized authority. However, a differential approach was followed in the treatment of family versus non-family managers. All respondents were in almost complete agreement over the fact that there was no performance -based compensation or performance evaluation of family (member) managers on an annual basis, while the same was done for non-family managers and employees *(Refer to Table 2 on Pg. 63).*

Extant family business literature suggests that family firms in their initial life-cycle stages (founder-entrepreneur stage) are more likely to be characterised by informal managerial systems, little planning and coordination activities, and centralized decision-making processes (Songini, 2006). However, our study reveals that as the next generation enters the business, while there are positive developments in human control systems, with the setting up of human resource teams responsible for HR processes and documentation, the 'family' influence still looms large. What is considered as a desirable practice for non-family managers is not seen as necessary for family managers.

Extant literature also contains a reference to a specific kind of agency conflict arising within family firms due to "different interests of dominant (family) and minority (non-family) shareholders, different roles played by family members, asymmetric altruism, and conflicts between owners and lenders" (Songini et al., 2015, p. 89). Within the family firms studied, there seems to be little evidence of intra-family agency conflicts of this type however. Thus, all respondents agreed that the relationship with the Family Head did not determine the compensation received by family members on a monthly basis. The lack of such agency conflicts may also have to do with the fact that most family firms studied are only the second generation.

Non-Family involvement in Governance Mechanisms

As regards our analysis of non-family involvement in governance systems and mechanisms, we exclude Family Firm 10 (FF10) for analysis, since the family recently sold a significant stake to a global private equity firm. Besides Family Firm 10, most other family firms are clearly those with large family involvement in ownership, management and governance. In most family firms, the Board of Directors comprises largely family members. There are a few firms where external members are present in the Board. Such external members however are those connected to the family and seen as friends. Most family firms do not have a non-family CEO. In fact, non-family managers are not employed at levels higher than that of family managers, even though most family firms attest to the fact that non-family professionals are employed in high positions within the business.

Most family firms did not have a formal family board, which could help coordinate the interests of the family members with that of the family business at the corporate board level. The absence of a formal family board could be because of most of the family firms were in the second generation.

CONCLUSIONS

This study explored the dimensions of professionalization and managerialization in family firms especially after the induction of the next-generation into the family businesses. The results suggest that the induction of the next-generation into family firms is associated with a change in the way family firms view the issues of professionalization and managerialization. The study shows that the next -gen does consider professionalization as critical to scaling up and business longevity. However, the scions do not equate professionalization with the mere hiring of professionals. They see it a means of adopting systems and processes and involving a mindset change.

Similarly, within managerialization, family firms have moved in the direction of putting finance control systems in place. While HR practices and mechanisms have also been put in place to select, recruit, train, evaluate and compensate non-family managers, family firms have not been able to overcome the bias between family and non-family human resources, which may hamper talent attraction and retention.

The results of this study may be of interest to research scholars and practitioners in the domain of family business, besides being of interest to controlling families and management professionals. The study confirms the multi-dimensional view of professionalization held by scions of family firms. While most scions see professionalization as a necessary condition for scaling up, not all are convinced about the need for hiring professionals. They would need to understand that the family influence led bias in treating non-family members and the existence of differential systems and processes for family managers versus non-family managers may prevent talent from getting on-boarded.

The study may offer valuable advice to professionals wishing to join family firms. The study shows that they will need to work hard to demonstrate the same levels of commitment and passion as owners. Professionals may also need to understand that delegation of authority may remain restricted largely to operational/functional roles and strategic decision-making, especially financial decision making and controls, may continue to rest with the family members.

The study may also provide valuable insights to family firm advisors to understand the apparent contradictions in family firms which seek to transition into professionally managed firms, through integrating professionals into their management teams and implementing systems and processes within family firms. They can use the study to escort family firms through such transition from family owned and managed to family owned and professionally managed firms.

With professionalization and managerialization acting a key success factor in the growth of family firms, this study may indicate the path that the next-generation will need to take to ensure the success of these strategies.

Table 1. Demographics of The Family Firms and Scions Studied

Characteristic	FF1	FF2	FF3	FF4	FF5	FF6	FF7	FF8	FF9	FF10
Personal Information										
Age of the scion	32	38	26	24	29	38	36	36	35	35
Years in Business	10	5	9	7	5	16	10	12	12	14
Generation to which respondent belongs	2nd	2nd	2nd	2nd	2nd	3rd	2nd	3rd	3rd	2nd
Business Information										
Type of Business	Manufacturing, service	Service & Manufacturing	Service	Real Estate, Manufacturing	Manufacturing, Construction & Trading	Manufacturing	Manufacturing	Manufacturing	Manufacturing	Manufacturing
Age of Business (in years)	7	35	19	9 (They had a steel trading business prior to this)	28	45	30	35	90	40
No. of employees	250	76 (services) + 550 (Mfg)	15	350	200	180	55	3500	180	600
No. of locations where business present	1	4	1	5	2	3, Also multiple sales/service offices pan India	2	11	2	8
Status of the business	Small (MSME)	Medium	Micro (MSME)	Small (MSME)	Medium	Small (MSME)	Medium (MSME)	Large	Small (MSME)	Large

Table 2. Human Control Systems, Business Practices and Decentralization of Authority

Human Control Systems	FF1	FF2	FF3	FF4	FF5	FF6	FF7	FF8	FF9	FF10
Presence of formal recruitment system	Agree	Neutral	Neutral	Strongly agree	Strongly agree	Agree	Agree	Agree	Agree	Strongly agree
Presence of a formal training system	Agree	Neutral	Disagree	Strongly agree	Agree	Neutral	Agree	Neutral	Agree	Neutral
Presence of a system of performance-based incentive pay for non-family members	Agree	Agree	Disagree	Strongly agree	Agree	Agree	Agree	Neutral	Agree	Agree
Presence of a performance-based compensation for family members	Disagree	Disagree	Disagree	Disagree	Agree	Disagree	Disagree	Disagree	Strongly Disagree	Strongly Disagree
Presence of a regular (annual) performance evaluation system for non-family employees	Agree	Agree	Disagree	Agree	Agree	Agree	Agree	Agree	Agree	Neutral
Presence of a regular (annual) performance evaluation system for family employees	Disagree	Neutral	Disagree	Neutral	Neutral	Neutral	Disagree	Disagree	Strongly Disagree	Strongly Disagree
Presence of formal scheduled staff meetings regularly	Agree	Strongly agree	Strongly agree	Neutral	Strongly agree	Agree	Agree	Agree	Agree	Strongly Agree
Differential compensation of different family members based on their relationship with the Family Head	Strongly Disagree	Neutral	Agree	Strongly Disagree	Strongly Disagree	Disagree	Strongly Disagree	Disagree	Strongly Disagree	Strongly Disagree
All business decision-making rests with 1-2 individuals (senior family members)	Disagree	Agree	Agree	Strongly Disagree	Neutral	Disagree	Agree	Disagree	Disagree	Disagree
All authority rests with 1-2 individuals (senior family members)	Disagree	Agree	Disagree	Strongly Disagree	Neutral	Disagree	Strongly agree	Disagree	Disagree	Disagree

Table 3. Non-Family Involvement in Governance Control Systems

Governance Control Systems	FF1	FF2	FF3	FF4	FF5	FF6	FF7	FF8	FF9	FF10
Board of Directors largely comprises of family members.	Agree	Strongly Agree	Strongly Agree	agree	Agree	Strongly Agree	Strongly Agree	Neutral	Agree	Strongly Disagree
There is presence of external members in the Board of Directors	Disagree	Disagree	Disagree	Agree	Strongly Agree	Disagree	Disagree	Agree	Disagree	Strongly Agree
High Family involvement in the management of the business	Strongly Agree	Strongly Agree	Agree	Agree	Strongly Agree	Agree	Agree	Agree	Agree	Disagree
Family involvement only in ownership, management is left to professionals.	Disagree	Strongly Disagree	Disagree	Neutral	Neutral	Strongly Disagree	Disagree	Neutral	Disagree	Neutral
Employment of non-family professionals (managers/supervisors) in responsible positions in the family business	Strongly Agree	Strongly Agree	Strongly Agree	Agree	Strongly Agree	Agree	Disagree	Strongly Agree	Agree	Strongly Agree
Employment of professionals at same/higher levels than family managers within the family business	Disagree	Disagree	Disagree	Neutral	Neutral	Agree	Disagree	Agree	Disagree	Strongly Agree
Non-family CEO in the family business	Disagree	Neutral	Strongly Agree	Disagree	Disagree	Disagree	Disagree	Neutral	Agree	Strongly Agree

REFERENCES

Dekker, J., Lybaert, N., Steijvers, T. and Depaire, B. (2015). "The effect of family business professionalization as a multidimensional construct on firm performance", *Journal of Small Business Management*, Vol. 53, No. 2, pp. 516–538.

Dekker, J. C., Lybaert, N., Steijvers, T., Depaire, B. and Mercken, R. (2012). "Family firm types based on the professionalization construct: Exploratory research", *Family Business Review*, Vol. 26, No. 1, pp. 81–99.

Eisenhardt, K.M. (1989). "Building theories from case study research", *Academy of Management Review*, Vol. 14, No. 4, pp. 532–550.

Gimeno, A. and Parada, M. (2014). "Professionalization of the family business: Decision making domains", In P. Sharma, P. Sieger, R. Nason, A. Cristina, & K. Ramachandran (Eds.), *Exploring Transgenerational Entrepreneurship Research: The role of Resources and Capabilities.* Northampton, MA: Edward Elgar Publishing Inc.

Hiebl, M. R.W. (2013). "Non family CEOS in family businesses: Do they fit?", *The Journal of Business Strategy*, Vol. 34, No. 2, pp. 45-51

Klein, S. and Bell, F.-A. (2007). "Non-family executives in family businesses: A literature review", *Electronic Journal of Family Business Studies*, Vol. 1, No. 1, pp. 19–37.

Madison, K., Daspit, J. J., Turner, K. and Kellermanns, F. W. (2018). "Family firm human resource practices: Investigating the effects of professionalization and bifurcation bias on performance", *Journal of Business Research*, Elsevier, Vol. 84(C), pp. 327-336.

Petrolo, D., Gnan, L., Voordeckers, W. and Lambrechts, F. (2019). "Defining Professionalization and Managerialization in Family Firms: A Bibliometric Analysis and Systematic Literature Review", Fourteenth International Conference on European

Integration –InnovatingEurope. https://pdfs.semanticscholar.org/d569/d9840dded7b67acccf6bcad88a0154610570.pdf

Songini, L. (2006). *The professionalization of family firms: theory and practice. Handbook of research on family business.* Cheltenham: Edward Elgar.

Songini, L., Morelli, C., Gnan, L. and Vola, P. (2015). "The why and how of managerialization of family businesses: evidences from Italy", *Piccola Impresa/Small Business,* Vol.1, pp. 86-115.

Stewart, A. and Hitt, M. A. (2012). "Why can't a family business be more like a nonfamily business? Modes of professionalization in family firms", *Family Business Review,* Vol. 25, No. 1, pp.58–86.

Thomas, D.R. (2006). "A general inductive approach for analyzing qualitative evaluation data", *American Journal of Evaluation,* Vol. 27, No. 2, pp. 237-46.

2.2 Self Help Groups and youth empowerment: A Study of Union Territory of Jammu and Kashmir

Dr. Syed Javed Iqbal Kamili and Prof. (Dr) Mohi Ud Din Sangmi

"In my experience, poor people are the world's greatest entrepreneurs. Every day, they must innovate in order to survive. They remain poor because they do not have the opportunities to turn their creativity into sustainable income"

Mohammad Yunus

ABSTRACT

There is an emerging need to promote youth empowerment through skill development. SHGs are proving effective in empowering women and transforming lives and as a result enhancing self-reliance, replicating them among youths could also yield positive results. The government of India has allocated funds to youths who are finding it convenient to join groups and access government funds. This study provides an enhanced understanding of SHG Scheme in Union Territory of Jammu and Kashmir.

Keywords: *Microfinance, Empowerment, Self-Help Group, Youth*

INTRODUCTION

The gap between penury and opulence is increasing day in, day out and the world is seriously contemplating to minimize the gap and to reach to those who have not been reached yet by the formal financial institutions. In this backdrop, microfinance has been accepted as a viable approach and accepted across the globe. Microfinance is a small loan that helps poor people inclined to start or expand their small business. It is helping millions of poor people, especially poor rural women, with tiny loans so that they can start small business, create self-employment and improve their lives. It is the supply of loans, savings and other financial services to the poor. (Khan A Nafees 2010). After the successful launch of Grameen Bank in Bangladesh, microfinance got impetus. It is spreading very fast across the globe. It provides financial services such as credit, savings and insurance for low-income clients that are being considered an indispensable tool to fight poverty. It has been evolving as an economic development approach intended to benefit low-income women and men. The term refers to the provision of financial services to low-income clients including the self-employed (Lilitha N 2003). If poor people have access to financial services, they can earn more, build their assets and cushion themselves against external shocks. Poor households use microfinance to move from everyday survival to planning for the future. They invest in better nutrition, housing, health and education which are key indicators of socio-economic empowerment (Kureel and Gazala (2015).

The World Bank estimates that 1.4 billion people worldwide live on less than $1.25 a day and in this scenery of penury, the philanthropist and altruist's contemplation across the globe made a significant development to reach the penurious class to reduce poverty and bring them under the umbrella of national economies and in this respect, microfinance emerged as an important tool to fight poverty. It is a form of service such as saving and uncollateralized credit extended to the poor. It has been lauded as a powerful vehicle for reducing global poverty and empowering women. From its inception in the 1970s with the Grameen Bank in Bangladesh, it has continued to be the primary instrument to reduce poverty. In countries around the world NGOs, governments and private individuals supply funds to around 7000 domestic MFIs that have expanded their outreach from a few thousand clients from 1970s to over 150 million beneficiaries today by some estimates. For poverty alleviation the world has now established microfinance an indispensable tool and in this connection countries around the world are in serious deliberation for reducing poverty through microfinance sources and over the last few decades the microfinance field has stretched out substantially. Considering microfinance an in-dispensable tool to reduce poverty, countries across the globe created various schemes and microfinance models to fight poverty and the achievements are significant. In Bangladesh, 48% poor households rose above the poverty line when provided access to micro finance. Additionally, 5% of the Grameen Bank graduated out of poverty each year by participating in micro finance programmes (Kandker, 2003). In Brazil almost 1.5 million people work in the informal sector as micro-entrepreneurs, and of them, 93% run profitable business with micro-credit (Murdoc & Haley 2001). In Bolivia, micro-credit loan clients doubled their income in two years. They were more likely to access health care and send their children to school with the help of micro-credit (Mosley & Paul, 2011).

International micro finance is related with providing institutional financial services to the deprived community of the whole world, commonly termed as poor. The microfinance aims at providing several financial services to the poor people. The services of micro finance include microcredit, micro savings, and micro insurance and so on. Again, microfinance also encourages micro enterprise, micro banking and micro business. In today's modern world the alleviation of poverty is a primary concern of every nation. Again, the developing countries across the world are facing a real challenge in this respect. The inflation and several other factors are also adding to this problem. In such a situation, the international micro finance proves to be of great help. The basic conception of microfinance is to extend the financial facilities to the poorest of the poor. These people do not have the proper employment and not even any property to produce as collateral to the banks against which the commercial banks can provide any kind of financial help. On the other hand, the banks are also not interested in processing small loans because the cost of such loans is high in comparison to other loans. The risks involved in these loans are assumed to be very high. Through micro-finance, poor people are provided with financial loans on very easy terms and nominal interest rate. Through this financial assistance these people are doing very well and the whole scenario of these countries is changing very rapidly. Another important factor is the repayment rates of these loans are very high. The microfinance assistance is very helpful in providing practical solutions to the problems like housing and urban services.

Microfinance in Asian Countries

The Asian region is comprised of seven countries in East Asia and five in South Asia, covering the bulk of the microfinance market in the region. From fourth place in 2011, Asia now ranks third among the five microscopic regions in overall score, mainly owing to substantial improvements in the *Supporting Institutional Framework* scores. It is encouraging that Asia has produced two big Micro Financial Models that include Grameen Bank in Bangladesh *(founder Prof Mohd Yunus who received Nobel Prize in 2006)* and SHG Bank-Linkage Model by NABARD in India who achieved the status for the creation of largest number of SHGs in the World. At present, Asia as a whole improved only slightly in *Regulatory Framework and Practices*, ranking third behind Sub-Saharan Africa and East Asia. On average, East Asia's regional score is higher than South Asia. Asia's political stability scores experienced a significant drop in Vietnam, India and Bangladesh, placing the region in second to last place, ahead of only the Middle East and North Africa. India, in particular, is still recovering from a full-blown crisis within the microfinance sector of Andhra Pradesh[1] (AP)—the most important MF market both in terms of outreach and portfolio— that began in October 2010.

Microfinance in India

Like other countries, particularly in developing countries, where microfinance has been taken as an indispensable tool to fight the poverty, many gigantic institutions in India took the responsibility upon their shoulders to reach the deprived class particularly the ones living in extreme conditions of poverty. Major initiatives came in 1969 by

---

[1] Andhra Pradesh is the Southeast coast of Indian Peninsula that suffered crises due to series of suicides by borrowers of microfinance beneficiaries in the year 2010 because of the exorbitant rate of interest by microfinance profitable institutions.

nationalization of commercial banks bank branches got extended in the rural area. India has over 35,000 rural branches of commercial banks and regional rural banks and around 15,000 cooperative bank branches to bring the people under the purview of banking system.

SHG Bank-Linkage Program and its progress in India

At present microfinance in India is being experimented with the help of different models and various schemes. One of the successful approaches of reducing poverty and reaching the penurious class is based on SHG-bank linkage model and SGSY Schemes. The breakthrough of Indian poverty alleviation is seen when NABARD presented SHG-bank linkage model which created the largest number of SHGs in the world. With model beginning by financing 255 SHGs during 1992-93, the program reached 620 SHGs in 1994-95 (Ratna Kishore 2011). Since then, the programme has been progressing and cumulative number of SHGs finance increased from 4.61 lakhs in 2002 to 10.73 lakhs in 2004 and further to 29.25 lakhs in 2007. As on March 2001, these were more than 61 lakhs saving linked SHGs and more than 42 lakhs credit linked SHGs which covers about 8.6 million SHGs crore household in India (Sangmi & Kamili, 2010. At present 59.6 million SHGs are currently linked with banks and 267 million are borrowers. The present growth rate of outreach SHGs during 2009 -10 has reached to 8.5% with 18% growth rate of MFIs to reach to the Indian poor. Loan outstanding with SHGs has remained 272.66 lakhs by the end of March 2010. The increase in number of SHGs has resulted in the increase in the flow of institutional credit to the weaker sections of population. The significant success of the programme was due to active involvement of 700 NGO's, 27 public sector commercial banks, 28 private sec-tor commercial banks, 86 regional rural banks, 31 state cooperative banks, 371 district central cooperative banks as well as policy support from the Government of India, Reserve Bank of India, increased participation from State Government and capacity building of partner agencies by NABARD (Khan, 2010). With the tremendous progress of Grameen Bank Model to empower women and most vulnerable strata of population, the concept of group lending got impetus and in recent years, the self-help group concept gained distinction in various developing countries. In Indonesia Bank of Rakyat (RBI), in Thailand Bank of Agriculture and Agriculture Cooperatives (BAAC), in Bangladesh Grameen Bank and Bangladesh Rural Advancement Committee (BRAC), in Malaysia Amanah Iktiar Malaysia (AIM) and in Nepal Agricultural Development Bank (ADBN), all these have shown a significant progress in poverty alleviation programmes with respect to income and employment generation and have distributed millions of dollars among various microfinance beneficiaries.

In India, the adaption of the new microfinance approach by rural financial institutions assumed the form of the "Self Help Group – Bank Linkage program." After an initial pilot study[2], the RBI set up a working group that recommended for internalization of SHG concept as a potential intervention tool in the area of banking with the poor. The RBI was quick to accept the recommendations and advised the banks to consider mainstreaming lending to SHGs as part of their rural credit operations. The SHG-Bank linkage program is gaining increasing acceptance amongst NGO community and bankers. The NABARD envisions covering one third of the rural population in India by establishing more one million SHGs. Under the SHG bank linkage program, NGOs and banks interact with the poor, especially women, to form small homogeneous groups. These small groups are encouraged to meet frequently and collect small thrift amounts from their members and are taught simple accounting methods to enable them to maintain accounts. Although individually these poor could never have enough savings to open a bank account, the pooled savings enable them to open a formal bank account in the name of the group. This is the first step in establishing links with formal banking system. Groups then, meet often and use the pooled thrift to impart small loans to members for meeting their small emergent needs. This saves them from usurious debt traps and thus begins their empowerment through group dynamics, decision-making and funds management. Gradually

---

[2] A Pilot Study on 500 SHGs of poor during the year 1992-93 for financial assistance has now become the largest micro-finance programme in the world.

the pooled thrift grows and soon they are ready to use for SHGs for their empowerment. The SBLP has now completed more than 21 years of existence. The Self-Help Group-Bank Linkage Programme (SBLP) was originated in GTZ-sponsored project in Indonesia. NABARD has set up a task force with the APRACA[3] to identify the existence of SHGs. Starting from a modest scale as a pilot in the year 1992, the SHG-Bank linkage programme has turned into a solid structure with more than 73.18 lakh savings-linked Self-Help Groups (SHGs) covering over 9.50 crore poor households as on 31 March 2013. The total savings of these SHGs with banks amounted to Rs. 8,217.25 crores. The number of credit-linked SHGs under the programme stood at 44.51 lakh. NABARD expended a sum of Rs. 50.44 crore during 2012-13 from Micro Finance Development and Equity Fund and Women Self Help Group Development Fund for various micro finance related activities such as formation and linkage of SHGs through SHPIs, training and capacity building of stake-holders, livelihood promotion, documentation and awareness etc.

NABARD continued to extend support to NGOs, RRBs, CCBs, Farmers Clubs[4] and Individual Rural Volunteers (IRVs) for promoting and nurturing SHGs. During 2013-14, grant assistance of Rs. 36.33 crore was sanctioned to these agencies. The cumulative assistance sanctioned to various agencies was Rs. 262.83 crore for promoting 7.46 lakh SHGs. Cumulative assistance of Rs. 79.04 crore was released for formation of 4.99 lakh SHGs as on 31 March 2014. The NGOs were the most dominant SHPI[5], forming more than 3.79 lakh SHGs. Grant assistance of Rs. 76.74 crore was sanctioned for promotion of 3.99 lakh JLGs across the country as on 31 March 2014. During 2013-14, Rs. 1,392.58 crores were disbursed by banks to around 1.29 lakh JLGs and the cumulative loan disbursement as on 31 March 2014 was Rs. 6,075.91 crores to 6.58 lakh JLGs.

---

[3] Asia-Pacific Rural and Agricultural Credit Association
[4] Farmers Clubs are organized by rural branches of banks with the support and financial assistance of NABARD for mutual benefit of the banks concerned and the village farming community/rural poor.
[5] Self Help Group Promoting Institutions, to promote and facilitate credit linkage of Self Help Groups with banks and provide continuous hand holding support.

Microfinance and Self-Help Groups

Self-Help Group (SHG) is an organization formed by members of the same socio-economic status, usually low-income households having similar objectives, aims and aspirations. All members of the group belong to families below poverty line. Group members usually create a common fund by contributing their small savings on a regular basis. They are unemployed and belong to the low-income households' lack access and ownership of property hence, the need for empowerment. Group evolves flexible system of working sometimes with the help of Self-Help Promotion Institutions and manage pooled resources in a democratic manner. As women were the main founders, these groups were mainly associated with women but SHGs are no longer a domain of women, due to economic repression in developing countries. Presently youths and male adults are joining these groups for empowerment purposes. SHG is generally an economically homogeneous group promoted and created with the help of VLWs[6], NGOs and officials of DRDAs[7]. They usually start by making voluntary thrift on a regular basis, which are a form of contractual savings ought to function democratically and accountably to achieve a common goal. Members support each other in solving common problems, share resources and find solutions together. SHGs broadly have three stages of evolution viz. (a) Group formation to evolve into a self-managed people's organization at grassroots level (b) Linkage with banks and capital formation through the revolving fund, skill development for management and activity and (c) Taking an economic activity for income generation. The SHG concept emerged

---

[6] Village Level Workers

[7] District Rural Development Agencies has traditionally been the principal organ at the district level to oversee the implementation of anti-poverty programmes of the Ministry of Rural Development. This agency was created originally to implement the Integrated Rural Development Programme (IRDP). Subsequently the DRDAs were entrusted with number of programmes of both state and central governments. From April 1999 a separate DRDA Administration has been introduced to take care of the administrative costs. The aim is to strengthen DRDAs and make them more professional in managing the anti-poverty programmes and be an effective link between the ministry and the district level.

from Bangladesh after the inception of Grameen Bank. Though, it is also observed that such groups were also created in Kenya and Vietnam. In the areas of urban development and housing, self-help takes the form of neighbourhood groups, tenant groups, slum development committees and so on whereas in rural development, it is through credit groups, development committees, user groups etc. Group oriented efforts in the form of micro-credit groups in different countries of Latin America, Africa and Asia are examples of current self-help efforts. The famous Grameen groups in Bangladesh and the Self-help groups (SHGs) in countries like Thailand, Nepal, Sri Lanka and India are forms of micro-credit groups. (Tapan Neeta 2010)

SCOPE OF THE STUDY

The Union Territory of Jammu and Kashmir is having huge problems of unemployment due to which the government has launched many programmes so as to involve the youth in these programs to generate employment. The present study gives emphasis to the Self-Help Group scheme introduced in the Union Territory of Jammu and Kashmir so that our youth can aspire to being job seekers and job creators.

OBJECTIVES

The study has been conducted mainly to:

- To analyse the impact of microfinance on SHGs.
- To analyse the emphasis of SHGs in Jammu and Kashmir.

METHODOLOGY

The study is focused on primary and secondary data sources. The primary data was collected by administering a questionnaire to 50 youths who were assisted by the government under various Skill Development Programmes. The secondary data was collected from various published and unpublished sources from various journals, magazines, articles and media reports and from various departments including the department of census, department of economics and statistics, district commissioner's office. Keeping in view the set objectives, this research design was adopted to have greater accuracy and in-depth analysis of the research study. Available secondary data from Convenor of Union Territory Level Banker's Committee (UTLBC) in UT of Jammu and Kashmir was extensively used for the study.

DATA ANALYSIS

A great progress is observed under SHG Scheme in Union Territory of Jammu and Kashmir as of the year 2021 given in the table below. In Public Sector Banks, there are 2757 SHGs formed for all and 2581 SHGs for woman. 2410 SHGs saving linked accounts are present for all in which 2.65 amount is available whereas 2243 SHGs saving linked accounts are present for women in which 2.55 amount is available. 1394 SHGs credit linked accounts are present for all in which 11.37 amount in crores is disbursed whereas 1274 SHGs credit linked account are present for women in which 11.03 amount in crores is disbursed.

In Private Sector Banks, there are 63381 formed for all and 28588 SHGs for woman. 62771 SHGs saving linked accounts are present for all in which 42.88 amount is available whereas 28984 SHGs saving linked accounts are present for women in which 21.22 amount is available. 46615 SHGs credit linked accounts are present for all in which 674.86 amount in crores is disbursed whereas 28550 SHGs credit linked account are present for women in which 398.26 amount in crores is disbursed.

In Regional Rural Banks, there are 10271 SHGs formed for all and 9693 SHGs for woman. 10025 SHGs saving linked accounts are present for all in which 25.13 amount is available whereas 9447 SHGs saving linked accounts are present for women in which 23.37 amount is available. 9006 SHGs credit linked accounts are present for all in which 128.1 amount in crores is disbursed whereas 8487 SHGs credit linked account are present for women in which 119.95 amount in crores is disbursed.

In Cent. /State Coop. Banks, there are 421 SHGs formed for all and 361 SHGs for woman. 421 SHGs saving linked accounts are present for all in which 0.11 amount is available whereas 361 SHGs saving linked accounts are present for women in which 0.10 amount is available. 403 SHGs credit linked accounts are present for all in which 1.4 amount in crores is disbursed whereas 354 SHGs credit linked account are present for women in which 0.77 amount in crores is disbursed.

The grand total is observable as 76830 SHGs formed for all and 41223 SHGs for woman. 75627 SHGs saving linked accounts are present for all in which 70.77 amount is available whereas 41035 SHGs saving linked accounts are present for women in which 47.24 amount is available. 57418 SHGs credit linked accounts are present for all in which 815.73 amount in crores is disbursed whereas 38665 SHGs credit linked account are present for women in which 530.01 amount in crores is disbursed.

Table 1. Cumulative Progress Under Self Help Group (Shg) Scheme As On 31.12.2021 In UT of J&K

Amount Rupees (INR) in Crores

SR.NO	NAME OF BANK	POSITION AS ON 31.12.2021										
		NO OF SHGs FORMED		SHGs SAVING LINKED				SHGs CREDIT LINKED			
		ALL	WOMEN ONLY	ALL NO OF A/Cs	AVAILABLE AMT	WOMEN ONLY NO OF A/Cs	AVAILABLE AMT	ALL NO OF A/Cs	AMOUNT DISBURSED	WOMEN ONLY NO OF A/Cs	AMOUNT DISBURSED
	PUBLIC SECTOR BANKS										
1	SBI	602	602	602	0.77	602	0.77	339	9.35	339	9.35
2	PNB	1772	1689	1426	1.53	1351	1.52	939	0.55	852	0.54
4	CBI	218	151	218	0.24	151	0.18	44	0.56	22	0.36
5	CANARA BANK	74	61	74	0.03	61	0.02	1	0.01	1	0.01
6	P&S BANK	34	28	33	0.05	28	0.03	18	0.17	15	0.14
8	UBI	57	50	57	0.03	50	0.03	53	0.73	45	0.63
11	BOM	0	0	0	0.00	0	0.00	0	0.00	0	0.00
	SUB TOTAL	2757	2581	2410	2.65	2243	2.55	1394	11.37	1274	11.03
	PRIVATE SECTOR BANKS										
13	J&K BANK	63381	28588	62771	42.88	28984	21.22	46615	674.86	28550	398.26
14	ICICI BANK	0	0	0	0.00	0	0.00	0	0.00	0	0.00
15	HDFC BANK	0	0	0	0.00	0	0.00	0	0.00	0	0.00

	SUB TOTAL	63381	28588	62771	42.88	28984	21.22	46615	674.86	28550	398.26
	REGIONAL RURAL BANKS										
24	JKGB	8423	8423	8177	19.18	8177	19.19	7351	99.73	7351	99.73
25	EDB	1848	1270	1848	5.95	1270	4.18	1655	28.37	1136	20.22
	SUB TOTAL	10271	9693	10025	25.13	9447	23.37	9006	128.1	8487	119.95
	CENT./STATE COOP.BANKS										
26	JCCB	262	262	262	0.09	262	0.09	262	0.07	262	0.07
27	BCCB	73	66	73	0.00	66	0.00	73	0.36	66	0.33
28	ACCB	86	33	86	0.02	33	0.01	68	0.97	26	0.37
29	CCB	0	0	0	0	0	0	0	0	0	0
30	JKSCB	0	0	0	0	0	0	0	0	0	0
	SUB TOTAL	421	361	421	0.11	361	0.10	403	1.4	354	0.77
	GRAND TOTAL	76830	41223	75627	70.77	41035	47.24	57418	815.73	38665	530.01

Source: Convenor of Union Territory Level Banker's Committee (UTLBC) in UT of Jammu and Kashmir

DISCUSSION

Empowerment is to give authority and enable a person or group of persons to gain power in order to make one's voice heard, to control one's own greed, power to nurture, heal, care for others, power to fight for justice, ethics, morality, power to achieve inner growths leading to wisdom and compassion. Youth empowerment provides enabling environment for youths to develop their true potentials so that they can contribute to the development of the society. The major instrument needed to empower youths is education. It can be regarded as an attitudinal, structural and cultural process whereby young people gain the ability, authority and confidence to make decisions and implement change in their own lives and the lives of other people including both youth and adults. It gives them hope for tomorrow in that their skills are sharpened and hence allowing them to access the future economic opportunities. They have increased interpersonal power to influence their future. It is about supporting to bring change and increasing opportunities thereby enable the potentials of these youth to be realized.

Microfinance plays a significant role in developing women across the globe. Women make up a large proportion of microfinance beneficiaries. Traditionally, women (especially those in underdeveloped countries) have been unable to readily participate in economic activity. Microfinance provides women with the financial backing they need to start business ventures and actively participate in the economy. It gives them confidence, improves their status and makes them more active in decision-making, thus encouraging gender equality.

REFERENCES

Baljit Singh. (1983). Economics of Indian Education. New Delhi: Meenakshi Prakashan

CS Nagpal and AC Mittal. (1993). Economics of education. New Delhi: Anmol Publications

Daryl Collins, Jonathan Morduch, Stuart Rutherford and Orlanda Ruthven (2009). Portfolio's of the poor: How the world's poor live on $ 2 a day. Princeton: Princeton university press,

Doan Tinh, Gibson John and Holmes Mark. (2014). "Impact of household credit on education and healthcare spending by the poor in Peri-Urban areas, Vietnam." *Journal of Southeast Asian Economies* 31, no.1

Epstein, Marc J and Yuthas, Kristi (2012). "Redefining education in the developing world." *Stanford Social Innovation Review* 10, no.1

Gow, Kathryn M. (2001). "How access to microfinance and education through technology can alleviate poverty in third world countries." *International Journal of Economic Development* 3, no.1

Pham, Thi Thu Tra and Nguyen, Kien Son. (2019). "Does microcredit influence parent's decision to send child to school or to work? Evidence from Vietnamese rural households." *The Journal of Developing Areas* 53, no. 3

2.3 Assessment of Financial Literacy across various Demographic Groups in India

Ms. Sana Bala and Prof. Farooq Ahmad Shah

ABSTRACT

Financial literacy may be understood as the ability of an individual to understand various finance related concepts which enable him/her to make informed decisions with respect to management of personal finances. Besides the financial knowledge, yet another important component of financial literacy is applying the financial knowledge through appropriate behaviour in effective management of financial resources and to avoid financial distress. Hence, the term financial literacy mainly has two components- financial knowledge and financial behaviour.

Financial literacy has assumed tremendous importance in the contemporary times as it has been linked with various positive outcomes like savings, retirement planning, debt management etc. Financially literate individuals are less likely to get trapped in financial frauds. It is being regarded as an important skill in the contemporary times which helps individuals to navigate through prevalent complex financial landscape. Keeping in view the benefits of financial literacy, attempts are being made by governments and various institutions globally to improve the level of financial literacy among the populations. In line with these efforts, a lot of academic interest has evoked with regard to this concept. A number of surveys have been conducted world over to assess the financial literacy levels among the populations. The empirical data from these surveys has consistently revealed prevalence of poor financial literacy across the globe particularly among the developing countries (see, for example; Van Rooij et al. (2011); Atkinson and Messy (2012); Klapper et al. (2012); Kebede and Kuar (2015); Naidu (2017); Garg and Singh (2018); Grohmann (2018) and Niu et al. (2020). In the Indian context, however, the scenario is particularly dismal as financial literacy levels among Indian masses are even lower when compared to global averages (see, for example; S&P Global FinLit Survey,

2014; VISA International Financial Literacy Barometer, 2012; Mastercard's Financial Literacy Index, 2013). The present study has been conducted in this backdrop. The main aim was to assess the financial literacy levels among individual investors in India and to assess if financial literacy has an impact on financial well-being.

The study has been conducted on a sample of 1100 individuals investors in India. The sample was chosen to give adequate representation to various socio-demographic groups. Financial literacy measurement instrument used in the study consisted of 22 items covering two dimensions- financial knowledge and financial behaviour. The findings of the study revealed that financial literacy levels among the individual investors in North India are not satisfactory with only 10.8% respondents scoring high on financial knowledge. Females, elderly (above 55 years age), youngsters (below 35 years age), lower income groups and those living in rural areas exhibit particularly low levels of financial literacy.

Keywords: Financial literacy, financial behaviour, personal finance,

FINANCIAL LITERACY- AN INTRODUCTION

Financial literacy is a frequently used term in the area of personal finance. It may be understood as the ability of an individual to understand various finance related concepts in order to make informed decisions with respect to management of personal finances. Mere possession of financial knowledge doesn't make an individual financially literate. An important component of financial literacy is applying the financial knowledge through appropriate behaviour in effective management of financial resources and to avoid financial distress. The term financial literacy is wider in scope and encompasses the knowledge of financial matters, behaviour, attitude and perception of an individual towards financial matters. However, in the literature the term is interchangeably used with terms like financial education, financial capability, debt literacy, financial knowledge, and economic literacy

Financial literacy among individuals is considered as a key factor in making informed financial decisions which would help them in improving their financial position. It is therefore regarded as a life skill. Financial literacy is often related to positive outcomes like savings, retirement planning, debt management etc. Besides this, financially literate individuals are less likely to get trapped in financial frauds. Financially educated consumers are considered as a pre-requisite in to ensure that a vital contribution is made by the financial sector to the economic growth and also in alleviating the poverty. Given these benefits associated with financial literacy, the concept has gained a lot of significance particularly in contemporary times marked with complex financial landscape and manifold increase in the number of financial products available.

Importance of Financial Literacy

Financial literacy has assumed immense importance in the contemporary times. As a matter of fact, there are many factors that have added to the significance of financial literacy and made it a centre of attention especially for researchers. Over the years, there has been a tremendous increase in the number and type of financial products available in the market. As a result, the financial landscape is becoming increasingly complex and thus it is imperative for an individual to have knowledge about the basic financial concepts so as to be able to operate in such a complex environment. Xu and Zia (2012) state that the main goal of organizing financial literacy programmes is to ensure that individuals can easily comprehend the basics of myriad number of financial products that are available in the contemporary times and make sound financial decisions. Remund (2010) and Mandell and Klein (2009) opine that for making investment decisions, an individual must understand the terminology associated with various financial products. As a matter of fact, the increasing complexity of the financial markets coupled with the deregulation has made financial decision-making tricky particularly for the financially unsophisticated individuals. Al-Tamimi (2009) state that due to these developments in financial markets, the importance of improving financial literacy has increased manifold. Highlighting the importance of financial literacy, Lusardi (2008) states that given the complexity of financial environment, it is impossible for an individual to operate efficiently without being financially literate.

Almenberg and Save-Soderbergh (2011) point out that in the contemporary times there has been a shift in decision making power from the government and employers to the individuals themselves This change has been brought in through liberalization of markets and introduction of various structural reforms in pension schemes. It is in this context that the MetLife Study (2011) and Rooij et al. (2011) conclude that the responsibility for financial well-being now lies largely with the individuals themselves. The individuals are therefore required to actively manage their own finances which cannot be achieved without having financial knowledge.

Experts assert that the increased emphasis on financial literacy emerged in the backdrop of the sub-prime mortgage crisis which is largely attributed to the financial unsophistication on the part of investors (see, for example; Debbich, 2015; Gerardi et al., 2010; Mandell and Klein, 2009). Mandell and Hanson (2009). Mandell and Klein (2009) raise concerns that the inability on the part of the individuals to make self-beneficial financial decisions not only harms an individual's interest but also entails negative consequences for the economy in general.

In the Indian context, financial literacy has become all the more important as it may prove highly beneficial in providing spurt to economic growth and help in achieving financial inclusion which is being aggressively pursued by the government. Financial literacy infuses confidence in an individual to easily navigate complex array of financial products available in the market and make a prudent investment decision. The goal of financial inclusion can also be achieved by improving the financial awareness among the individuals. To bring the individuals within the ambit of formal financial system, it is necessary to acquaint them with the basic financial education. Given the importance of financial literacy, the government through various institutions is making interventions at multiple levels to improve financial education levels among the masses as it would not only benefit individuals but also prove highly rewarding for the overall economy.

Schmeiser and Seligman (2013) point out that poor financial knowledge and money management skills among individuals remain a cause of concern among policy-makers as they deem them important for ensuring financial security. Jappelli and Padula (2013) state that the benefits of that improving financial literacy levels would also yield outcomes liked increased savings among individuals and improve financial security. Huston (2010) stresses that in current complex financial scenario financial literacy is increasingly being acknowledged as a core skill among consumers essential for making personal financial decisions. For the same reason the concept has evoked a lot of academic interest. A lot of research has been focused on measuring financial literacy and suggesting means for its improvement.

Despite all this, a little attention has been given to developing standardized measures of financial literacy and academic literature lacks a unanimously accepted definition for the concept. Infact as pointed out by Huston (2010), majority of research studies done in this area (72%) lacked a definition of financial literacy. Schmeiser and Seligman (2013) and Remund, (2010) state that owing to this, organisations as well as individuals doing research in this area continue to use the definitions and measures of financial literacy developed on their own as a standard definition and measurement approach for same is not available in the literature. Across literature, financial literacy is interchangeably used with terms like financial education, financial knowledge and financial sophistication, financial competency and an explicit definition is lacking as confirmed by many studies (see, for example; Aren and Aydemir, 2014; Huston, 2010; Al-Tamimi, 2009; Moore, 2003)

Financial Literacy scenario in India

Keeping in view the significance of financial literacy, governments and institutions across the globe endeavor to improve financial literacy levels among the masses. However, such interventions can be made only after an assessment of currently prevalent financial literacy levels among the individuals. In this regard, a number of surveys have been carried out across the world to measure financial literacy levels among the populations. These surveys mainly conclude that the overall financial literacy levels across the globe are low. In the Indian context, however, the scenario is particularly dismal as financial literacy levels among Indian masses are even lower when compared to global averages (see, for example; S&P Global FinLit Survey, 2014; VISA International Financial Literacy Barometer, 2012; Mastercard's Financial Literacy Index, 2013).

Standard and Poor, world's leading provider of independent credit risk research and benchmarks, conducted an extensive research across 140 countries in 2014, covering 1,50,000 adults to get an insight into financial literacy scenario across the globe. The findings of the survey reveal that three quarters of Asian adults and two-thirds of worldwide adults do not possess financial literacy.

Among the Asian countries, Singapore reportedly has the highest percentage of financially literate adults (59 percent), followed by Hong Kong and Japan (both with 43 percent). China fares poorly with less than one-third of adults being financially literate. In the Indian context, 76% of the Indian adults were found to be lacking understanding of key financial concepts like risk diversification, inflation and compound interest. This places India way below the worldwide average of financial literacy though almost at par with other South Asian and BRICS nations.

As per the study findings, only 56% of Indian adults could correctly answer the question related to inflation, while only 14% could answer risk diversification related question. As regards to compound interest concept, only half of the participants surveyed could correctly answer the question. Notably, the survey highlights a vast gap in financial literacy in

India with respect to gender. A difference of seven percentage points is reported with 73% males and 80% females not being financially literate.

Similarly, the findings of VISA's International Financial Literacy Barometer 2012 study conducted across 28 countries on 25,500 respondents also bring to fore the poor financial literacy scenario in India. It places India at 23rd rank out of 28 countries surveyed, with only 35% of its population being financially literate. Indian adults also fared poorly when asked if they could endure personal financial emergency spanning over three months, with only 30% respondents answering it in affirmation. Similar findings have been reported by Mastercard's Financial Literacy Index (2013) conducted between April 2013 and May 2013 based on the responses of 7756 participants, aged 18-64 years, across 16 countries. The financial literacy index was calculated by seeking responses from consumers on three parameters i.e., "basic money management" (50% weight), "financial planning" (30% weight) and "investment" (20% weight). For overall financial literacy index, India scored 59 points which is quite low. Only Japan fared poorer than this by scoring 57 points. Agarwalla *et al.* (2013) also confirm prevalence of low financial literacy among Indian masses. The authors report that on various dimensions of financial knowledge, Indian adults fare poorly compared to other countries surveyed by OECD. The findings of their study reveal that only 24% of Indians possess high financial knowledge which is lower than South Africa (33%), the lowest scoring country in OECD survey.

The poor financial literacy rates prevalent in India present a worrisome situation as it negatively affects the financial security of the population which may subsequently lead to lesser prosperity. Poor financial literacy in India is also proving to be a hurdle in government's endeavor of financial inclusion. The ambition of bringing large section of population within the ambit of formal financial system by providing them easy access to financial products and services would remain unfulfilled until financial literacy rates are improved. In addition to this, financial literacy has particularly become important in the current times owing to the complexity of the financial scenario and its role in augmenting economic prosperity of nations.

Research gap

The need of financial literacy in current times has already been emphasized. Given its significance in view of the current complex financial scenario and the benefits it has for an individual as well as economy as a whole, the subject of financial literacy has evoked a lot of academic and research interest. Research studies have shown that average financial literacy levels across the world are low. This is particularly true in case of developing countries like India. However, in the Indian context, research studies conducted in this area seem to be far inadequate. These studies have either limited geographical scope or lack adequate representation of various socio-demographic groups. To overcome this limitation, the present research study aims to assess financial literacy levels among individuals, giving adequate representation to various socio-demographic groups so as to make the study more inclusive and representative. The study aims to identify various groups within the population that possess less financial awareness so that attention is devoted to improve financial education scenario in India. The present study has also tried to take a more inclusive measure of financial literacy by adopting both financial knowledge as well as financial behaviour dimension while assessing an individual's financial literacy score.

OBJECTIVES OF THE STUDY

The present study has been undertaken to achieve the following objectives:

- To measure the level of financial literacy among individual investors and identify the weak areas where investors need to improve their knowledge.
- To assess if any differences exist in financial literacy levels among different demographic groups

Hypotheses

To achieve the study objectives and give a proper direction to the study, the following hypothesis has been framed:

1. **HO_1:** There is no significant difference in the financial literacy levels of individuals across various demographic variables.

    This major hypothesis is sub-divided into following sub-hypotheses:

    HO_{1a}: There is no significant difference in the financial literacy of individuals across age.

    HO_{1b}: There is no significant difference in the financial literacy of individuals across income level.

    HO_{1c}: There is no significant difference in the financial literacy of individuals across education level.

    HO_{1d}: There is no significant difference in the financial literacy of individuals across various occupations.

    HO_{1e}: There is no significant difference in the financial literacy of individuals based on place of residence.

    HO_{1f}: There is no significant difference in the financial literacy of individuals across gender.

    HO_{1g}: There is no significant difference in the financial literacy of individuals across family structure.

Population and sampling design

An individual investor for the purpose of this study was defined as any individual with a regular source of income having made any investment in any form of financial instrument e.g. shares, debentures, bonds, gold, saving bank account, insurance, mutual funds, derivatives etc.

The study is based on a sample of 1100 individual investors which was drawn using quota sampling technique Five areas were chosen from North India on geographical basis which included Delhi, Chandigarh, Srinagar, Anantnag and Udhampur. These areas were chosen to adequately represent metropolitan, urban and rural areas. From amongst the chosen areas, the sample was selected to ensure ample representation to individuals across varied demographic characteristics like age, income, education, gender etc. The respondents for the study were chosen from educational institutions, hospitals, banks, business establishments and private offices.

DATA COLLECTION

The data for the study was collected using a structured questionnaire. A total of 1522 individual investors were contacted for the purpose of this study. These individual investors were contacted through their workplaces and were allowed a sufficient time to fill the questionnaires. The area-wise break-up of the questionnaire distribution is given in Table 1.1. Of these 1522 questionnaires a total of 1182 questionnaires were returned indicating a decent response rate of 77.66%. The highest response rate was from Delhi (80.25%), while the lowest response rate was in Udhampur (73.65%).

Table 1.1. Break-up of response rates (Region-wise)

Region	Questionnaires distributed	Questionnaires received	Questionnaires discarded	Usable questionnaires
Delhi	319	256 (80.25%)*	16	240 (21.81%)**
Chandigarh	317	249 (78.55%)*	16	233 (21.18%)**
Srinagar	327	259 (79.20%)*	12	247 (22.45%)**

Anantnag	282	214 (75.89%)*	17	197 (17.91%)**
Udhampur	277	204 (73.65%)*	21	183 (16.64%)**
Total	1522	1182 (77.66%)*	82	1100

* Figures in brackets represent response rates
** Figures in brackets represent percentage of total sample comprised

A preliminary analysis of questionnaires revealed that out of total 1182 questionnaires received, only 1100 could be used for actual data analysis as the remaining 82 questionnaires had to be rejected on account of being outliers or incomplete or inconsistent. Thus, the final data analysis of the study is based on 1100 questionnaires. The detailed account of the area-wise questionnaire distribution is given in Table 1.1.

Demographic profile of respondents

The first part of the research instrument used required the respondents to fill in a detailed account about their demographic profile. All demographic factors which were considered consequential for the study were included in the profile. These include age, educational qualification, family structure, gender, income, marital status, occupation etc. The detailed demographic profile of 1100 respondents whose responses were finally used to arrive at various results of the study is presented in Table 1.2.

Table 1.2. Demographic profile of the respondents

Demographic factor	Group	Frequency	Percentage
Age	<35 years	337	30.6
	36-55 years	470	42.7
	>55 years	293	26.6
Gender	Male	584	53.1
	Female	516	46.9

Income	Upto 1,50,000	165	15
	1,50,001-3,00,000	223	20.3
	3,00,001-5,00,000	239	21.7
	5,00,001-8,00,000	260	23.6
	Above 8,00,000	213	19.4
Educational qualification	Upto 10+2	227	20.6
	Graduation	406	36.9
	Post-graduation	400	36.4
	Higher qualification	67	6.1
Occupation	Business	290	26.4
	Govt. service	219	19.9
	Pvt. service	318	28.9
	Professional	273	24.8
Location	Delhi	240	21.81
	Chandigarh	233	21.18
	Srinagar	247	22.45
	Anantnag	197	17.91
	Udhampur	183	16.64
Family structure	Joint	428	38.9
	Nuclear	672	61.1
Marital status	Unmarried	330	30
	Married	770	70

Research instrument: Description and development

The study was undertaken using a research instrument which represent a compilation of the items used to measure similar constructs in some previously published works. Wherever required, the items have, however, been suitably modified in accordance with the context and needs of the current study. The research instruments used in the present study have are briefly explained in the following sections.

Financial Literacy instrument

Following definition of the financial literacy as proposed by Australian Unity (2014) has been adopted in this research study:

"Financial Literacy is a person's understanding of financial concepts and options in the context of their personal economic situation, combined with their behaviour and judgment to apply the knowledge to achieve a desired level of financial wellbeing"

In line with the above definition and to ensure comprehensiveness of measurement instrument, study has relied on use of both the constructs viz., financial knowledge and financial behaviour for measuring financial literacy among the individuals.

Financial Knowledge:

Financial knowledge is the knowledge about the financial concepts and products (Zait and Bertea, 2015).

Financial knowledge construct was measured using 16 items which tested the individual investors on their understanding and comprehension of various financial concepts. These items were compiled from different instruments that have been used in various financial literacy surveys conducted across the world. For each correct response the respondent was given a score of "1" and for incorrect response a score of "0". The score for 16 items was summed up to arrive at the overall score for financial knowledge.

Financial Behaviour

Financial behaviour refers *to the way an individual deals with his financial matters and takes the financial decisions. It seeks to understand how an individual uses his financial knowledge in managing personal finances.*

Financial behaviour of the respondents has been assessed by seeking information from them regarding the way they dealt with finance related matters in their routine life. For this purpose, the study has mainly relied upon the questionnaire used by OECD for their international studies. A total of seven items were employed to gain insight into some vital areas of financial behaviour like assessing affordability of products and expenditures, behavior regarding timely payment of bills, keeping watch over financial affairs, maintaining and adhering to household budget, making efforts to evaluate financial products and active saving habits, setting long-term financial goals. These items enquired respondents if they exhibited particular behaviour in managing their finances. The response to each question was measured on a 5-point likert scale, ranging from 1→ strongly disagree; 2→ disagree; 3→ neutral; 4→ agree; 5→ strongly agree. For each item, a score of one was given if respondent agreed to statement by indicating 4 or 5 as response which would mean a desirable financial behaviour. For the responses 1, 2, or 3, zero score was given. Of these 7 statements used for measuring financial behaviour construct, the first item *"While making any purchases, I carefully consider if I can afford it"* had to be dropped given its poor loading in CFA conducted on the final data. As such financial behaviour was eventually measured using 6 items only. A respondent could thus score a maximum of 6 for financial behaviour construct. Respondents were categorized based on financial behaviour score in the similar way as was done for financial knowledge. This classification is quite similar to that adopted by OECD (2012). Respondents scoring 5 or 6 were categorized as the ones demonstrating positive financial behaviour; Respondents with scores of 3 or 4 were categorized as those depicting average financial behaviour and the remaining were classified as demonstrating indifferent financial behaviour. It is however pertinent to mention here that to ensure comparability of financial behaviour with other constructs and to ensure ease in data analysis, the financial behaviour score was converted to 5-point scale.

Assessment of Financial Knowledge

Each respondent's financial knowledge score was calculated on the basis of number of correct responses given by the individual respondent. For each correct response, a score of one was given and for an incorrect response or where respondent had chosen "Don't know" option a score of zero was given. The aggregate score for financial knowledge was calculated by summing up the number of correct responses given by an individual respondent. The respondents scoring 12 or above were categorized as those possessing high financial knowledge, those scoring between 8 and 11 were grouped as possessing average financial knowledge and the rest were categorized into poor financial knowledge group (as adopted by Agarwalla *et al.*, 2013; Atkinson and Messy, 2012).

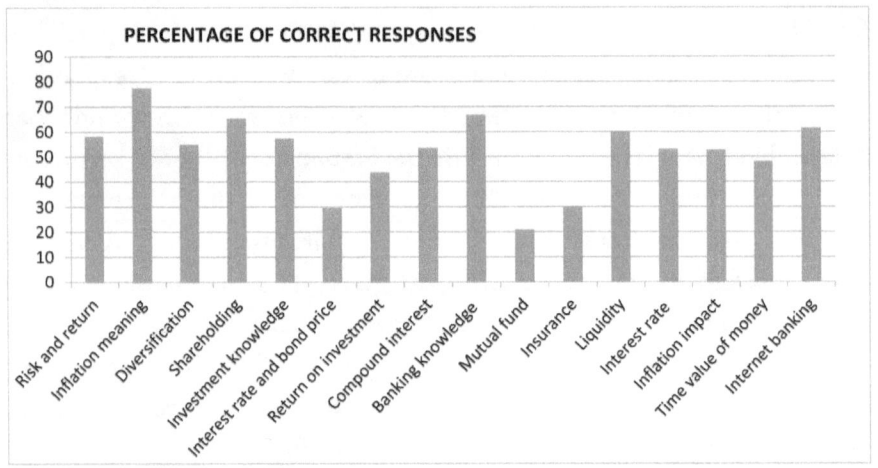

Figure 1.1: Summary statistics for Financial Knowledge questions

The summary of the correct response rate obtained on various items of the financial knowledge questionnaire is presented in the bar graph in Fig 1.1. Also Table 1.3 presents summarized statistics of the various questions pertaining to financial knowledge dimension based on the survey responses. It also ranks various concepts in the order of correct response percentage reported.

It can be inferred from the table results that the highest correct response rate is for ***inflation*** related question (77.45%). This question sought to check if the respondents understood the meaning of inflation. Inflation is frequently talked as an issue and therefore gets a lot of coverage in print media. It seems to be a possible reason for widespread awareness about this concept among the individuals. The other items where respondents fared well were ***banking knowledge*** (66.64%), ***shareholding*** (65.45%), ***internet banking*** (61.45%), ***liquidity of assets*** (60%) ***and risk and return*** (58.18%). The rank score for risk and return knowledge is at par with the countries like Norway but is way behind the percentages reported in countries like UK (77%), Hungary (82%) and Malaysia (86%) as reported in OECD financial survey (2012) conducted across 14 countries in the world.

The understanding of **risk and return** concept is also not up to mark as only 58.18% respondents could answer the question regarding this concept correctly. When compared with the global scenario as presented in the findings of OECD financial literacy survey of 2012, these scores are below the average as 13 of the 14 countries surveyed by OECD report better scores than the present one. The overall unsatisfactory level of awareness as exhibited by the respondents regarding various aspects of investment particularly stocks as reported in this study can thus become a stumbling block preventing individuals from investing in stocks.

With regard to other financial products like **mutual funds** and **insurance**, the respondents of the current study exhibited correct response rate of 20.82% and 30% respectively. Mutual funds are emerging as a popular means of investment in current times.

Table 1.3. Financial Knowledge items and their related correct scores

Item code	Percentage of respondents who answered it correctly	Percentage of respondents who gave incorrect answer	Percentage of respondents who gave "Don't know" as answer	Rank
FK1	58.18	27.64	14.18	6
FK2	77.45	13.92	8.63	1
FK3	55	36.28	8.72	8
FK4	65.45	15.55	19	3
FK5	57.45	32.82	9.73	7
FK6	29.64	49.27	21.09	15
FK7	43.64	34.18	22.18	13
FK8	53.45	34.73	11.82	9
FK9	66.64	24.82	8.54	2
FK10	20.82	57.64	21.54	16

FK11	30	63.55	6.45	14
FK12	60	29.91	10.09	5
FK13	52.91	29.82	17.27	10
FK14	52.64	28.72	18.63	11
FK15	48	34.37	17.63	12
FK16	61.45	24.91	13.64	4
Overall	52.05	33.63	14.32	

However, such a poor level of knowledge being exhibited by individuals regarding this is a cause of concern. This rate is quite low when compared to the findings of the study by Chen and Volpe (1998) where the recorded correct response rate stood at 47.08%.. The scenario is no better in case of awareness about the insurance as an investment option. Only about one-third of respondents of the survey sample could correctly answer when asked the reason for buying insurance, while Chen and Volpe (1998) record far better score of 64.94% for this concept

Table 1.3 also ranks different financial knowledge items in the order of highest response rate achieved with the item getting highest correct response rate getting rank one. It can thus be inferred from the table that the respondents demonstrate satisfactory level of knowledge about the concepts like inflation, banking, internet banking, and liquidity of assets while highly inadequate level of knowledge is possessed about the concepts like mutual funds, insurance, impact of inflation on bond prices, and return on investment.

Table 1.4 portrays the overall scenario of financial knowledge levels in the survey sample. As laid down in the previous chapter, respondents answering less than half of the questions correctly have been grouped as possessing poor financial knowledge, individuals answering between 50-74.99% questions correctly have been grouped as possessing average financial knowledge, while others are said to demonstrate high financial knowledge.

From Table 1.4, it is clear that only a small fraction (10.81%) of the survey sample demonstrate high financial knowledge which is quite dismal. It is way behind the scores (24%) as reported by Agarwalla *et al.* (2013) in their study conducted on urban working youth in India.

Table 1.4. Classification based on financial knowledge

Financial knowledge level	Frequency	Percentage
Poor	440	40
Average	541	49.18
High	119	10.82

It is, however, pertinent to mention that this deviation in scores as reported by Agarwalla *et al.* (2010) may be attributed to the fact that the survey sample for their study included educated urban working youth while the current study has taken an inclusive group of individuals with varied educational, income and age profile.

Assessment of Financial Behaviour

The behaviour statements mentioned in Table 1.5 form an important part of financial literacy as per OECD as they stress that the outcomes of financial literacy are reflected in the form of positive financial behaviour. The first statement seeks to check organisational skills among the respondents so that they fulfil their financial commitments in time and thus avoid penalty for delayed payment.

From table 1.5, it can be inferred that 46.54% of respondents have answered the statement *I always make sure to pay all my bills in time* in affirmative. It is, however, quite low when compared with the findings of the international survey conducted by OECD where positive response rate for this statement is 83%. The poor response compared to the international scores may be attributed to multiple reasons like non-availability of money, lack of access to electronic payment facilities, unwillingness to meet commitments on time as is pointed out by OECD 2012 report. The same holds true for all other statements used to assess financial behaviour as depicted in the table 1.5. The percentage of respondents answering in affirmative for various behaviour statements is quite low in comparison to global figures.

Table 1.5. Summary statistics for Financial Behaviour

Item code	Statements	Percentage of respondents exhibiting positive behaviour
FB2	I always make sure to pay all my bills in time	46.54
FB3	I keep a personal watch on all my financial affairs	46.10
FB4	I maintain a household budget and adhere to it	42.64
FB5	I purchase a financial product only after comparing it with similar products from other companies	47.27
FB6	I try to regularly save a portion of my monthly income	41.54
FB7	I set long-term financial goals and strive to achieve them	49.45

From Table 1.5, it can be inferred that only 46.18% individuals exhibit positive financial behaviour which is quite low compared to the international average. These scores are lower even when compared with the figures reported by Agarwalla et al. (2013) based on their study in India. The study findings reveal that 68% respondents to be demonstrating positive financial behaviour while Atkinson and Messy (2012) report 60% respondents to be exhibiting positive financial behaviour in their survey across 14 countries conducted under the aegis of OECD.

Table 1.6. Classification based on Financial Behaviour

Financial behaviour	Frequency	Percentage
Positive	508	46.18%
Average	467	42.45%
Indifferent	125	11.36%

The overall financial literacy score has been calculated by summing up financial knowledge and financial behaviour score for an individual. The maximum score that an individual could achieve was 22 (16 for financial knowledge and 6 for financial behaviour). The average score for the survey sample of this study was 11 which is quite low when compared to scores reported by OECD surveys (which also had maximum score of 22). The average scores as calculated in the OECD survey ranged between 12.4 to 15.1 with an overall average for all countries taken together being 13.7.

Impact of demographics across various constructs

One of the main objectives of the study undertaken was to ascertain the impact of various demographic factors like age, gender, income, educational qualification, etc on respondents' financial literacy levels. To achieve this research objective, one-way ANOVA was used to assess the difference in the mean score of various constructs of financial literacy with regard to various demographic factors and to establish if this difference is statistically significant or the difference is merely attributable to random variations.

The hypothesis framed with regard to this include:

HO_1: There is no significant difference in financial literacy level of individuals across various demographic variables like age, gender, income, educational qualification, marital status, family structure etc.

Age-wise comparison across various constructs

One-way ANOVA test is used to compare the group means in case of categorical variables. Since age is a categorical variable so One-way ANOVA test was used to compare the difference between means across various constructs to test the following hypothesis:

HO_{1a}: There is no significant difference in financial literacy of individuals across age.

Table 2.1. One-way ANOVA results across age

Variable	Age(in yrs)	Mean Score	Overall mean	ANOVA /F-value	Sig*
FK	Less than 35	2.53	2.60	62.872	.000*
	36-55	2.87			
	Above 55	2.27			
FB	Less than 35	2.22	2.28	22.652	.000*
	36-55	2.52			
	Above 55	1.97			
FL	Less than 35	2.44	2.51	54.435	.000*
	36-55	2.77			
	Above 56	2.19			

Note: * indicates p<.05; ns = not significant; FK = Financial knowledge; FB = Financial behaviour; FL = Financial literacy

Table 2.1 presents the results of One-way ANOVA test for age across various constructs of financial literacy and financial well-being. Age has been categorized into three groups- Less than 35 years; 36-55 years and above 55 years. The results reveal that age has a significant impact on all the constructs of financial literacy thereby rejecting the null hypothesis. Across both the constructs of financial literacy i.e. financial knowledge and financial behaviour, there are significant differences in the mean scores across the three age categories with mean score being highest for 36-55 years' age group (FK_{mean}=2.87; FB_{mean}=2.52), followed by less than 35 years' age group (FK_{mean}= 2.53; FB_{mean}= 2.22) and least mean score being reported by above 55 years' age group (FK_{mean}= 2.44; FB_{mean}= 1.97). Similar results are reported for the overall mean score of financial literacy. Differences in the mean values for FK, FB and FL are statistically significant with p-values being < .05 for all the three and hence the null hypothesis is rejected. It can thus be inferred that with respect to age financial literacy follows an inverted U-shaped curve with financial literacy levels peaking at middle and being low for younger and older age groups. These findings are in line with the findings of other studies conducted in the area including Atkinson and Messy (2012); Xu and Zia (2012); Almenberg and Soderbergh (2011); Lusardi and Mitchell (2011);

ANZ Survey (2008). The prevalence of better financial literacy levels in 36-55 years' age group compared to the younger and older age groups can be due to the fact that individuals in this age group are largely responsible for managing financial affairs and therefore are more keen to acquire financial knowledge to discharge this responsibility in a better way.

Income-wise comparison across various constructs

The results of one-way ANOVA for testing the below mentioned hypothesis have been presented in Table 2.2.

$H0_{1b}$: There is no significant difference in the financial literacy of individuals across income levels.

It can be inferred from Table 2.2 that the mean scores for various constructs of financial literacy vary significantly across various income classes as p-values for all constructs are less than .05. It leads to the rejection of null hypothesis stated above with regard to financial literacy. Annual income has been categorized into five groups and each successive group reports higher mean score than the prior group for financial knowledge construct

Table 2.2. One-way ANOVA results across income groups

Variable	Income(in Rs)	Mean Score	Overall mean	ANOVA /F-value	Sig*
FK	Upto 1,50,000	2.36	2.60	15.633	.000*
	1,50,001-3,00,000	2.40			
	3,00,001-5,00,000	2.61			
	5,00,001-8,00,000	2.75			
	Above 8,00,000	2.82			
FB	Upto 1,50,000	2.06	2.28	5.112	.000*
	1,50,001-3,00,000	2.11			
	3,00,001-5,00,000	2.29			
	5,00,001-8,00,000	2.43			
	Above 8,00,000	2.43			

FL	Upto 1,50,000	2.27	2.52	13.101	.000*
	1,50,001-3,00,000	2.32			
	3,00,001-5,00,000	2.51			
	5,00,001-8,00,000	2.66			
	Above 8,00,000	2.72			

Note: * indicates $p<.05$; ns = not significant; FK = Financial knowledge; FB = Financial behaviour; FL = Financial literacy

Similar trend is seen in case of financial behaviour and overall financial literacy score. This is in line with the findings of the study conducted by Agarwalla et al. (2013) who state that higher income levels among individuals are associated with higher financial literacy levels. The 5L-8L and above 8L income groups record mean way above the overall mean across both the constructs of financial literacy. Similar findings have been reported by other studies conducted in the area of financial literacy (see, for example; Atkinson and Messy, 2012; Klapper et al., 2012; Xu and Zia, 2012; Lusardi and Mitchell, 2011; ANZ Survey, 2008). However, contrary to these studies, Ramasawmy et al. (2013) report that income levels do not significantly affect financial literacy levels among individuals. It is however pertinent to mention that their study is based on undergraduates so the results cannot be generalized.

Qualification-wise comparison across various constructs

In the present study, the difference in the financial literacy levels has been studied across individuals with varying educational qualification levels using one-way ANOVA. The individuals were grouped in four categories based on their educational levels and subsequently following hypotheses were tested:

$H0_{1c}$: There is no significant difference in the financial literacy of individuals across the education levels.

The results in Table 2.3 indicate that there are significant differences in the financial literacy level of individuals across various educational qualification categories (p<.05). These findings are coherent with the results obtained by other researches in the area (see, for example; Atkinson and Messy, 2012; Klapper *et al.*, 2012; Xu and Zia, 2012; Lusardi and Mitchell, 2011; ANZ Survey, 2008). In the Indian context, similar results have been reported by Agarwalla *et al.* (2013) who state that higher educational attainment has a significant positive relation particularly with the financial knowledge component of financial literacy. The mean scores for financial literacy constructs show an increasing trend with better educational qualification levels. However, beyond the post-graduation level, the financial literacy levels show a slight dip. A possible explanation for positive association between higher educational level and financial literacy may be better comprehension of financial concepts among highly educated individuals.

Table 2.3. One-way ANOVA results for educational qualification

Variable	Educational Qualification	Mean Score	Overall mean	ANOVA /F-value	Sig*
FK	Upto 12th	2.47	2.60	6.166	.000*
	Graduation	2.55			
	Post-graduation	2.72			
	Higher qualification	2.70			
FB	Upto 12th	2.17	2.28	2.866	.036*
	Graduation	2.21			
	Post-graduation	2.40			
	Higher qualification	2.39			
FL	Upto 12th	2.39	2.51	5.660	.001*
	Graduation	2.46			
	Post-graduation	2.63			
	Higher qualification	2.61			

Note: * *indicates p<.05; ns = not significant; FK = Financial knowledge; FB= Financial behaviour; FL = Financial literacy*

Occupation-wise comparison across various constructs

Differences in financial literacy and financial well-being have been studied across the occupational profile of respondents using One-way ANOVA test. The following comprised the relevant hypothesis for this test:

HO_{1d}: There is no significant difference in the financial literacy of individuals across various occupations.

The results of One-way ANOVA test with respect to the occupation are presented in Table 2.4. Occupation is one of the important demographic factors and is expected to influence multiple areas like job security, income stability, retirement related concerns etc. People in government jobs are expected to feel financially secure because of stable income and they are also expected to experience less financial stress regarding their future compared to their counterparts in private sector. The Table reveals that individuals pursuing business and those with government employment report higher level of financial literacy compared to overall financial literacy score for all the groups taken together. The differences in the mean scores across various occupations are highly significant (p = 0.000) for all constructs of financial literacy. These findings are however contradictory to those reported by Bhushan and Medhury (2013) based on their study conducted in Himachal Pradesh reveal state that salaried people in non-government jobs exhibit better financial literacy compared to their counterparts in government jobs.

Table 2.4. One-way ANOVA results for occupation

Variable	Occupation	Mean Score	Overall mean	ANOVA /F-value	Sig*
FK	Business	2.84	2.60	21.585	.000*
	Govt. service	2.73			
	Pvt. service	2.43			
	Professional	2.45			

FB	Business	2.46	2.28	8.793	.000*
	Govt. service	2.45			
	Pvt. service	2.06			
	Professional	2.21			
FL	Business	2.74	2.52	18.829	.000*
	Govt. service	2.65			
	Pvt. service	2.33			
	Professional	2.38			

Note: * indicates p<.05; ns = not significant; FK = Financial knowledge; FB = Financial behaviour; FL = Financial literacy

Differences across various constructs based on gender

For the purpose of this study, gender has been categorized into two groups i.e., male and female. It may be noted that independent sample t-test has been used to study differences across various constructs based on gender. The following hypothesis have been tested using independent sample t-test and results thereof have been presented in Table 2.5:

HO_{1f}: There is no significant difference in the financial literacy of individuals across gender.

The results presented in Table 2.5 make it amply clear that significant differences exist across financial literacy constructs among males and females (p<.05). The findings of the study bring out that males report far better levels of financial literacy compared to females. These findings are consistent with the findings of numerous other similar studies, for example, Boisclair *et al.* (2014); Agarwalla *et al.* (2013); Schmeiser and Seligman (2013); Atkinson and Messy (2012); Xu and Zia (2012); Almenberg and Soderbergh (2011); ANZ Survey (2008); Lusardi (2008); Chen and Volpe (1998).

Table 2.5. Gender-wise comparison across various constructs

Variable	Gender	Mean	Mean difference	t-value	Sig*
FK	Male	2.74	.285	6.256	.000*
	Female	2.45			
FB	Male	2.43	.307	4.498	.000*
	Female	2.12			
FL	Male	2.65	.291	6.104	.000*
	Female	2.36			

Note: * indicates p<.05; ns = not significant; FK = Financial knowledge; FB = Financial behaviour; FL = Financial literacy

Xu and Zia (2012) state that prevalence of low financial literacy among females compared to males is a matter of concern as it makes the former economically more vulnerable given their longer life spans and low wealth holdings.

SUGGESTIONS AND RECOMMENDATIONS

In light of the findings of the study, a number of suggestions are put forth. These suggestions, mainly aimed at improving financial literacy scenario in India and having implications for various entities including government, financial regulatory bodies, financial institutions, policy-makers as well as individual investors, are listed below:

1. The results of the study clearly indicate a lack of adequate financial knowledge among the individuals with 40% of the respondents exhibiting poor financial knowledge levels, lacking knowledge of even some basic concepts with regard to finance. Hence, there is an urgent need to educate people about basic financial concepts which would improve their ability to make prudent personal financial decisions.

2. Financial knowledge is found to be low among youngsters i.e., individuals with less than 35 years of age. Poor financial knowledge

has been responsible for poor debt management particularly among youngsters. This necessitates initiatives to improve financial awareness among the youngsters to ensure that they make well-informed financial decisions and are safeguarded against financial frauds. It may be partly achieved by introducing financial education as a part of curriculum at the college level.

3. The prevalence of low financial knowledge among the elderly is also a cause of concern. This age group is particularly vulnerable because of low income coupled with high medical expenses. It is therefore highly desirable that steps are taken to improve their financial awareness about the options which can help them to plan better for their retirement without getting trapped in debt. This would go long way in improving their financial-wellbeing levels.

4. A general financial literacy program ignores the differences existing among the individuals based on their income, education level, gender or age groups. These groups vary in their comprehension level, financial goals and aspirations, financial concerns etc. Thus a common financial literacy programs may not be effective. The content of such programmes should be designed after considering the differences existing among the various demographic groups so that it suits their requirements and they can comprehend it properly.

5. Similarly, prevalence of varying levels of financial literacy among individuals also calls for devising different financial education programs for them. For the beginners, programs covering basic financial concepts can be designed, while for those exhibiting basic level of financial knowledge, programs with advanced concepts with regard to investing and financial management may be introduced.

6. Financial literacy is particularly low among the women. Additionally, low income, lack of ownership rights and high life expectancies compared to men are other factors which increase the vulnerability of women with regard to financial matters. Therefore, imparting financial

education among women may equip them with necessary knowledge to take well informed financial decisions. Imparting financial knowledge among them may instill confidence in them to plan for their finances in future and thus reduce their vulnerability.

7. Keeping in view the importance of financial literacy and its positive impact on financial well-being, it is recommended that financial education be integrated with general education curriculum at an earliest stage. Basic finance related concepts, if introduced at the school level, are expected to be better assimilated by individuals and prepare them well for better management of personal finances ahead.

8. Financial literacy programmes, highlighting the benefits of positive financial behaviours, should also be conducted so that individuals are encouraged to adopt the behaviours like paying bills on time, keeping an eye on financial markets, saving regularly, maintaining a household budget etc. It would ensure better money management, inculcate saving and investing habits among individuals.

LIMITATIONS OF THE STUDY

Although adequate care has been taken in designing and conducting the present study, yet the study of this nature and magnitude is still bound to suffer from certain limitations. These limitations in the study restrict the applicability of the results of this work and leave a scope for more research to be carried out in this field. These limitations must therefore be kept in mind while deriving any conclusions based on the findings of this study. Some major limitations of this research are enumerated below:

- As the sampling unit for this study was "individual investor", the findings of this study can be generalized for investors only unlike the findings of other financial literacy surveys which are generalized for whole population.

- Due to constraint of time and resources, the study could not be made more comprehensive through inclusion of more areas for data collection. The study is based on data collected from only five regional areas which seems inadequate given the scope of the study. Thus, there are concerns about the generalisation of the results of the study.
- Though a large number of concepts were covered in financial literacy questionnaire yet, in order to contain the length of the questionnaire, some equally important concepts could not be included. This has limited the comprehensiveness of the instrument and hence the reliability and generalisability of the findings.

REFERENCES

Agarwalla, S. K., Barua, S. K., Jacob, J., & Varma, J. R. (2013). Financial literacy among working young in urban India. *Indian Institute of Management Ahmedabad, WP,* (2013-10), 02.

Almenberg, J., & Säve-Söderbergh, J. (2011). Financial literacy and retirement planning in Sweden. *Journal of Pension Economics & Finance,* 10(4), 585-598.

Al-Tamimi, H. A. H. (2009). Financial literacy and investment decisions of UAE investors. *Journal of Risk Finance.*10(5),500-516.

Aren, S., & Dinç Aydemir, S. (2014). A literature review on financial literacy.

Atkinson, A., & Messy, F. A. (2012). Measuring financial literacy: Results of the OECD/International Network on Financial Education (INFE) pilot study.

Bank, A. N. Z. (2008). ANZ survey of adult financial literacy in Australia.

Bhushan, P., & Medury, Y. (2013). Financial literacy and its determinants.

Boston College Center for Work and Family. (2011). *The MetLife study of financial wellness across the globe: A look at how multinational companies are helping employees better manage their personal finances.* New York, NY: Metropolitan Life Insurance Company.

Chen, H., & Volpe, R. P. (1998). An analysis of personal financial literacy among college students. *Financial services review,* 7(2), 107-128.

Debbich, M. (2015). Why Financial Advice Cannot Substitute for Financial Literacy?

Garg, N., & Singh, S. (2018). Financial literacy among youth. *International Journal of Social Economics.*

Gerardi, K., Goette, L., & Meier, S. (2010). Financial Literacy and Subprime Mortgage Delinquency: Evidence from a Survey Matched to Administrative Data. Federal Reserve Bank of Atlanta: *Working Paper Series.*

Grohmann, A. (2018). Financial literacy and financial behavior: Evidence from the emerging Asian middle class. *Pacific-Basin Finance Journal,* 48, 129-143.

Huston, S. J. (2010). Measuring financial literacy. *Journal of consumer affairs,* 44(2), 296-316.

Jappelli, T., & Padula, M. (2013). Investment in financial literacy and saving decisions. *Journal of Banking & Finance,* 37(8), 2779-2792.

Kebede, M., & Kuar, J. (2015). Financial Literacy and Management of Personal Finance: A Review of Recent Literatures. *Research Journal of Finance and Accounting,* 6(13), 92-106.

Klapper, L. F., Lusardi, A., & Panos, G. A. (2012). *Financial literacy and the financial crisis* (No. w17930). National Bureau of Economic Research.

Lusardi, A. (2008). *Financial literacy: an essential tool for informed consumer choice?* (No. w14084). National Bureau of Economic Research.

Lusardi, A., & Mitchell, O. S. (2011). *Financial literacy and planning: Implications for retirement wellbeing* (No. w17078). National Bureau of Economic Research.

Mandell, L., & Hanson, K. O. (2009). The impact of financial education in high school and college on financial literacy and subsequent financial decision making. In *American Economic Association Meetings, San Francisco, CA* (Vol. 51)

Mandell, L., & Klein, L. S. (2009). The impact of financial literacy education on subsequent financial behavior. *Journal of Financial Counseling and Planning, 20*(1).

Moore, D. L. (2003). *Survey of financial literacy in Washington State: Knowledge, behavior, attitudes, and experiences.* Washington State Department of Financial Institutions.

Naidu, J. G. (2017). Financial literacy in India: A review of literature. *International Journal of Research in Business Studies and Management, 4*(6), 30-32.

Niu, G., Zhou, Y., & Gan, H. (2020). Financial literacy and retirement preparation in China. *Pacific-Basin Finance Journal, 59,* 101262.

Ramasawmy, D., Thapermall, S., Dowlut, S. A., & Ramen, M. (2013). A study of the level of awareness of financial literacy among management undergraduates. In *Proceedings of 3rd Asia-Pacific Business Research Conference* (pp. 25-26).

Remund, D. L. (2010). Financial literacy explicated: The case for a clearer definition in an increasingly complex economy. *Journal of consumer affairs, 44*(2), 276-295

Schmeiser, M. D., & Seligman, J. S. (2013). Using the right yardstick: Assessing financial literacy measures by way of financial well-being. *Journal of Consumer Affairs, 47*(2), 243-262.

Van Rooij, M., Lusardi, A., & Alessie, R. (2011). Financial literacy and stock market participation. *Journal of Financial Economics, 101*(2), 449-472.

VISA (2012). Visa's international financial literacy barometer, 2012.

Xu, L., & Zia, B. (2012). *Financial literacy around the world: an overview of the evidence with practical suggestions for the way forward.* The World Bank.

Chapter 3
Contemporary Issues in Technology Management

3.1 Blockchain Technology in the Financial Sector: A Bibliometric Analysis of the Dimensions AI Database

Dr. Rachana Jaiswal

ABSTRACT

Blockchain technology could unlock new financial products and rally existing industry commitments to reduce manual paperwork in an effort to reduce carbon emissions by establishing new financing product platforms (OECD 2020), resulting in a total transformation of the financial sector. It is currently regarded as one of the most cutting-edge innovations in the finance industry, with the potential to reduce financial fraud, instil a secure transaction system, and manage risk within an interconnected global financial system, ultimately fostering confidence in the transaction ecosystem. After the spread of the Coronavirus, the increasing popularity of blockchain technology creates jargon for all academicians, researchers, and scholars. Consequently, this research paper focuses on existing publications in the field of Blockchain technology and its application in the field of finance, as provided by the dimension AI database, for the purpose of a comprehensive analysis and extensive discussion. From 2014 to 2022, a total of 3321 publications are collected for bibliometric analysis. The VOS viewer visualises the cooperation relationship between publications, the bibliometric network, the foundational characteristics, and the citation structure. Through cluster analysis, this research also provides insights into the various levels of institutions, authors, publications, and countries/regions networking. The findings indicate that there has been a tremendous interest in publishing over the past three years. In addition, India ranks third in documentation after the United States and China, but lacks citation and networking. The implications of the findings provide a substantial understanding of the journal and author who are prominent in citation and occupying more space in publishing research in this field, thereby assisting future researchers in comprehending the literature and conducting a systematic review.

Keywords: *Digital Finance, Blockchain, Covid-19, VOS Viewer, Networking analysis*

INTRODUCTION

The ongoing pandemic has provided a powerful impetus for the widespread adoption of digital technology in the financial services industry, as well as a surge in the use of internet-based, mobile, and online-based systems. According to Crossman's report (2020), which polled American bankers, there has been a 35 percent increase in the number of customers using online banking. Another study, conducted by Allison (2020), came to the conclusion that during the pandemic, there was a growth of more than forty percent in the number of contactless transactions worldwide. There is a digital financial infrastructure that establishes trust and governance to perform and provide the operations in an online mode. These operations can be performed and provided by the infrastructure. According to Bohme et al. (2015), Iansiti and Lakhani (2017), and Yli-Huumo et al. (2016), blockchain technology is at the center of such infrastructure. The phrase "blockchain technology stack" is currently a buzzword that refers to interconnected platforms of trust that carried an immutable and unhackable distributed ledger of users and their information for the purpose of creating transparency and maintaining the provenance of all transactions, as well as providing the foundation for crypto currencies within the digital world economy (Swan, 2015; Naughton, 2016). It offers the parties a tamper-proof platform with the unaltered historical data of users and real-time access benefits, which helps to reduce risk and fraud by enforcing trust within the ecosystem (Mendling et al., 2018). One way to think of it is as a distributed ledger for keeping track of transactions, with the data being stored in blocks. The header, which contains meta information, and the contents section, which contains information such as the transactions made, the address of the parties, etc., are considered to be two of the most important parts of the paper by Swan (2015) and Naughton (2016). (White, 2017; Mendling et al., 2018). Customers' demographic information can be safely and accurately stored in a private manner using the blockchain technology that underpins the digital finance infrastructure. This information can then be made available to all participants in the network without invading the customers' privacy (Agbo et al., 2019; Crosby et al., 2016). Due to the fact that this information will be distributed and stored in a distributed manner, it will be possible to avoid the creation of duplicate records, which will in turn reduce the amount of money and effort required to maintain these records (Agbo et al., 2019; Yli-Huumo et al., 2016).

BACKGROUND WORK

According to the precedents of the literature, Bitcoin was the first instance in which blockchain technology came to the attention of people all over the world (Nakamoto, 2008). In addition, there has been a rise in crypto-based lending and borrowing in the previous half decade, to the point where BlockFI, a centralized crypto financing unit, has acquired a retail customer base of more than 4 lakhs. Those who want to take out loans in this environment are required, much like in a traditional bank, to keep their digital assets on deposit as collateral. Once the process of collateralizing crypto currencies is complete, the borrower will continue to own the collateral, but they will not be able to trade with it or conduct any other transactions with it (Time of India, 2021). The blockchain is becoming an innovative technology that is embedded with cryptography, resilience, and encrypted distributed ledger technology DLT with the real-time proven transaction to facilitate fast, secure, and greater transparency on low fees being charged with zero intermediaries or middlemen. Blockchain is evolving as a decentralized digital ledger that can be used to record and verify transactions (Bohme et al., 2015; Iansiti and Lakhani, 2017; Yli-Huumo et al., 2016). The gradual progression of blockchain technology, which has attracted the attention of researchers and academicians in recent years, can be observed from the various publications that are currently available (Forni & Meulen, 2016; Tandon et al., 2020). The growing popularity motivated me to conduct the research on this topic with the following objective:

RESEARCH OBJECTIVES

1. To explore the major field of blockchain publication and its trend.
2. To analyze the influential authors' organizations, countries, and journals with their networking and collaboration work.

RESEARCH METHODS

The Dimension AI database is one of the largest databases currently available and is openly and without charge to the entire academic and research community. The database contains the most influential journals and publishing houses across a variety of fields. For the purpose of transporting out the bibliometric analysis, researchers therefore prefer to select only this database. The process of retrieving the data from this source starts with the subject of Blockchain, which is the first step in the process.

The terms "Blockchain" and "Financial Institution" or "Financial Sector" or "Banking Services" in the article's title and abstract are two of the search criteria that can be used in the data source. Because there is already such a large body of work (4968 pieces) on Blockchain technology, our search has been restricted to the fields of research in management, tourism and services, banking finance and investment, and only business management. The conclusion reached from the analysis of previously published material spans the years 2014 to 2021 and the first three months of 2022. Initially, 2022 was not taken into consideration; however, due to the publication in the early quarter (i.e. 311) that is approximately equivalent to the publication in 2018, this instigated to consider the publication in 2022, which offers greater insight into how there is a gradual increase in the publishing.

Through bibliometric analysis, a total of 3312 already-existing publications are used to capture some foundation characteristics. These characteristics include the total number of publications, top journals that are more inclined towards the publishing blockchain concept, total citation, and the average (mean) citation of author, funding organisation, and country, respectively. Bibliometric analysis is a method that was developed by Pritchard in 1969 as a scientific approach to comprehend the gradual pattern, scope, temporal evolution, and coverage through the lens of multidisciplinary aspects and views (Caviggioli & Ughetto, 2019; Bhatt et al., 2020; Khanra et al., 2021).

It gives an all-encompassing view of the research topic, its respective influential author with citation, the affiliation for funding, and the researchers' networking in various regions and countries, complete with mapping (Donthu et al., 2020; Leung et al., 2017; Xu et al., 2018). This bibliometric review is an approach that is widely accepted in many different fields of research, including manufacturing Caviggioli & Ughetto, (2019), marketing Gurzki & Woisetschlager, (2017), and finance Corbet et al. (2018), in addition to technology and innovation (Li et al. 2018; van Oorschot et al. 2018).

RESULTS AND DISCUSSION

The foundational characteristics of the published documents in the area of Blockchain application in the financial sector.

This section deals with the foundational characteristics of 3312 publications in various ways such as research direction, an annual presentation of publication, co-author citation, country, organization, and author wise and also visualize the networking among these areas.

Figure 1 provides an insight into the top 10 fields of publication in which commerce, management, tourism, and services have the highest number of publication (3312) whereas information and computing science (772) and economics (291) is also popular among the mind of academicians and researchers. Despite wide coverage of Blockchain it still has less publication in other fields such as studies in human society (104), followed by Mathematical sciences (66) Law and legal studies (62), engineering (61), technology (38), built environment and design (23), and psychology and cognitive sciences (9). Besides these publications, there are some other fields apart from these top 10, where the research direction takes place such as medical and health science, physical science, and environmental science.

Figure 1: Depicts the top 10 fields for publication in the area of Blockchain Application Source: Generated using Dimension data

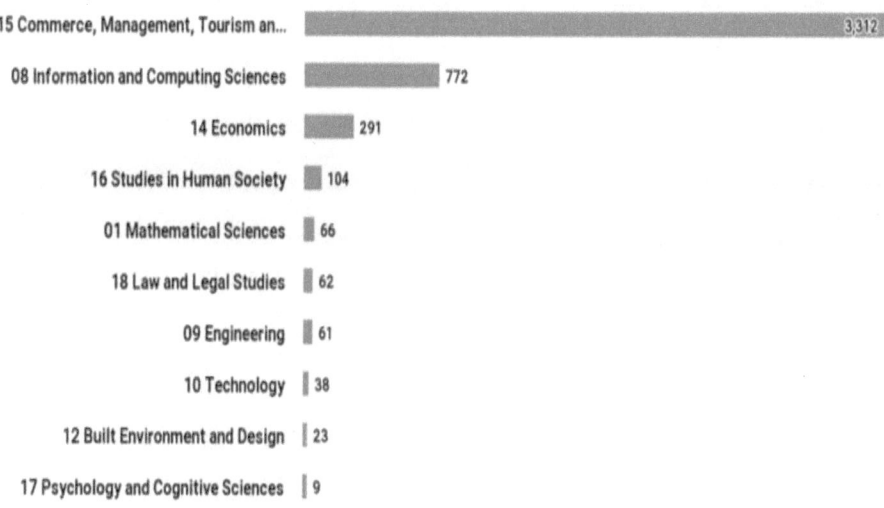

Figure 2 presents the trend line of the publication from 2013 to 2022(1st quarter). The focus reason to go with the 1st quarter of 2022 data was the figure is very close to the annual data of 2018. Which can provide a great insight that how Blockchain become more popular in the past three years which can be seen in the figure that how the publication is gradually increased year on year as in 2019 (604), 2020 (812), and 2021 (1138). The result indicates that researchers are getting more inclined toward Blockchain technology and their publication as there is tremendous scope of work which is associated with this technology.

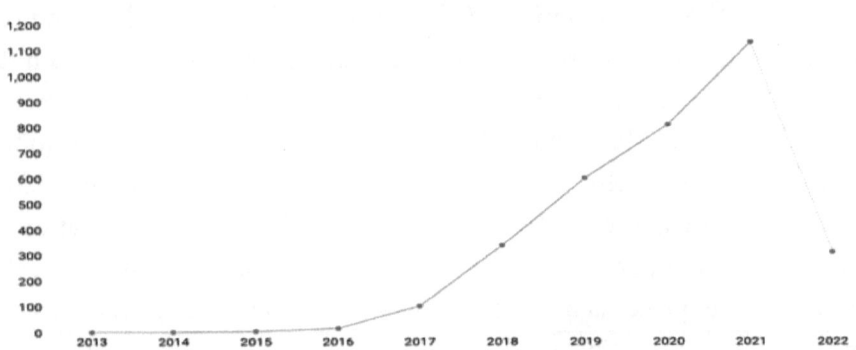

Figure 2: Trend line of the publications from 2013 to 2022(1ˢᵗ quarter)
Source: Generated using Dimension data

Productive countries in the field of blockchain technology and its application in the financial institution

Table 1. Depicts the top 10 countries with the highest Publication

ID	Country	TP	TC	AC	% of TP	CC	TLS	Links	Cluster
16	China	305	2260	7.40	21.049	1141	131	43	2
87	United States	277	3530	12.74	19.1166	1402	173	48	6
34	India	205	1048	5.11	14.1477	781	73	41	3
86	United Kingdom	189	2427	12.84	13.0435	1318	179	48	1
40	Italy	104	565	5.43	7.17736	357	45	39	1
30	Germany	100	1007	10.07	6.90131	381	51	41	1
3	Australia	74	768	10.37	5.10697	373	52	41	4
67	Russia	73	161	2.20	5.03796	45	30	18	4
29	France	63	815	12.93	4.34783	572	68	42	5
83	Turkey	59	253	4.28	4.07177	204	46	32	7

Source: Generated using Vos-viewer on Dimension data

Table1, provide the insights that China, the United States, and India are the top most productive countries with a total (of 305), (277) and (205) publication followed by the United Kingdom (189), Italy (104), and Germany (100). Albeit, the United Kingdom has lesser publications in comparison to India and china but occupies more space in the citation

(2427) which is more than double of India and higher than China. In the same vein, the total publication of Germany is (100) which are half of the publication of India but it has citation approximately close to India. Another interesting fact that can derive from this table is that France which has very fewer publications (63) has the greatest figure in an average citation (12.9365) which opens more room for citations from other countries. United Kingdom has the greatest total link strength (179) followed by the USA (173) and China (131). Although China has the maximum number of total publications and citations still it stands in the sixth position as far as an average citation (7.40) is concerned, way behind France (12.93), the United Kingdom (12.84), United States (12.74), Australia (10.37) and Germany (10.07).

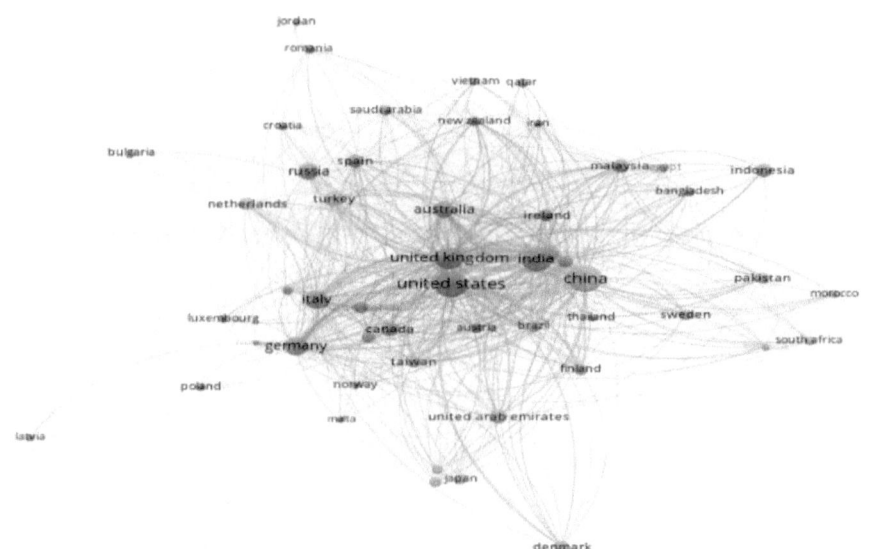

Figure 3: Collaborative networks of the countries in the field of blockchain technology.

Source: Generated using Vos-viewer on Dimension data

Next, the characteristics of cooperation between countries are investigated. For that, the criteria for filtration are chosen by considering only those authors who's having a minimum of two documents and a minimum citation must be 10. The whole cooperation network among the 88 countries and the closest visualization network of connected countries consisting of 52 were selected. The total strength of the co-authorship links with other countries will be visualized by Vos-viewer are illustrated in Figure 3, the node denotes the country which is associated with the research domain, the size of the node represents the total number of published documents, the connection between two nodes means that there is a cooperative relationship/networking. The thickness of the connection line represents more strength of the cooperation. From this picture, we can visualize that the United States, China, and United Kingdom, and India have high networking and degree of cooperation with other countries. The result stated that the United States is the most cooperative country, and often cooperates with China, the United Kingdom, and India. Specifically, the indicators, i.e., Total Publication (TP), Total Citation (TC), Citation of cooperation (CC), links denote the number of cooperating countries/regions with the target one, total links strength (the weight of links) and cluster, are used to describe cooperation countries/regions, as shown in Table 1.

Productive Organization/Institution as per total Publication and citation

Table 2. Depicts the top 10 organizations with citation cooperation

ID	Organization	TP	TC	TLS	AC	%TP	L	C
357	Hong Kong polytechnic university	32	766	492	23.94	35.96	151	2
1354	Worcester polytechnic institute	10	469	255	46.9	11.24	113	6
977	Universidade paulista	7	378	307	54	7.865	131	10
256	Eth Zurich	10	353	169	35.3	11.24	106	3
942	Toulouse business school	9	291	281	32.33	10.11	117	10
1111	University of Kassel	4	252	119	63	4.494	96	4
565	Macquarie University	4	249	85	62.25	4.494	68	1
123	California state university, Bakersfield	6	242	90	40.33	6.742	63	4

| 77 | Beijing institute of technology | 5 | 230 | 116 | 46 | 5.618 | 85 | 14 |
| 1237 | University of Sheffield | 2 | 229 | 81 | 114.5 | 2.247 | 64 | 2 |

Source: Generated using Vos-viewer on Dimension data

Table 2 provides a brief insight into the top 10 organizations/institutions as per the total number of citations. Hong Kong polytechnic university has the highest number of citations (766) followed by Worcester polytechnic institute (469), Universidade Paulista (378), and Eth Zurich (353) but they are lagging in terms of average citation and come after the University of Sheffield (114.5) which carry highest average citation despite having only (2) publication followed by University of Kassel (63) average citation with (4) publication, Macquarie University (62.25) with (4) publication which reflects that Hong Kong polytechnic university should work on improving their average citation(23.94). Moreover, Hong Kong polytechnic university has the highest total link strength (29) followed by Eth Zurich (20), California state university, Bakersfield (13), and, Toulouse business school (13).

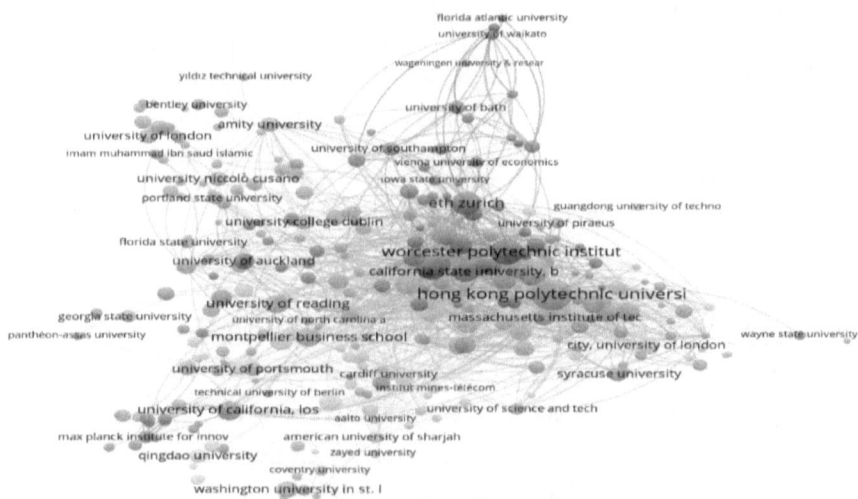

Figure 4: Collaborative networks of the Citation with organization/institutions

Source: Generated using Vos-viewer on Dimension data

Next, the characteristics of cooperation between citation and organization are investigated. Out of the 1396 organizations, only 338 meet the threshold on the selected criteria of filtering i.e. minimum no. of documents of an organization must have 2 or more than 2 documents with a minimum of 10 or more than 10 citations should be there. The largest set of connected items consists of 317 organizations which represent a degree of cooperation and networking which can be visualized by Vosviewer shown in figure 4.

Table 3. Depicts the top 10 organizations with the highest Publication

ID	Organization	TP	TC	TLS	AC	%TP	Links	Cluster
357	Hong Kong polytechnic university	32	766	29	23.94	21.77	19	14
22	Amity university	22	95	7	4.318	14.97	6	12
989	University college London	15	101	13	6.733	10.2	10	9
1162	University of Mumbai	13	50	4	3.846	8.844	4	4
269	Financial university	13	12	2	0.923	8.844	1	5
698	O. P. Jindal global university	11	90	17	8.182	7.483	12	19
1306	Universität Hamburg	11	25	6	2.273	7.483	5	1
1354	Worcester polytechnic institute	10	469	11	46.9	6.803	4	21
256	Eth Zurich	10	353	20	35.3	6.803	15	16
612	Modul university Vienna	10	102	7	10.2	6.803	6	18

Source: Generated using Vos-viewer on Dimension data

Table 3 exhibits the Top 10 Organizations/Institution according to the total number of documentation published. Hong Kong polytechnic university is on top with the (32) highest number of total publications followed by Amity University (22) and University College London (15). Moreover, Amity University and University College London have lesser citations 95 and 101, and average citations of 4.318 and 6.733 respectively in comparison to Worcester polytechnic institute (469) and Eth Zurich (353) with average citations of 46.9 and 35.3, which depicts that despite having a good number of publication these organization lacking to improve their citation which opens a room to work more on citation of the published documents.

Next, the characteristics of cooperation between co-authorship and organization are investigated. Out of the 1396 organizations, only 338 meet the threshold on the selected criteria of filtering i.e. minimum no. of documents of an organization must have 2 or more than 2 documents with a minimum of 10 or more than 10 citations should be there. The largest set of connected items consists of 258 organizations which represent a degree of cooperation and networking which can be visualized by Vos-viewer shown in figure 4.

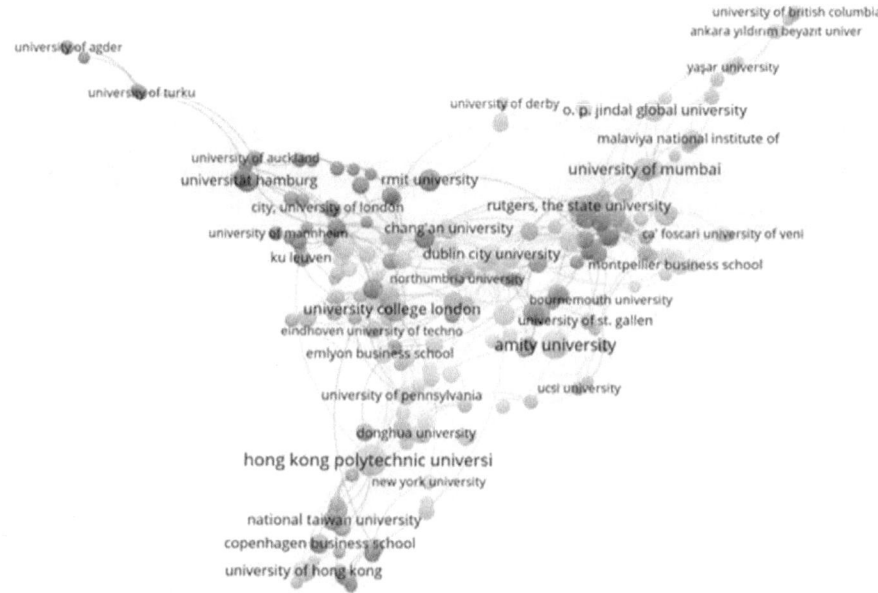

Figure 5: Collaborative networks of the co-authorship with organizations/institutions

Source: Generated using Vos-viewer on Dimension data

Productive Journals based on citation

Table 4. Depicts the top 10 productive journals with the highest citation

ID	Source	TP	TC	CC	TLS	L	C
6091	SSRN electronic journal	106	1757	5757	56644	450	2
3601	International journal of production research	20	1464	24671	90195	446	3
3474	International journal of information management	18	1185	16359	65927	447	1
3600	International journal of production economics	17	1101	19418	69883	433	6
2897	IEEE access	23	953	8509	38640	443	1
6215	Technological forecasting and social change	43	933	11448	52375	449	5
3938	Journal of cleaner production	12	858	14506	49903	440	3
6161	Supply chain management an international journal	8	777	11832	45492	442	3
4714	Management science	9	608	5816	29274	446	6
6164	Sustainability	16	596	9424	30943	441	3

Source: Generated using Vos-viewer on Dimension data

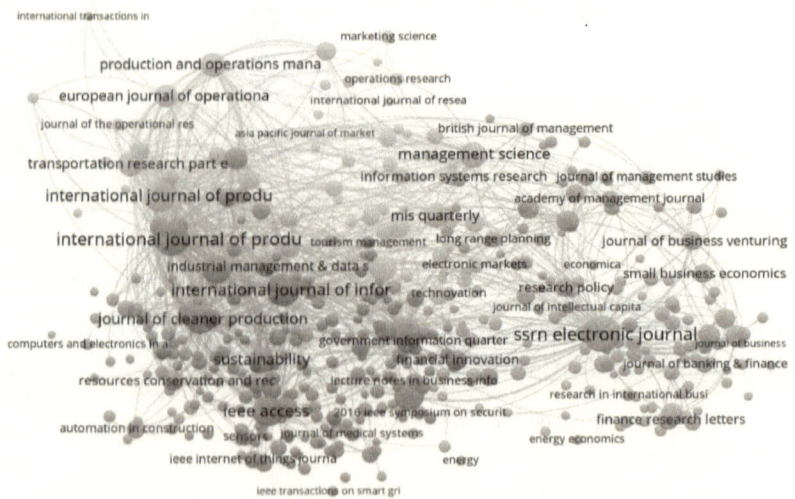

***Figure 6:** Collaborative networks of Productive journals*
Source: Generated using Vos-viewer on Dimension data

Next, the characteristics of cooperation between co-citation and source are investigated. For that out of 6756 sources, 451 meet the threshold criteria after filtering criteria applied which is the minimum number of citations must be 20 or greater than 20. The node and its size denote the journal and the number of citations, respectively. The link represents that the linked two journals are cited in the same paper at the same time. For more details, in the top 10 most productive journals (see Table 4) International journal of production research has the highest Co-author citation (24671) followed by the International journal of production economics (19418), and the International Journal of information management (16359). Another interesting fact that comes out from this table is that these four journals also have more than 1000 citations according to total citations.

Productive Authors based on citation

Table 5 represents the top 10 influential authors in the field of blockchain technology and its application in financial institutions. The highest number of publications and citations of work is Choi, tsan-ming(14) and (631) respectively, followed by Sarkis, Joseph with (11) publications and (494) citations. Besides this, Telles, Renato and Seuring, Stefan has lesser publication (2) but their average citation is greatest among all the authors (118.5) and (112.5) respectively.

Table 5: Depicts the top 10 productive Authors with total citation and link strength

ID	Author	TP	TC	TLS	AC	% of TP
902	Choi, tsan-ming	14	631	6	45.07	24.5614
4269	Sarkis, joseph	11	494	16	44.91	19.29825
3901	Queiroz, maciel m.	5	362	6	72.4	8.77193
5175	Wagner, stephan m.	6	340	12	56.67	10.52632
2451	Kouhizadeh, mahtab	4	324	7	81	7.017544
5189	Wamba, samuelfosso	7	289	7	41.29	12.2807

4303	Schmidt, christoph g.	4	242	8	60.5	7.017544
4842	Telles, renato	2	237	3	118.5	3.508772
4366	Seuring, stefan	2	225	0	112.5	3.508772
4159	Saberi, sara	2	201	4	100.5	3.508772

Source: Generated using Vos-viewer on Dimension data

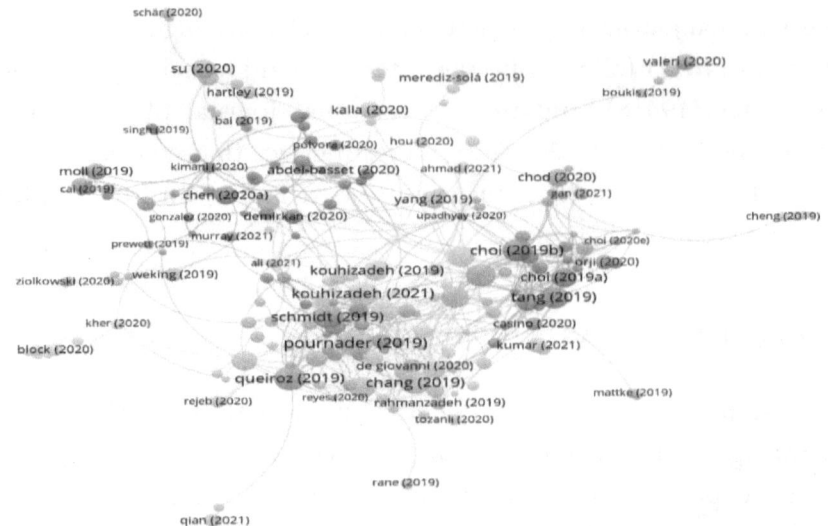

Figure 7: Collaborative networks of Productive documents

Source: Generated using Vos-viewer on Dimension data

Next, the characteristics of cooperation between citation and authors are investigated. Out of the 2500 authors, only 306 meet the threshold on the selected criteria of filtering i.e. minimum no. of citation should be 10 or more than 10. The largest set of connected items consists of 212 authors which represent a degree of cooperation and networking which can be visualized by Vosviewer shown in figure 6. We can see from the figure itself that the most popular documents with the greatest networking are Pournader (2019), Schmidt (2019), Kouhizadeh (2021), Choi (2019b) and chang (2019).

CONCLUSION

As a result of the ongoing pandemic, there is an urgent requirement to relocate business structures, and digitalization has emerged as an important goal. This is helping to achieve key watchwords such as agility and resilience by harnessing the usage of Blockchain in the movement of various financial products and securities in an effort to achieve a sustainable recovery with contactless connectivity. This study provides a detailed insight into the existing publication as well as the strong cooperation and networking among the author's countries, as well as organisation wise for the purpose of analysing the productiveness and its competitiveness in the market. It is anticipated that the current crisis will significantly accelerate the shift toward utilising cutting-edge technologies in order to organically shake up the business landscape. It's possible that Covid-19, which jolted humanity to an inflection spike where embracing technology is an indispensable item to succeed and thrive by converting the crisis into an opportunity, is the primary reason for the gradual increase in the number of publications. Therefore, it would not be an exaggeration to say that Blockchain has the potential to significantly strengthen the financial infrastructure in such a way as to improve transparency, enhance security, lower the operating costs for any financial institution, and assist in the prevention of money laundering and the financing of terrorism.

REFERENCES

Agbo, C. C., Mahmoud, Q. H., & Eklund, J. M. (2019). Blockchain technology in healthcare: a systematic review. In *Healthcare* (Vol. 7, No. 2, p. 56). Multidisciplinary Digital Publishing Institute.

Allison, P. (2020). Mastercard's Contactless Transactions Jump More Than 40% Amid Coronavirus Crisis. Wall Street Journal. https://www.wsj.com/articles/mastercards-profit-falls-though-ceo-says-spending-is-stabilizing-11588164791

Beck, R., Stenum Czepluch, J., Lollike, N., & Malone, S. (2016). Blockchain–the gateway to trust-free cryptographic transactions. In: 24th European Conference on Information Systems, ECIS 2016.

Bhatt, Y., Ghuman, K., & Dhir, A. (2020). Sustainable manufacturing. Bibliometrics and content analysis. *Journal of Cleaner Production, 260*, 120988.

Böhme, R., Christin, N., Edelman, B., & Moore, T. (2015). Bitcoin: Economics, technology, and governance. *Journal of economic Perspectives, 29*(2), 213-38.

Bracamonte, V., & Okada, H. (2017). An exploratory study on the influence of guidelines on crowdfunding projects in the ethereum blockchain platform. In *International conference on social informatics* (pp. 347-354). Springer, Cham.

Caviggioli, F., & Ughetto, E. (2019). A bibliometric analysis of the research dealing with the impact of additive manufacturing on industry, business and society. *International journal of production economics, 208*, 254-268.

Chanson, M., Bogner, A., Wortmann, F., & Fleisch, E. (2017). Blockchain as a privacy enabler: An odometer fraud prevention system. In *Proceedings of the 2017 ACM International Joint Conference on Pervasive and Ubiquitous Computing and Proceedings of the 2017 ACM International Symposium on Wearable Computers* (pp. 13-16).

Christidis, K., & Devetsikiotis, M. (2016). Blockchains and smart contracts for the internet of things. *Ieee Access, 4*, 2292-2303.

Corbet, S., Meegan, A., Larkin, C., Lucey, B., & Yarovaya, L. (2018). Exploring the dynamic relationships between cryptocurrencies and other financial assets. *Economics Letters, 165*, 28-34.

Crosby, M., Pattanayak, P., Verma, S., & Kalyanaraman, V. (2016). Blockchain technology: Beyond bitcoin. *Applied Innovation, 2*(6-10), 71.

Crosman, P. (2020). Digital Banking is surging during the pandemic. Will it last?https://www.americanbanker.com/news/digital-banking-is-surging-during-the-pandemic-will-it-last

Donthu, N., Kumar, S., & Pattnaik, D. (2020). Forty-five years of journal of business research: a bibliometric analysis. *Journal of Business Research, 109,* 1-14.

Forni, A., & Meulen, R. (2016). Gartner's 2016 hype cycle for emerging technologies identifies three key trends that organizations must track to gain competitive advantage. *Gartner Newsroom.* https://www.gartner.com/en/newsroom/press-releases/2016-08-16-gartners-2016-hype-cycle-for-emerging-technologies-identifies-three-key-trends-that-organizations-must-track-to-gain-competitive-advantage (Accessed 12.13.19)

Gazali, H. M., Hassan, R., Nor, R. M., & Rahman, H. M. (2017). Reinventing PTPTN study loan with blockchain and smart contracts. In *2017 8th international conference on information technology (ICIT)* (pp. 751-754). IEEE.

Gurzki, H., & Woisetschläger, D. M. (2017). Mapping the luxury research landscape: A bibliometric citation analysis. *Journal of business research, 77,* 147-166.

Haferkorn, M., & Quintana Diaz, J. M. (2014). Seasonality and interconnectivity within cryptocurrencies-an analysis on the basis of bitcoin, litecoin and namecoin. In *International Workshop on Enterprise Applications and Services in the Finance Industry* (pp. 106-120). Springer, Cham.

Iansiti, M., & Lakhani, K.R. (2017). The truth about blockchain. Harvard Business Review 95 (1), 118–127.

IHS Markit, (2019). Blockchain in Finance Report. https://news.ihsmarkit.com/prviewer/release_only/slug/technology-finance-industry-blockchain-market-reach-462-billion-2030-ihs-markit-says

Khanra, S., Dhir, A., Kaur, P., & Mäntymäki, M. (2021). Bibliometric analysis and literature review of ecotourism: Toward sustainable development. *Tourism Management Perspectives, 37*, 100777.

Leung, X. Y., Sun, J., & Bai, B. (2017). Bibliometrics of social media research: A co-citation and co-word analysis. *International Journal of Hospitality Management, 66*, 35-45.

Li, M., Porter, A. L., & Suominen, A. (2018). Insights into relationships between disruptive technology/innovation and emerging technology: A Bibliometric perspective. *Technological Forecasting and Social Change, 129*, 285-296.

Lundqvist, T., De Blanche, A., & Andersson, H. R. H. (2017). Thing-to-thing electricity micro payments using blockchain technology. In *2017 Global Internet of Things Summit (GIoTS)* (pp. 1-6). IEEE.

Mendling, J., Weber, I., Aalst, W. V. D., Brocke, J. V., Cabanillas, C., Daniel, F., & Zhu, L. (2018). Blockchains for business process management-challenges and opportunities. *ACM Transactions on Management Information Systems (TMIS), 9*(1), 1-16.

Min, X., Li, Q., Liu, L., & Cui, L. (2016). A permissioned blockchain framework for supporting instant transaction and dynamic block size. In *2016 IEEE Trustcom/BigDataSE/ISPA* (pp. 90-96). IEEE.

Nakamoto, S. (2009). Nakamoto, S, Bitcoin: A peer-to-peer electronic cash system.

Naughton, J. (2016). Is Blockchain the most important IT invention of our age. *The Guardian, 24*.

Papadopoulos, G. (2015). Blockchain and digital payments: an institutionalist analysis of Cryptocurrencies. In *Handbook of digital currency* (pp. 153-172). Academic Press.

Pass, R., & Shelat, A. (2015). Micropayments for decentralized currencies. In *Proceedings of the 22nd ACM SIGSAC Conference on Computer and Communications Security* (pp. 207-218).

Peters, G. W., & Panayi, E. (2016). Understanding modern banking ledgers through blockchain technologies: Future of transaction processing and smart contracts on the internet of money. In *Banking beyond banks and money* (pp. 239-278). Springer, Cham.

Pritchard, A. (1969). Statistical bibliography or bibliometrics. J. Document. 25 (4), 348–349.

Swan, M. (2015). *Blockchain: Blueprint for a new economy.* "O'Reilly Media, Inc.".

Tandon, A., Dhir, A., Islam, A. N., & Mäntymäki, M. (2020). Blockchain in healthcare: A systematic literature review, synthesizing framework and future research agenda. *Computers in Industry, 122*, 103290.

Time of India. (September 2021). "Explained: Crypto-based lending and borrowing". https://timesofindia.indiatimes.com/business/cryptocurrency/blockchain/explained-crypto-based-lending-and-borrowing/articleshow/86171187.cms

Van Oorschot, J. A., Hofman, E., & Halman, J. I. (2018). A bibliometric review of the innovation adoption literature. *Technological Forecasting and Social Change, 134*, 1-21.

White, G. R. (2017). Future applications of blockchain in business and management: A Delphi study. *Strategic Change, 26*(5), 439-451.

Xue, X., Wang, L., & Yang, R. J. (2018). Exploring the science of resilience: critical review and bibliometric analysis. *Natural Hazards, 90*(1), 477-510.

Yli-Huumo, J., Ko, D., Choi, S., Park, S., & Smolander, K. (2016). Where is current research on blockchain technology? —a systematic review. *PloS one, 11*(10), e0163477.

Zhu, H., & Zhou, Z. Z. (2016). Analysis and outlook of applications of blockchain technology to equity crowd funding in China. *Financial innovation, 2*(1), 1-11.

3.2 Cryptocurrency market in pandemic exhibited unusual behaviour

Anil Vishnu Vaidya

ABSTRACT

Cryptocurrency has been in discussion at various levels for the past few years. In India, many exchanges sprung up in the 2017-18 period. RBI announced an indirect ban overturned by the Supreme court in 2020. Since then, RBI has been talking about launching its own digital coin. As claimed by the exchanges, many in India have tried their hands at trading cryptocurrencies during this period.

The volatility in the prices of cryptocurrencies has been well known. A study by Zhao et al. [1] points out investor attention as a plausible cause of volatility. These researchers investigated Google search results as an indicator of investor attention. Wang & Chen [2] included sentiments from social networks to predict crypto prices. The herd mentality has also been pointed out as the cause of prices in the crypto market by Boxer & Thompson [3]. While these studies indicated possible causes, almost all researchers used data from a relatively stable period. The pandemic period has reportedly shown a great increase in prices and volumes on the crypto exchanges around the world. The demand and supply relationship has been generally accepted as influencing prices. The stock market prices also exhibit volatility; there is much to learn from those markets also.

This study examines the unusual behavior of cryptocurrency prices during the pandemic. For study purposes, bitcoin prices are used as indicators for the crypto market, specifically focusing on the pandemic period of Jan 1, 2020 to Dec 31, 2021. It was found that there was a high correlation between bitcoin price and the Sensex during the pandemic. Further, there was a serial correlation, the autocorrelation, in the consecutive prices of bitcoin. The herd mentality of investors was not evidenced.

INTRODUCTION

Cryptocurrency has been in discussion at various levels for the past few years. In India, many exchanges sprung up in the 2017-18 period. RBI announced an indirect ban, overturned by the Supreme court in 2020. Crypto exchanges in India claimed that many in India have tried their hands at trading cryptocurrencies and have made significant investments. Since then, RBI has discussed its intention to launch its own digital coin. Finally, in the budget speech of February 1, 2022, the Finance Minister announced that RBI would launch its digital currency during the financial year 2022-23. RBI Governor and others have been advocating a complete ban on cryptocurrency in India. However, the finance bill 2022 did not mention ban; instead, it included a tax regime for the income earned and transactions completed in cryptocurrency. On the other hand, El Salvador has accepted bitcoin as legal tender. However, IMF has urged the President to remove it, stating that it may pose difficulty for the country even seeking loans in the future, reported by BBC [4].

While there have been discussions on the volatility and risks of the cryptocurrency, the prices moved up significantly during pandemic. For instance, the bitcoin price around INR 0.50 million on April 1, 2020, moved to INR 3.45 million on December 31, 2021, almost six times growth in just 21 months. However, in the previous two years, the price did not significantly increase (from INR 0.44 million on April 1, 2018 to INR 0.50 on April 1, 2020). This paper attempts to explore the factors that contributed to such an increase.

REVIEW OF LITERATURE

The papers published over the past few years show various angles examined by researchers. It is interesting to view these from different perspectives. Here I group those under three classes:

Cryptocurrency market dynamics

The volatility in the prices of cryptocurrencies has been well known. A study by Zhao et al. [1] points out investor attention as a plausible cause of volatility. These researchers investigated Google search results as an indicator of investor attention. The LightGBM (Light Gradient Boosting Machine) algorithm was reported as giving good results for price prediction indicating that the risk can be mitigated (Xiaolie et al.) [5]. Caporale et al. [6] have argued persistence in the crypto market. The researchers established that the past and future values are positively correlated, although the degree of correlation changes over time. They suggest that this indicates market inefficiency. Liu & Tsyvinsky [7] concluded that there is a strong time-series momentum effect in the crypto market, bringing investor attention.

Interconnectedness of markets

The pandemic period has reportedly shown a significant increase in prices and volumes on the crypto exchanges around the world. The demand and supply relationship has been generally accepted as a factor influencing prices. The stock market prices also exhibit volatility; there is much to learn from those markets also. Iyer [8], in her study, has indicated a strong interconnection between the cryptocurrency market and the stock market. The spillovers from the price volatility of the cryptocurrency market in the stock markets reflect the changes in the market indices. Gita Gopinath, in 2022 tweeted that there is a strong correlation between the bitcoin price and the stock market movement. The relationship between financial markets and cryptocurrency prices is also suggested by Tobias et al. [9], stating that "There is interconnected between virtual assets and financial markets". The researchers further add that "crypto-assets are no longer on the fringe of the financial system". It means that the risk diversification benefits are limited as the two systems move together. The discussion on banning cryptocurrency was set to rest by the Government of India in the budget speech. Roychoudhury [10] reported Gita Gopinath's view that cryptocurrency could not be banned. He mentions that Indians have invested Rs 15,000 – 20,000 Crores in cryptocurrency markets at a conservative estimate, and regulating it is the way forward.

The Social and Behavior aspect

The herd mentality has also been pointed out as the cause of prices in the crypto market (Boxer & Thompson) [3]. While these studies indicated possible causes, almost all researchers' data was from a relatively stable period. Cryptocurrency has been posited as a social phenomenon by Limba et al. [11], stating that the broader adoption by the global population accords it legitimacy. Naf et al. [12] posited that sustainable cryptocurrency makes an economic and social contribution to the sustainable development of the world and has offered a methodology to assess the sustainability of cryptocurrency based on 13 categories. Researchers have proposed a holistic definition of sustainability in the context of cryptocurrency. Wang & Chen [2] have suggested that the social media comments show sentiments that become a significant factor in forecasting the crypto price.

RESEARCH QUESTION

Which factors influenced cryptocurrency prices during the pandemic?

RESEARCH METHODOLOGY

Being a comparatively newer area, the published cryptocurrency research has been limited, although there have been projects in the pipeline as presented in the recent technology-related conferences. My literature review brings forth interconnected of markets, especially the stock market and cryptocurrency market. The behavioral aspects were studied by researchers under the herd mentality concept besides the influence of social media. Thirdly the internal dynamics of the cryptocurrency market was also investigated as evidenced from the literature review. Based on these three dimensions, I offer the following research construct for my investigation.

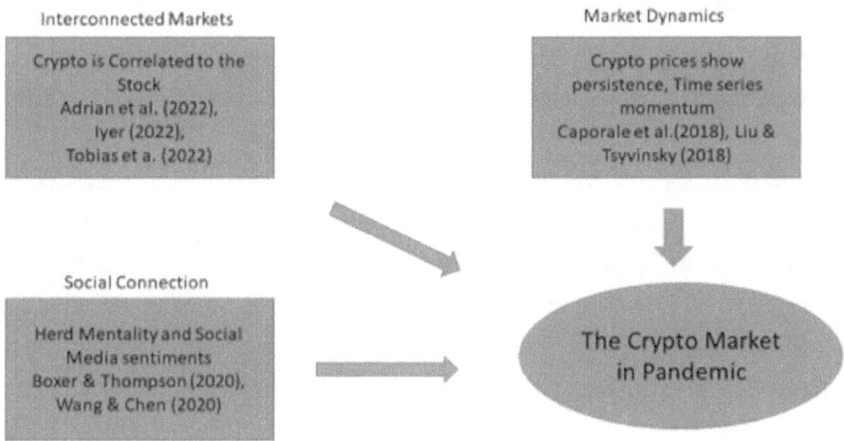

Figure 1: Research Construct

I studied crypto prices, considering the learning from the literature review. I aimed to investigate price movements during the pandemic period, as witnessed in India. For study purposes, I used bitcoin price focusing on the period of April 1, 2020 to December 31, 2021.

FINDINGS

The cryptocurrency market capitalization went from USD 20 billion in January 2017 to USD 3 trillion in November 2021, exhibiting a twentyfold increase in crypto assets in the pandemic months of March 2020 to November 2021 (Iyer) [8] (RBI) [13]. Before the pandemic, the bitcoin and ether prices showed little correlation with stock market indices. However, bitcoin and the stock market moved together during the pandemic, and the correlation coefficient of daily moves of 0.01 became 0.36 (Adrian et al.) [14].

I gathered data from the following two sources:

1. BSE Sensex data from BSE website bseindia.com
2. Bitcoin INR price data from Yahoo Finance website

The total data gathered ranged from January 1, 2017 to February 28, 2022, though my focus was on the pandemic period. The stock market in India showed significant gain during the pandemic despite the restrictions on movement and lockdowns that impacted businesses. While the economy contracted 7.3% in 2020-21 as reported by RBI in April 21 report, the BSE Sensex rose from a low of 28265 on April 1, 2020 to 58253 on December 31, 2021. In the same period, the Bitcoin price rose from INR 505,986 to INR 3,450,574. While the Sensex doubled, the Bitcoin price increased six-fold. Figure 2 shows the plot of BTC prices in INR for the pandemic period. It also shows a plot of the BSE Sensex movement for the same period. The Bitcoin price and BSE Sensex were highly correlated during the pandemic days.

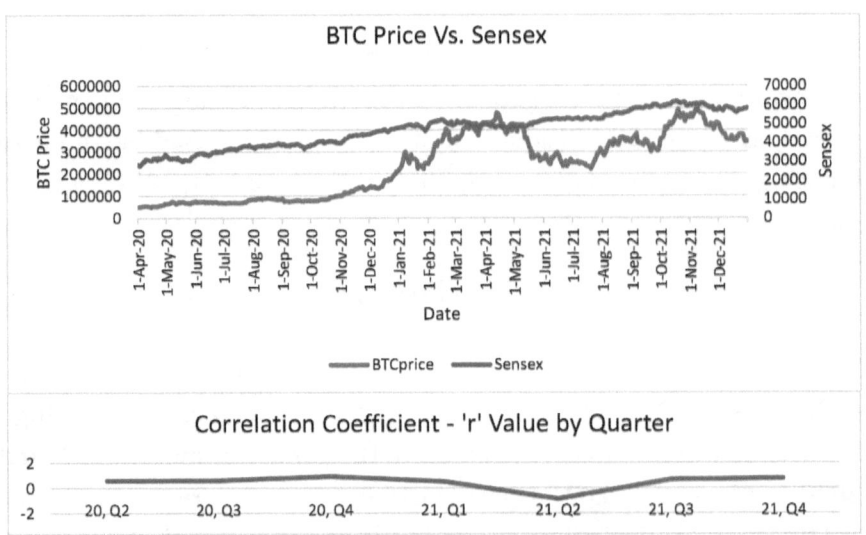

Figure 2: Correlation Charts – BTC Price Vs. Sensex

Figure 2 shows that the BSE Sensex and BTC prices moved together in the pandemic period. The direction of movement appears to have reversed for a brief period in quarter 2 of 2021. In order to get a clearer understanding, I computed correlation coefficients for seven quarters and plotted those against price movements.

For the period April 1, 2020 to December 31, 2021, the Pearson Coefficient 'r-value between daily Bitcoin price and corresponding BSE Sensex is found to be 0.888135 using excel, indicating a high positive correlation. Using Python NumPy 'r-value turned out to be 0.88798, confirming computation in excel. The p-value with python was extremely small, < 0.0000001. Pearson correlation assumes a linear relationship moving at a constant rate, while the Spearman correlation assumes a monotonic relationship among variables that may not move at a constant rate. Using python NumPy the Spearman coefficient gave a similar result of 0.888139. Table 1 here shows the computed value of Pearson correlation coefficients by quarter.

Table 1. Correlation Coefficients by Quarter

20, Q2	0.595957
20, Q3	0.61494
20, Q4	0.92929
21, Q1	0.518269
21, Q2	-0.86894
21, Q3	0.681309
21, Q4	0.741418

Spearman's coefficient for 2021 Q2 was -0.87760, similar to the Pearson coefficient of -0.86894.

Interestingly the correlation between BSE Sensex and the Bitcoin price varies for different periods. It is much lower in pre-pandemic and relaxed restrictions times compared to the pandemic period. Here are the 'r' values shown in Table 2.

Table 2. Correlation between BSE Sensex and Bitcoin price

	Phase	Period	'r' values
1	Pre-Pandemic	January 1, 2017 to December 31, 2019	0.57906
2	Pandemic	April 1, 2020 to December 31, 2021	0.88813
3	Relaxed restrictions	January 1, 2022 to February 28, 2022	0.31894

Autocorrelation

Caporale et al. [6] and Liu & Tsvinsky [7] suggested that the crypto prices show high time-series momentum. I tested the autocorrelation with the Durbin-Watson test in python using April 1, 2020 to December 31, 2021 data, the pandemic period. The test gave a result of 0.048 statistic indicating a very high positive serial correlation in the bitcoin prices during a pandemic. The Durbin-Watson test gives statistics from 0 to 4, with 2 indicating no correlation, 0 with high positive serial correlation, and 4 with high negative serial correlation.

Causality

Singh & Bhatnagar [15] have suggested unidirectional causality of Sensex with bitcoin price testing data for the period 2015 to 2019. The Granger causality test was conducted to determine if a given time series causes another time series. I ran the Granger causality test in python for the pandemic period of April 2020 to December 2021. F test was at 6.417 with a p-value of 0.0117 for one lag period, indicating the causal relationship between Sensex and bitcoin price. Although the test shows that changes in Sensex caused changes in the bitcoin price, intuitively, it is challenging to accept as the bitcoin price is a global phenomenon and the Sensex is local to India. Hamilton [16] suggested that while the Granger test has the word 'causality' embedded in it is best to consider the test as a way to explore whether the Sensex is a helpful measure to determine the direction of the bitcoin price rather than the cause of it. Further, he also suggested that the Granger causality test is applicable in the world of economics and of little use in the other fields. Eichler [17] still considers the Granger causality test as an empirical concept for causal inference.

Investors and Herd mentality

I had separately investigated the stock market rise during the pandemic; a related paper is currently under review. My study revealed that the Demat accounts increased substantially and that many more retail investors started dealing in the stock market. While checking whether the same phenomenon existed in the crypto market, I realized that little official data was available. Mahanta [18] reported that Coinswitch Kuber increased its user base from 1.5 million to 14.5 million in 2021. The average time spent by a user on the Kuber app was 27 minutes, up from 13 minutes in the beginning of the year.

RBI [13] Deputy Governor mentioned some figures in his speech. He declared that data informally gathered showed an average wealth of Indian investors to be only INR 1566 and that 4 out of 5 investors have put in less than INR 10,000 in cryptocurrencies. These numbers do not indicate mass investments by Indians in the cryptocurrency market. The herd mentality of cryptocurrency investors researched by Boxer & Thompson (2020) is not supported by these numbers in pandemic, specifically in Indian context.

ANALYSIS

My investigation using the bitcoin price as the representative of the cryptocurrency market throws some interesting results. Liu & Tsyvinsky [7] stated that they had found no correlation of the crypto market with the stock market. They were completely independent, further adding that cryptocurrency has no exposure to the stock and commodities market. On the other hand, Tobias et al. [9] emphasize that the crypto prices move in sync with stocks, meaning that cryptocurrencies cannot be considered as a hedge against risks in the stocks. My findings align with Tobias et al. [9] that there was a high correlation between the two markets, as shown in Figure 2.

Further, the serial correlation was computed using the Durbin-Watson test. It exhibited high autocorrelation in the cryptocurrency price movements.

Summarizing my findings:

1. There was a high correlation between the movement of the BSE Sensex and the price of bitcoin during the pandemic period up to December end 2021.
2. The correlation between Sensex and BTC price seems much lower in the pre-pandemic and the relaxation period of 2022.
3. Autocorrelation, the serial correlation of the Bitcoin prices was high during the pandemic period.
4. The Granger causality test indicated that the movement in Sensex causes bitcoin price movement. I find it hard to believe, considering that the bitcoin price is globally determined while Sensex is more local. I agree with Hamilton [16] that Granger test results may be used only to indicate direction and not causality.
5. The herd mentality of cryptocurrency investors does not seem to have occurred in India during a pandemic.

CONCLUSION

The findings show that there was a correlation between BSE Sensex and bitcoin price during the pandemic. However, it is equally valid that the bitcoin price is determined globally while the Sensex is the stock market index within Indian boundaries. It also clearly showed that the correlation was lower in the pre-pandemic dates, also this year after relaxation. In another study, the rise stock market could be traced to an increased level of retail investors and the SIP inflows. This phenomenon also points to the behaviour aspect of people. The Coinswitch report of increased accounts aligns with the same concept, meaning the number of people participating in the cryptocurrency increased during the pandemic. However, the concept of herd mentality in the cryptocurrency market is not supported in India during the pandemic.

Secondly, autocorrelation, the time-series momentum, was also high during the pandemic period. Interestingly, although the Granger causality test indicates Sensex being the cause of bitcoin price, it does not appeal to common sense because of geographical differences between the two markets. Further, Hamilton proposed earlier that the Granger causality test may, at best, point to only direction and not the cause-effect relationship.

LIMITATIONS AND WAY FORWARD

This study used bitcoin price as an indicator of the crypto market. It will be more appropriate to study an index of the cryptocurrency market, which includes other assets. No reliable index has been developed so far; it will be essential to formulate one should the research be more helpful. Further, there is little authentic data available on the cryptocurrency investors and the amount invested by them, as reported by RBI. We will need a mechanism to establish this. Such limitations for the Indian market may be overcome with the Indian Government's decision to tax the crypto transactions. The data available then will be more trustworthy.

REFERENCES

[1] **Zhao, C., Liu, F., Lim, E., Tan, C. & Zheng, Z. (2018).** Unraveling the effects of Google search on volatility of cryptocurrencies *Thirty Ninth International Conference on Information System, San Francisco*

[2] **Wang, U. & Chen, R. (2020).** Cryptocurrency price prediction based on multiple market sentiments *53rd Hawaii International Conference on Systems Sciences*

[3] **Boxer, M. & Thompson, N. (2020).** Herd behaviour in cryptocurrency market *ACIS 2020 Proceedings*

[4] BBC (2022) IMF urges El Salvador to remove bitcoin as legal tender *BBC News* accessed from https://www.bbc.com/news/

world-latin-america-60135552#:~:text=The%20International%20 Monetary%20Fund%20(IMF,transactions%2C%20alongside%20 the%20US%20dollar.

[5] **Xiao lei, S., Mingxi, L & Zegian, S. (2020).** A novel cryptocurrency trend forecasting model based on LightGBM *Finance Research Letters* (32) Science Direct

[6] **Caporale, G., Gil-Alana, L. & Plastun, A. (2018).** Persistence in cryptocurrency market *Research in International Business and Finance* 46 pp. 141-148

[7] **Liu, Y. & Tsyvinsky, A. (2018).** Risk and returns of cryptocurrency *National Bureau of Economic Research Working paper series*

[8] **Iyer, T. (2022).** Cryptic connections: Spillovers between crypto and equity markets *Global Financial Stability Notes* International Monetary Fund no. 2022/1

[9] **Tobias, A., Iyer, T. & Qureshi, M. (2022).** Crpto prices move more in sync with stocks, Posing new risks *IMF Blogs* January 11, 2022

[10] **Roychoudhury, A. (2021).** Banning of cryptocurrency poses challenges: IMF Chief Economist Gita Gopinath *Business Standard* December 16, 2021

[11] **Limba, T, Stankevicius, A. and Andrulevicius, A. (2019).** Cryptocurrency as disruptive technology: Theoretical insights *Entrepreneurship and Sustainability Issues* 6(4)

[12] **Naf, M., Keller, T. & Seiler, R. (2021).** Proposal for a methodology for the sustainability assessment of cryptocurrency *Proceedings of the 54th Hawaii Conference on System Sciences 2021*

[13] **RBI (2022)**. Cryptocurrency – An assessment *RBI Speeches & Interviews* February 14, 2022 accessed from https://m.rbi.org.in//Scripts/BS_SpeechesView.aspx?Id=1196

[14] **Adrian, T, Iyer, T & Qureshi, M. (2022).** Crypto prices move more in sync with stocks, posing new risks *IMFBlog* International Monetary Fund January 11, 2022

[15] **Singh, P. & Bhanagar, D. (2020)**. Bitcoins as a determinant of stock market movements: A comparison of Indian and Chinese stock markets *Theoretical & Applied Economics* XXVII 3(624)

[16] **Hamilton, J. (1994)**. Time Series Analysis *Princeton University Press* p. 306–308. ISBN 0-691-04289-6

[17] **Eichler, M. (2012)**. Causal Inference in Time Series Analysis in Berzuini, Carlo (ed.). *Causality: statistical perspectives and applications* (3rd ed.). Hoboken, N.J.: Wiley. pp. 327–352. ISBN 978-0470665565.

[18] **Mahanta, V. (2022)**. About 20 million Indians jumped onto crypto bandwagon in 2021 *The Economic Times* January 1, 2022

3.3 Role of ICT in Promoting Financial Inclusion Among Rural Households: Empirical Evidence from Kashmir Valley, India – A Case Study

Mohd Iqbal Dar[1], Irfan Ahmad Sheikh[2], Dr. Sugandha Chhibber[3]

ABSTRACT

The universe of study is Kashmir Valley where data was collected through a questionnaire. The total sample size of the study was 480 and data was collected from all the respondents. The objective of the study is to know the role of ICT in promoting financial inclusion. The study found rural population was not availing of branchless banking services up to the mark due to a lack of awareness and literacy. Data were analyzed through descriptive statistics and cross tab by using SPSS. The study found that 63.4%, 17.6%, 41.8%, and 44.9%, of respondents, were availing services of Debit cards, Credit Card, Internet Banking, and Mobile banking respectively. Also, it was found that only 18.6% of respondents were extremely aware of branchless banking. Results showed there was regional inequality in availing and using branchless banking services among rural households in the three selected districts of Kashmir Valley.

Keywords: *Financial Inclusion, Branchless Banking, Literacy, Awareness.*

INTRODUCTION

In India, the goal of inclusive and sustainable growth cannot be achieved without covering marginal sections of the population, rural areas, and disadvantaged groups under the mainstream financial system. The population of poor and deprived sections continues to be a challenge in front policymakers around the globe by covering them under the formal financial system. The term financial exclusion refers to the circumstances of people who remain excluded from the formal financial system by having no access to financial services and products such as bank accounts, debit cards, credit cards, the facility of education loans and insurance, etc. "People were poor, not because they were stupid or lazy. They worked all day long, doing complex physical tasks. They were poor because the financial institutions in the country did not help them widen their economic base." (Yunus, 2007). An equitable financial system provides equal opportunities to people who are economically and socially disadvantaged and play an active part in the growth of the economy (Thingalaya et al. 2010). Access to limited financial services like savings, remittances, loans, and insurance services to a majority of the population who live in rural and unorganized sectors acts as a constraint to growth impetus. Thus in achieving inclusive growth financial inclusion is considered an important factor in the contribution of growth as financial inclusion intends for people to connect with banks (Throat, 2006). "Financial inclusion refers to the process of ensuring access to financial services and timely and adequate credit where needed by vulnerable groups such as weaker sections and low-income groups at an affordable cost." (Rangarajan, 2008). Financial inclusion is the service of providing access to all members of the economy to financial services and products. However, with the help of existing literature, it was found that financial inclusion is not up to the mark in the UT of Jammu and Kashmir when compared to other States/UTs of India or the national benchmark. The study aims to know the role of ICT in promoting financial inclusion among rural households in the Kashmir Valley. We concluded after going through a vast number of studies that there was no study conducted on the role of ICT in promoting financial inclusion. Thus, the present study is an attempt to fill this gap, thus, making an original contribution to the existing literature.

REVIEW OF LITERATURE

Demirguc-Kunt and Klapper, (2012) found that 50% population of adults have bank accounts worldwide at the formal financial institution. Still, 50% adult population remains unbanked throughout the world among them 35% reported barriers to account use. The most common barriers were the high cost of financial services, low income, the distance of bank branches, and lack of documentation, although there were significant differences among regions and individual characteristics. The percentage of global non-account holders who were excluded from the formal financial system have cited low income (30%) most important reason for not having a bank account, the other reasons were too expensive financial services (25%), a family member has already an account (23%), bank branches too far away (18%), lack of trust on financial service providers (13%), and religion-related reasons (5%). Chandran, (2010) found there were various barriers to financial inclusion like the distance of bank branches, infrastructure, lack of awareness, and low income. He found that only 59% have bank accounts of all Indian adult population means still 41% are unbanked which is a serious matter, while in rural areas financial inclusion was only 39%. Demirguc-Kunt et al., (2018) found financial inclusion was rising globally. They concluded their study with a globally 69% population of adults having bank accounts in 2017, which is up 62% from the year 2014 and which was 51% in 2011. Raman, (2012) found in India 41% of the adult population of the country was unbanked. Sharma, (2016) found there was a positive and significant association between financial inclusion and economic growth. Fungacova and Weill, (2015) revealed the level of financial inclusion in China which they also compared with (BRICS) Brazil, Russia, India, China, and South Africa. They were of the view that higher income, better education, being a male, and being older contributed greater to financial inclusion. Pena et al., (2014) found the personal characteristics that influence financial inclusion was age, position in the household, and marital status, other research study also supports these findings Camara et al., (2014). The branch network has a positive and strong impact on financial inclusion. A Branch network was used in the study to capture branch density and access to banking (Kumar, 2013). Rakesh and Shilpa, (2013) focused on the initiatives taken by the banking fraternity to cover untapped and under-banked areas. They found various supply and demand-side barriers for poor people that could not access financial services, also affordable products and services were not offered to disadvantaged sections. The study suggested that there was a need to overcome constraints both from the demand and supply side to achieve an objective of greater financial inclusion to alleviate poverty.

Therefore, the researcher thought that by using technology the barriers to financial services can be reduced by promoting branchless banking services, thus in the present study researcher was interested to know the role of ICT in promoting financial inclusion.

RESEARCH METHODOLOGY

The study is descriptive and empirical. The present research paper attempted to know the role of ICT in promoting financial inclusion among rural households in the Kashmir Valley. To achieve the said objective, data were collected from the head of the family of rural households in the Kashmir valley through a questionnaire. The multistage sampling technique was applied for collecting primary data. In the first stage, three districts were selected purposefully district Baramulla was selected from North Kashmir, Budgam from Central Kashmir, and district Anantnag from South Kashmir. In the second stage from each selected district, 4 Blocks were randomly selected and finally, one village was chosen with a sample size of 40 respondents from selected Blocks. The total sample size of the study was fixed at 480 but data was collected from 492 respondents as we got extra questionnaires filled from Block Singhpora under Baramulla District. Hence our updated sample size of the study is 492. The data collection was started in October 2020 and completed in January 2021. The data were analyzed with help of SPSS. The tools and techniques of descriptive statistics and cross tab were applied for analyzing data. The questionnaire variables and statements were framed based on existing literature mentioned under the literature review above.

RESULTS AND DISCUSSION

As you know the world is becoming technology friendly with the advancement in technology there is a rapid move to use technology in every sector. The financial sector has also taken steps to adopt technology and to provide financial services to the users which saves time and cost of financial services to both parties' one is the user of financial services and the other party is the provider/seller of financial services. With the advancement in the financial sector banking institutions also started to provide technology-friendly services to their clients which helped banks to widen their customer penetration. Banking institutions have launched different IT-enabled products for their customer's such popular products are called branchless banking services to customers of banking institutions. Branchless banking has made banking services convenient to its clients also the usage of banking services got increased as the customers don't need to visit physical banking institutions for their services which saves their time however customers can avail of such services at home by using the electronic mode of banking.

Branchless banking has made it possible to include the customers who were financially excluded due to certain reasons like distance of bank branches and cost of financial services etc.

The results of the study show that 63.4% of rural household (HH) respondents are using ATM card facilities of the banks which help them in accessing banking services whenever they require them. The results of the study show that there is regional inequality in using ATM card services among the selected districts of rural households in the Kashmir Valley. District Anantnag shows better results than the other two districts where 132 respondents (83.0%) out of a total of 159 respondents HHs are using ATM Card services which is quite high than other districts. It is to be noted that there are 177 respondents (36.6%) out of a total of 483 respondents in the selected districts who do not use ATM card facilities for banking. The respondents who were availing of ATM cards their behavior of using ATM Cards show 56.5% of respondents HHs are using their ATM Cards monthly followed by 37.3% weekly and 6.2% of respondents are using ATM cards even quarterly which is not a good sign for the complete financial inclusion scheme launched by central govt. as mere availing of banking services by all people of the country does not mean we have achieved complete or 100% financial inclusion one should use financial services frequently as you know dormant accounts of people in the banking institutions are not counted as financially included people. Results show there is a difference in the behavior of users of ATM Cards among rural HHs of selected districts. No respondent was using their ATM card yearly which is a good sign. The researcher has taken four categories to measure the usage of ATM cards. The categories to measure the usage of ATM cards were taken as weekly, monthly, quarterly, and yearly. The respondents who were not using ATM Card facility due to certain reasons are 71.7% respondents were not aware of such facility followed by 15.5% respondents due to distance of ATMs and 12.8% respondents by other reasons.

Only 17.6% of respondents are availing of credit card services which means still 82.4% of respondents are excluded from such facilities. There is regional inequality in availing such facilities among three selected districts. Mostly 58.7% of respondents were of the opinion that due to poor financial records at the bank they could not avail credit card facility followed by 15.5% of respondents who were not aware of such facility.

Respondents were asked about internet banking and it was found that 58.2% of respondents are not using the Internet Banking facility which means only 41.8% of respondents are enjoying this service. The frequency of usage for those who are availing of internet banking services is 43.3% of respondents Weekly, 54% Monthly, and 3% Quarterly. The respondents who were not using Internet Banking due to various reasons such as not being aware of internet banking (51% respondents), followed by due to illiteracy or not being well educated (32.5% respondents), and other reasons. With the increasing trend of using smartphones, respondents were asked about using the Mobile Application Banking facility and it was found that only 44.9% of respondents are using Mobile application banking. It means that still rural masses may not have in their possession smartphones or they may not be able to use smartphones due to illiteracy and other reasons. Also, it was found that only 18.6% of respondents were extremely aware of branchless banking which is quite low.

If we summarize the whole study, we find that rural households of Kashmir Valley are very much reluctant in availing of branchless banking services and the households are not aware of such technology-based services offered by banking institutions in Kashmir valley. The rural population of Kashmir valley was illiterate or less educated and economically weaker which can be the solid reason for not availing and enjoying branchless banking services. The findings of the study will help policymakers to frame such policies that can overcome the problems of rural India in availing and using technology-based banking services and push awareness drive to educate people about different IT products of banking and their use.

REFERENCES

Camara, N. & Tuesta, D. (2014). Measuring financial inclusion: A multidimensional index. *BBVA Working Paper, 14* (26), 1-39.

Chandran, J. (2010). Challenges for India in moving towards financial inclusion. *Journal of Contemporary Research in Management, 5* (2), 47-56.

Demirguc-Kunt, A. & Klapper, L. (2012). Measuring financial inclusion: The Global Findex Database. Policy Research Working Paper 6025, Washinton, DC. World Bank, 1-43.

Demirguc-Kunt, A., Klapper, L., Singer, D., Ansar, S., & Hess, J. (2018). The Global Findex Database 2017: Measuring financial inclusion and the Fintech revolution. Washington, DC: World Bank, 1-151.

Fungacova, Z. & Weill, L. (2015). Understand financial inclusion in China. *China Economic Review, 34*, 196-206, http://dx.doi.org/10.1016/j.chieco.2014.12.004.

Kumar, N. (2013). Financial inclusion and its determinants: Evidence from India. *Journal of Finance Economic Policy,* 5 (1), 4-19, doi: 10.1108/17576381311317754.

Pena, X., Hoyo, C. & Tuesta, D. (2014). Determinants of financial inclusion in Mexico based on the 2012 national financial inclusion survey (ENIF) (No. 1415). *BBVA Working Paper,* 14 (15), 1-32.

Rakesh, H. M. & Shilpa, R. (2013). Financial inclusion in Karnataka: A study on banker's initiative. *International Journal of Commerce, Business Management,* 2 (6), 344-352.

Raman, A. (2012). Financial inclusion and growth of the Indian Banking system. *Journal of Business and Management,* 1 (3), 25-29.

Rangarajan, C. (2008). *Report of the committee on financial inclusion,* Ministry of Finance, Government of India, 1-178.

Sharma, D. (2016). Nexus between financial inclusion and economic growth: Evidence from the emerging Indian economy. *Journal of Finance Economic Policy,* 8 (1), 13-36, doi:10.1108/JFEP-01-2015-0004.

Thingalaya, N. K., Moodithaya, M. S., & Shetty, N. S. (2010). *financial inclusion and beyond: Issues and Challenges.* Academic Foundation.

Thorat, Y. S. P. (2006). Financial Inclusion in Readings on Financial Inclusion. *Indian Institute of Banking and Finance, Mumbai.*

Yunus, M. (2007). *Creating a world without poverty: Social business and the future of capitalism.* Public Affairs.

3.4 Mental Health Apps: Using technology to accelerate the curve on acceptability amongst college students

Ms. Karishma Khadiwala

ABSTRACT

Mental health is crucial at all stages of life, from birth to adolescence to adulthood and old age. High-intensity classes, pressure to excel in academics, career planning, living on a budget, family concerns, awkward social settings, increasing social media use, and less stigma around seeking help are all stressors that students encounter. Students' energy levels, attentiveness, reliability, mental capacity, and optimism can all be affected by mental health issues, resulting in poor performance. While many institutions provide on-campus mental health support, many students who can be benefited from them do not obtain them. Mobile mental health apps are technological advances that fall under the umbrella of mobile health (mHealth). The use of mobile devices for the practise of public health is referred to as mHealth, which is a subset of electronic health (eHealth). Anxiety, panic, and depression are among the topics addressed by mental health apps for college students. Cognitive development, personal growth, and mental health enhancement can all be aided by well-designed mental health mobile apps that deliver knowledge in interactive, engaging, and exciting ways. The goal of the study is to learn more about how college students use Mental Health Apps, their perceived needs, and the acceptability of app-based interventions. The paper analyses the numerous apps available, their benefits, and the implications for educators and app developers who would like to target their products' untapped potential. Finally, app aggregators will be given recommendations on how to promote these apps among college students.

Key Words: mHealth, Mental Health Apps(MHAs), aggregators

Mental Health Apps: Using technology to accelerate the curve on acceptability amongst college students.

"Mental health… is not a destination but a process. It's about how you drive, not where you're going."

Noam Spencer, PhD.

INTRODUCTION

As per the World Health Organization, minimum 7.5 percent of total population of India, roughly 90 million individuals, suffers from mental illness and need medication. Going to a therapist or a psychiatrist is still frowned upon in India; this is astonishing to believe, given that the country was one of the first to implement an organized National Mental Health Program in the early 1980s. According to the World Health Organization, mental health issues create a burden of 2443 disability adjusted life years (DALYs) per 100,000 persons, with a suicide rate of 21.1 per 100,000. Between 2012 and 2030, the organization estimates that the country will lose $1.03 trillion.

In India, more than 3 crore people are enrolled in colleges. Students at these universities have to balance strong academic duties with peer relationships, financial pressure, and rapid environmental changes. Emerging adult individuals (ages 18–25) have a high-risk developmental period linked to the start of mental health disorders (Jones, 2013; Conley et al., 2014). Moreover, starting college at any age is a critical and often stressful time in an individual's life since they must build career by taking professional classes while also studying. Many college students experience mental health issues as a consequence of high level of stress. Despite the fact that many colleges have on-campus mental health services, many students who could get an advantage from them do not receive the attention and assistance they require. Students who haven't been able to leave their houses for therapy or meet face-to-face with their therapists to discuss how they've been feeling during coronavirus outbreaks have faced another challenge as a result of the lockdown.

Virtual doors for online sessions have been opened by therapists across the country. Meanwhile, mental health apps abound thanks to technological advancements. The use of digital mental health services, such as those offered through smartphone apps, is on the rise. There are a wide range of mental health apps available on both Android and Apple.

Mental health apps are solutions for enhancing many elements of mental health and well-being that may be accessible through your smartphone or mobile device. Relaxation, managing stress, and sleep are examples of areas where such tools could be helpful. They may also provide self-help resources, therapeutic activities, and referrals to qualified mental health experts for therapy. Availability, Confidentiality, Simplicity, and Participation are just a few of the potential advantages that make mental health apps appealing to a wide spectrum of users.

REVIEW OF LITERATURE

Due to an increase in its prevalence and the destructive impact it has on the individual, their dear ones, and society as a whole, mental health disorders have been a significant matter of discussion in our society in recent years.

"Mobile apps for Mental Health: a content analysis" by Md. Aminul Islam published in Indian Journal of Mental Health, August, 2020: The main objective of this paper was to look into several components of mental health apps. It states that the mobile phone is unquestionably one of the world's most widely used and adopted technologies. There was a total of 837 Apps about mental illness accessible on the Google Play Store throughout the study period. According to the findings, mental health apps are most commonly used to treat depression, anxiety, general mental health, stress, and post-traumatic stress disorder. Apps, on the other hand, provide a variety of ways to promote mental health. Some of the techniques utilized include relaxation, managing stress, symptom monitoring, calming music, journaling, interacting with mental healthcare, interpersonal support, mindfulness, and emotion monitoring. Relaxation was a popular method for dealing with certain mental health issues. On average, a thousand people download the most popular apps. App developers should think about the findings of this study while developing a health-related app. Furthermore, the findings of the research point to the reasons behind the popularity of free mental health apps. Looking at the rating and the quantity of individuals who evaluated these apps made it difficult to anticipate their dependability. According to the report, future research should focus on the Apps' usefulness in improving mental health.

The Research Paper published by JMIR Res Protoc: "Effectiveness of Using Mental Health Mobile Apps as Digital Antidepressants for Reducing Anxiety and Depression: Protocol for a Multiple Baseline Across-Individuals Design": The research paper has analyzed that there is a growing amount of individuals that are adopting mental health mobile applications to manage stress and despair. Majority of these apps, as per evaluations, lack documented validation of efficiency. Standard randomized controlled trials take too long to conduct in this profit-driven market, which is one reason for the lack of research. Furthermore, if such applications demonstrate to be as beneficial as expected, this will contribute to the body of facts supporting their effectiveness. It may also assist individuals residing in regional areas, those from economically disadvantaged categories, and children and youth by increasing access to care. Improved capacity to enhance face-to-face treatment with electronic homework tasks which could be finished online and exchanged with a therapist immediately.

STATEMENT OF PROBLEM

Several developments are influencing the utilization of mhealth applications. The pressure to conform to quicker developments and the increasing obstacles are fueling the creation of these apps. As a result, the researcher is concerned in people's awareness and inclinations for mhealth apps, as well as their overall satisfaction.

RESEARCH OBJECTIVES

1. To investigate the various Mental Health apps available for college students in Mumbai.
2. To analyze the awareness and usage of the existing Mental Health apps amongst college students in Mumbai.
3. To examine the various challenges faced in penetration and acceptance of Mental Health apps across Mumbai.
4. To make suggestions and recommendations to the Mental Health apps for sustainable growth

METHODOLOGY

This research is both descriptive and analytical.

- Data sources: The study is collected from both primary and secondary data.
- Sampling Design: The study's population is made up of college students (Junior college to degree college students). The method utilized is a simple random sampling technique.
- Sample Size: The study's sample size is 100 participants.
- Study's geographical scope: The study's scope is limited to Mumbai only.

ANALYSIS AND INTERPRETATION

- **Demographic profile of respondents**: According to gender wise classification it was observed that 89% were females and rest were males.

- **Awareness of Mental Health apps**: The study states that 84.2% of students are aware of Mental Health Apps whereas remaining 15.2% were not aware of these apps.

With respect to knowing how they are aware researcher found that 84.2% of students are aware about these apps through social media, 36.8% through advertisements on TV, 31.6% are aware through personnel marketing done through app service providers and 21% through friends or colleagues.

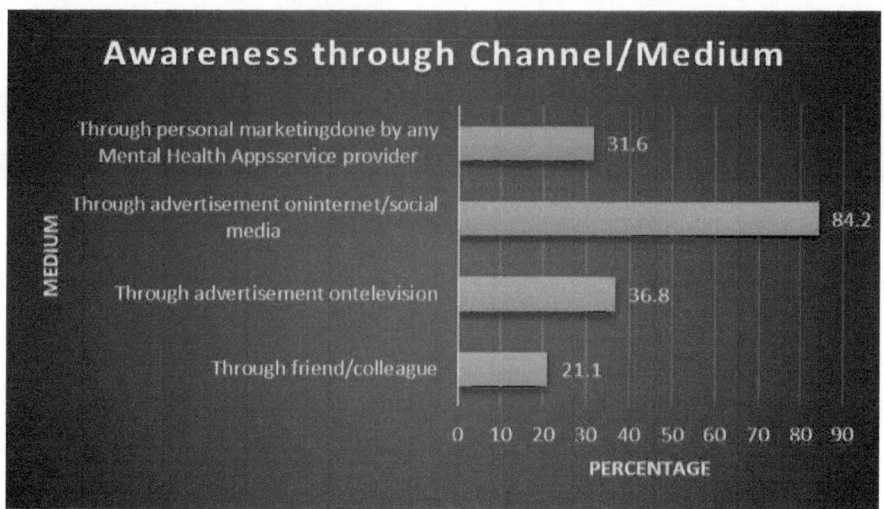

Figure 1: Awareness through channel/medium
Source: Primary Data

- **Usage of Mental Health Apps:** 15.8% of students say they are very useful, 78.9% says some-what useful whereas 5% of students answered they are not useful. This means growth of MHAS is still in the nascent stage. Result establishes the fact that 42% of students download these apps for tracking their habits/activities, 14% to face depression, 13.5% for personality disorders, 12.1% to calm and meditate and 20.4% to get counselling during exams or any hypertension.

- **Apps used more frequently**: The chart clearly depicts that students use more Apple health for overall well-being, followed by Calm an app for anxiety and stress, Healthify me for weight management, Mood-fit and Happify to manage their emotions and least is Head Space. Also, to be noted that 7% have said other apps apart from these popular ones as the choices are many.

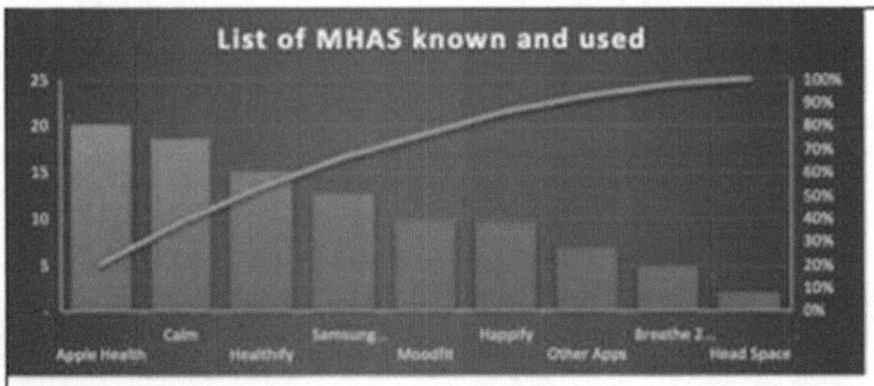

Figure 2: List of MHAS known and used

Source: Primary Data

- **Significance:** With the result researcher develops an impression that these apps are very useful to students for multiple reasons. Users like apps that are easy to use, have a range of functions and choices, are customized, economical, insightful, trustworthy, and protected. They also prefer apps that provide interpersonal help, consumer support, or emergency assistance. Many of them have mentioned about the chatbots as one of the best services what they like.

- **Challenges faced:** The study reveals that were quite a few challenges faced by students in using these apps. 48% of students face usability issues in terms of bugs and poor UI design, Internet connectivity issues and lack of guidance and clear explanation. 28% of students pointed out poor regulation of quality and lack of control. 85% of students raised privacy issues and lack of security. 45% stated that they are overpriced, 36% of students find Poor customer service and 57% pointed that it lacks personalization.

- **Preferences of end users in an app**: It was found that majority of the students said that it is very important for app to be easy to use, should be updated with information, should be easily accessible and top of all should be cost effective. Daily reminders with positive messages and daily progress tracker would be preferred.

SUGGESTIONS

1. **Research collaborations among software creators and medical organizations** could help them to enhance the efficiency of the business and their services. Health care experts must be included in the development of apps since they will offer factual insight during the creation of the application's material and workflows.
2. **Marketing Techniques:** Research clearly shows that many of the students are not aware and also don't know the benefits of apps. More students should be cognisant about the benefits of these apps so that it helps them in a positive way. Aggressive marketing techniques should be used. Social media should be used primarily as all the students are very much active on all social media sites. Even tie ups with colleges to promote apps would work.
3. There should be more focus on **tailormade programs**. Students would be more inclined to use and check-in if facilities and programs were customized for them.
4. App developers should make apps more **interactive, creative and interesting** by using animations and motivational stories

of people. App developers can optimise their interfaces by introducing apps in their regional languages too.
5. **Ethical and confidentiality** have always been the biggest concern. The approaches used to construct mental health apps should be properly disclosed to end consumers, by app creators. They should also be transparent about their security procedures. There is a need for a significant evidence basis to educate us on the effectiveness and safety of mental health apps.
6. Specific parameters must be developed in order to conduct a **standardized assessment** of mental health-related app **performance**. Clinical professionals should peer-review these apps. Several public and private stakeholders must be engaged in the implementation with the purpose of delivering verified information and accreditation for mental health applications that patients can use to judge their effectiveness and make meaningful selections.
7. To keep customers involved, programmers should present a number of **options, features, and content** from which they can choose, such as a number of meditations, exercises, and challenge categories.
8. In an emergency or crisis situation, there should be an **offline option** that enables customers to access the mental health app. Developers can capture and save user history and data while the consumer is offline, then upload the information whenever the user connects to the internet.
9. Some form of **legislation and control** of health apps is urgently needed to assure both efficiency and integrity. All main partners, including healthcare specialists and end consumers, should be involved in the regulatory process.

CONCLUSION

Mental health apps not only have the ability to enhance service quality, but also are playing a transformational role in improving access and affordability across India. The country has a severe shortage of professional psychologists. Under such a scenario, easy smartphone based digital apps are going to drive away the taboos and help people access the required mental health support in a safe, convenient and on-demand basis. It should be mentioned that a mental health app will never be able to substitute a consultation to a psychiatrist and is not intended to do so.

REFERENCES

Aggarwal NK (2012). Applying mobile technologies to mental health service delivery in South Asia. *Asian Journal of Psychiatry.*;5(3):225–230. 10.1016/j.ajp.2011.12.009 [PubMed] [CrossRef] [Google Scholar]

Brian RM, Ben-Zeev D (2014). Mobile health (mHealth) for mental health in Asia: objectives, strategies, and limitations. *Asian Journal of Psychiatry.*; 10:96–100. 10.1016/j.ajp.2014.04.006 [PubMed] [CrossRef] [Google Scholar]

Chadda RK (2014). Caring for the family caregivers of persons with mental illness. *Indian Journal of Psychiatry.*;56(3):221–227. 10.4103/0019-5545.140616 [PMC free article] [PubMed] [CrossRef] [Google Scholar]

Keyes, CLM. (2005). Mental illness and/or mental health? Investigating axioms of the complete state model of health. J Consult Clin Psychol; 73: 539–548.Google cholar | Crossref | Medline | ISI

Price M, Yuen EK, Goetter EM, et al. (2014). mHealth: a mechanism to deliver more accessible, more effective mental health care. *Clin Psychol Psychother*; 21:427-36. 10.1002/cpp.1855 [PMC free article] [PubMed] [CrossRef] [Google Scholar]

Srivastava Kalpana C K, Bhat PS (2016). Mental Health Awareness: The Indian Scenario. *Industrial Psychiatry Journal.*;25(2):131–134.

10.4103/ipj.ipj_45_17 [PMC free article] [PubMed] [CrossRef] [Google Scholar]

Technology and the Future of Mental Health Treatment. National Institute of Mental Health (2017). Available online:https://www.nimh.nih.gov/health/topics/technology-and-the-future-of-mental-health-treatment/index.shtml

World Health Organization (1992). The ICD-10 Classification of Mental and Behavioural Disorders: Clinical Descriptions and Diagnostic Guidelines; 1992. http://apps.who.int/iris/bitstream/10665/37958/8/9241544228_eng.pdf.

Chapter 4

Challenges brought up by Covid-19 Pandemic

4.1 Effect of lockdown on Consumer behavior with reference to usage of Fitness apps in Mumbai District

Ms. Sunita A. Panja and Ms. Nikita M. Tanksali

ABSTRACT

Constant technological evolution and the development of new mobile devices such as Smartphones or tablets loaded with a variety of applications that offer a higher level of comfort and practical use to consumers has become the center of life for consumers.

During this pandemic situation, India has witnessed the huge lockdown in the world—from March 25 to May 2020, where 130 crore Citizen were instructed to stay indoors. It was during this period, there was a huge surge in downloads of various apps all over the world. Amongst all, the fitness apps saw a upswing in daily active users (DAUs). India saw the upsurge in downloads of fitness apps. People had not only downloaded these apps but they actually used them.

Due to lockdown, the only option left for fitness industry was to increase their digital presence. Large number of fitness studios started offering online classes, letting members to access such services from their doorsteps. The pandemic also stimulated people to change their food habit, daily workout routine, their home gyms and invest more in fitness equipment. People have become more conscious about their health and fitness.

On the other hand, it raises a question in everyone's mind, whether people will sustain their daily workout routines and food habits post pandemic? With the ever multiplying variants of the Covid Virus, it becomes important to understand the effectiveness and efficiency of the Fitness App Industry in the long run.

The aim of this study is to observe the shift in consumer behavior relating to Fitness apps and food habits during the pandemic situation. Also a systematic review on the intention of the consumers to use these mobile applications related to the future of fitness post pandemic, mindfulness and undertaking physical activity by consumers in order to stay fit and healthy forever. The study will also throw light on the improvement to be made by the fitness industry to sustain in the market even after pandemic.

Keywords: Pandemic, Mobile applications, Fitness, Food habit, Consumer behaviour

INTRODUCTION

Fitness industries in India is growing and thriving exponentially. The state of wellness and to maintain a healthy lifestyle is desired by all. Many people in India are becoming increasingly concerned about their health as a result of sedentary work. People in India are suffering serious effects as a result of their unhealthy lifestyles and macro-environmental situations. Constant rise in obesity, stroke, diabetes, and heart ailment triggered the emphasis amongst people about their health. As a result, the future of fitness and health industries appears to be brighter.

Technological developments to the health and fitness business has resulted in an explosion of fitness apps in India. Every health and fitness app aspires to offer more unique and inventive features than previous versions.

During pandemic and also due to the high cost of subscriptions in health and fitness centres, there has been a boom in the health and fitness app sector in India. There was increase in the download of Fitness Apps in India by 156%- the highest in any country during the pandemic. Through a variety of fitness and wellness apps, fitness enthusiasts were not only meeting their daily workout targets but were also practicing mindfulness and meditation.

Those who are keen to live a healthy lifestyle embraced health and fitness applications in massive numbers. These apps are quite cost-effective for health-conscious people. Fitness applications also serve as a motivator, encouraging users to live a healthier and fitter lifestyle and increasing their health awareness. The main purpose of these mobile applications is to keep consumers updated about their health.

The most beneficial fitness applications have been those that track heart rates, calorie intakes, sleep cycles, daily water consumption and monitor glucose levels in the body due to the ease and efficiency with which these things may be measured, as opposed to conventional, ineffective physical activity trackers.

Modern fitness technology lead to the development of Metaverse due to which the fitness fans are able to achieve their fitness objectives with the help of extremely immersive and engaging exercise games in the future. The games are promoting movement-based cardio exercises, music-mapped routines, and innovative fitness activities like as boxing, sword fighting, and dance, among others, and will be produced using VR and AR technologies.

REVIEW OF LITERATURE

Sakitha Anna Joseph, Reshma Raj K., Sony Vijayan (March, 2020) in their paper *"User's Perspective about Mobile Fitness Applications"* analysed the impact of fitness application on users and the effectiveness of fitness application on improving user's fitness.

Salvador Angosto, Jeronimo Garcia-Fernandez, Irena Valantine and Moises Grimaldi-Puyana (August 2020) in their paper *"The Intention to Use Fitness and Physical Activity Apps: A Systematic Review"* identified the factors that lead to the intention to use technologies, Smartphones and Apps in sport category.

Qing Wang, Bjorg Egelansdal, Gro V Amdam, Valerie L Almli, and Marije Oostindjer (April, 2016) in their paper *"Diet and Physical Activity Apps: Perceived Effectiveness by App Users"* identified that Diet apps were more effective when they were frequently used and over a long period of time, compared to infrequent or short-term use.

OBJECTIVES OF THE STUDY

1) To study the importance of Fitness/Mindfulness in our life
2) To observe the shift in the consumer behavior relating to Fitness apps and food habits during the pandemic situation.
3) To understand the efficiency and effectiveness of the Fitness App Industry in the long run
4) To suggest measures on the improvement to be made by the fitness industry to sustain in the market even after pandemic.

LIMITATION OF STUDY

The primary data collected for study is limited to the Mumbai District only and restricted for the period of 3 years (1st April, 2019 to 31st March, 2022). Primary data may get biased and may be influenced by the behavior and mood of the respondents from whom data is collected.

RESEARCH METHODOLOGY

The present study has a sample of 35 respondents belonging to the working class across Mumbai District, who are selected on the basis of convenient sampling to know the effect of lockdown on their behavior towards fitness and mindfulness activity and schedule.

Data has been collected using primary and secondary methods of data collection. Primary data was collected through the structured questionnaire through Google forms to satisfy the objective of the research paper. Also Direct personnel interview method was followed to extract information from respondents.

Secondary data was collected from various journals, articles, newspapers, magazines and websites. The collected data were further analyzed by using simple statistical tool like percentage

DATA ANALYSIS & INTERPRETATION

- **Demographic Composition of the respondents:**

Table 1. Gender-wise composition of the Respondent

Gender	Number of Respondent	Percentage (%)
Male	21	60
Female	14	40
Total	**35**	**100**

Source: Primary Data

Table 2. Age-wise composition of the Respondent

Age	Number of Respondent	Percentage (%)
Below 30	18	51.4
30 – 40	2	5.7
40 – 50	9	25.7
50 – 60	5	14.3
Above 60	1	2.9
Total	**35**	**100**

Source: Primary Data

Table 3. Qualification of the Respondent

Qualification	Number of Respondent	Percentage (%)
Undergraduate	5	14.3
Graduation	5	14.3
Post-Graduation	18	51.4
Professional Qualification	7	20
Total	**35**	**100**

Source: Primary Data

Table 4. Occupation of the Respondent

Occupation	Number of Respondent	Percentage (%)
Homemaker	3	8.6
Self Employed	9	25.7
Service in Public Sector	2	5.7
Service in Private Sector	15	42.8
Retired	3	8.6
Professional	3	8.6
Total	**35**	**100**

Source: Primary Data

- **How do you take care of your Physical & Mental Well-being?**

Table 5. Care of Physical & Mental Well being

	Number of Respondent	Percentage
Yoga	6	17.1
Exercise	8	22.9
Gym	12	34.3
Diet	9	25.7
Others	0	0
Total	**35**	**100**

Source: Primary Data

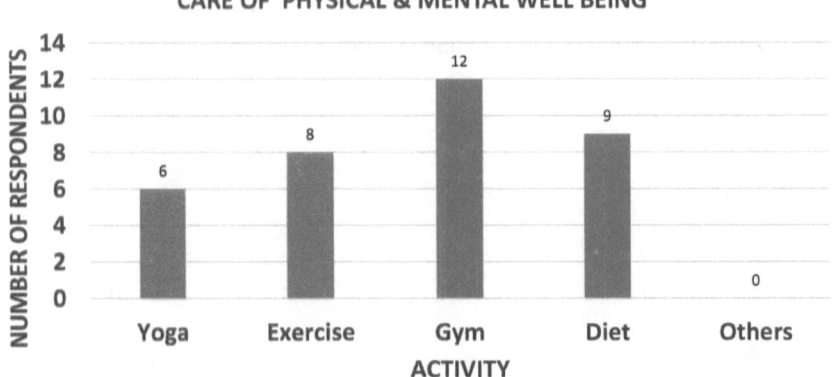

Figure 1: Care of Physical & Mental Well being

Source: Primary Data

Out of the total respondents, around 17% of respondents take care of their health and mental well-being through yoga, whereas approx. 23% of the respondents are engaged in regular

workout/exercise activities, 34% of the respondents regularly visit gyms and fitness centres and around 26% of the respondents follow a diet to stay physically and mentally fit.

- **Did the current pandemic situation affect your routine mindfulness/ fitness activity?**

Table 6. Effect of current pandemic situation on routine mindfulness/ fitness activity

	Number of Respondent	Percentage (%)
Yes	27	77.1
No	8	22.9
Total	**35**	**100**

Source: Primary Data

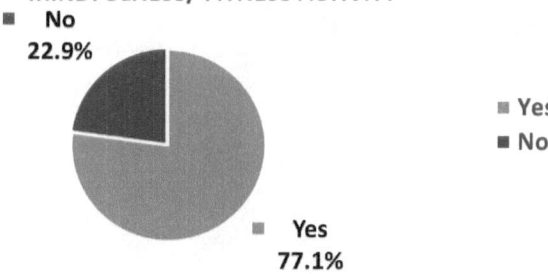

Figure 2: Effect of current pandemic situation on routine mindfulness/ fitness activity

Source: Primary Data

The above chart and table shows that the current pandemic situation has affected the majority of the respondents (77%) in their routine fitness activity whereas 23% of the respondents claimed that the pandemic has no effect in their routine mindfulness/fitness activity.

- If Yes, how did it affect your mindfulness/ fitness activity?

Table 7. Time Effect on mindfulness/ fitness activity

	Number of Respondent	Percentage (%)
Devoted More Time	19	54.3
Devoted Less Time	5	14.3
No Time	3	8.6
No Change in schedule	8	22.8
Total	**35**	**100**

Source: Primary Data

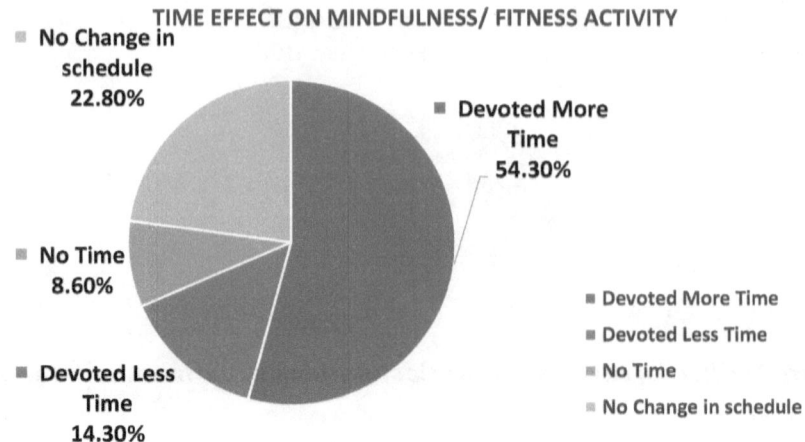

Figure 3: Time Effect on mindfulness/ fitness activity

Source: Primary Data

Majority of the respondents (54.3+14.3+8.6) = 77.2% say that owing to the current pandemic situation, there is a change in their mindfulness/ fitness schedule. Nearly 54.3% respondents could

spend more time for their fitness activity, whereas only 14.3% respondents complained of having less time for such activity, very few respondents (8.6%) said that they could not devote any time at all for their fitness. On the other hand, almost 23% of the respondents said that there is no change in their fitness activity schedule during the pandemic situation.

- **How have you managed to sustain the existing Fitness/ Mindfulness activity during the lockdown?**

Table 8. Sustenance of existing Fitness/ Mindfulness activity during the Lockdown

	Number of Respondent	Percentage (%)
Yoga at Home	9	25.7
Home Gym Set up	8	22.9
Installed Fitness Apps	13	37.1
Not applicable	5	14.3
Other	0	0
Total	**35**	**100**
Source:	*Primary*	*Data*

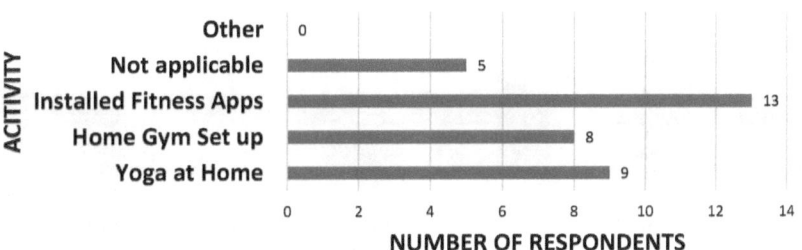

Figure 4: Sustenance of existing Fitness/ Mindfulness activity during the Lockdown Source: Primary Data

On inquiring about the sustenance of existing fitness/mindfulness activity, 25.7% of the respondents started performing yoga at their home itself, approximately 23% of the respondents have installed gym at home to perform their daily work out, 37.1% of the respondents have installed various fitness apps to have a track on their fitness activity.

- **What is the effect of the change in the fitness activity on your health?**

Table 9. Effect of the change in the fitness activity on respondent's health:

	Number of Respondent	Percentage (%)
Change in weight	12	34.3
Change in Food habits	10	28.6
Change in health conditions	6	17.1
Not applicable	0	0
No effect	7	20
Total	35	100

Source: Primary Data

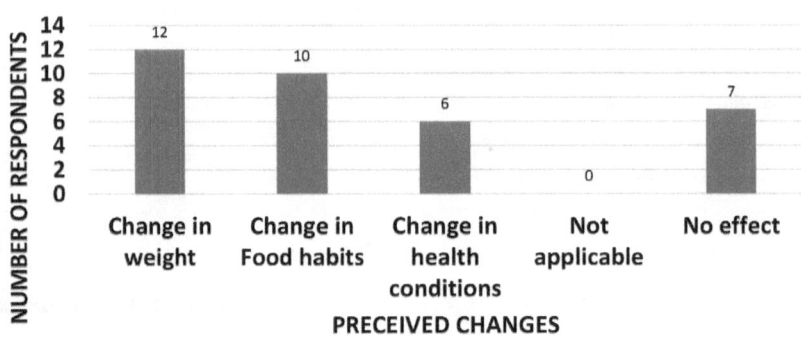

Figure 5: Effect of the change in the fitness activity on respondent's health

Source: Primary Data

Around 80% of the respondents observed change in them owing to the change in the scheduled of fitness activity with respect to change in their weight (34.3%), change in food habits (28.6%) or change in their overall health condition (17.1%). Nearly 20% of the respondents felt no change in them in this current pandemic situation.

- **Are you aware of the following Fitness Apps?**

Table 10. Awareness regarding Fitness Apps

	Number of Respondent	Percentage (%)
Fitelo	5	14.3
Cure.Fit	6	17.1
Fittr	8	22.9
HealthifyMe	10	28.5
Aaptiv	1	2.9
Others	1	2.9
NA	4	11.4
Total	**35**	**100**

Source: Primary Data

The above table shows that almost 88.6% of the respondents are aware of some or the other fitness apps as these kinds of apps are more popular among the younger generations whereas only 11.4% of the respondents are not aware of any of the fitness apps. Amongst the well-known fitness app in India, HealthifyMe and Fittr are the most popular apps due to heavy digital marketing and brand endorsements by the Bollywood celebrities.

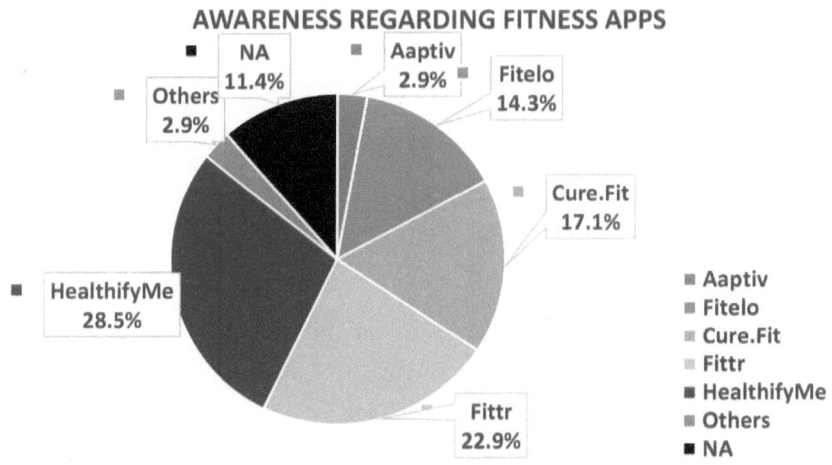

Figure 6: Awareness regarding Fitness Apps

Source: Primary Data

- According to you, which is the most important element in a Fitness/ Mindfulness Application?

Table 11. Most Important Element in a Fitness App

	Number of Respondent	Percentage (%)
Workout/ Yoga Routines	10	28.6
Recipes	3	8.6
Calorie Counting	7	20
Progress Charts	5	14.3
Running Tracker	6	17.1
Other NA	4	11.4
Total	**35**	**100**

Source: Primary Data

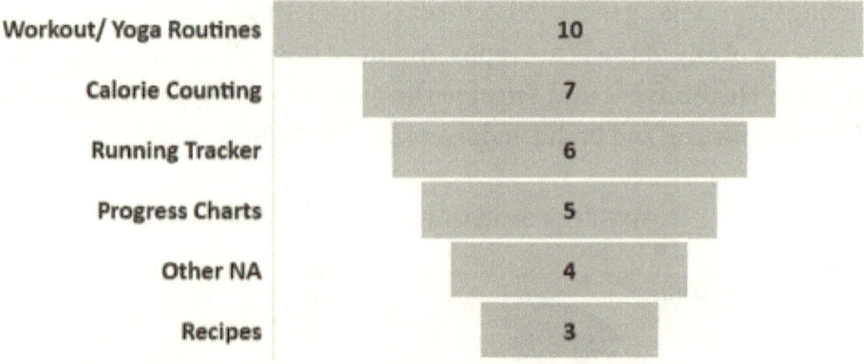

Figure 7: Most Important Element in a Fitness App

Source: Primary Data

From the above chart and Table, it can be said that majority of the respondents (28.6%) feels that workout/yoga routine is the most important element in Fitness apps which is primarily required by the users of apps followed by calorie counting (20%), Running tracker (17.1%), progress chart (14.3%), Diet Recipes (8.6%)

- **Do you use any of the above mentioned Fitness/ Mindfulness applications?**

Table 12. Use of Fitness/ Mindfulness applications

	Number of Respondent	Percentage (%)
Yes	27	77.1
No	8	22.9
Total	**35**	**100**

Source: Primary Data

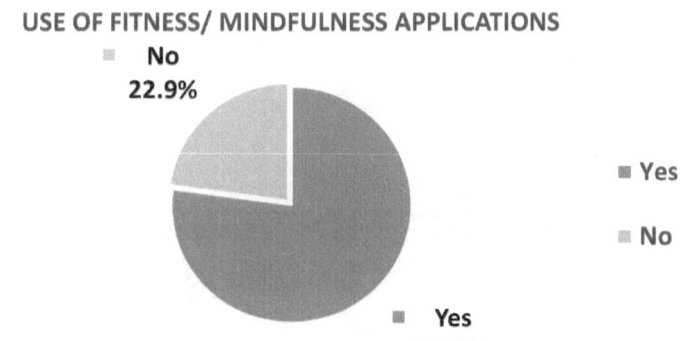

Figure 8: Use of Fitness/ Mindfulness applications

Source: Primary Data

Out of the respondents who are aware of the fitness apps, about 77% of them actually use these apps as these apps are highly cost effective and users can use it as per their convenience whereas 23% of the respondents have not yet personally used these apps maybe due to lack of awareness and lack of technical knowledge regarding usage of these apps.

- **If Yes, are these applications helpful to attain your fitness goal during the pandemic?**

Table 13. Attainment of Fitness Goals

	Number of Respondent	Percentage (%)
Yes	27	77.2
No	2	5.7
Can't Say	6	17.1
Total	35	100

Source: Primary Data

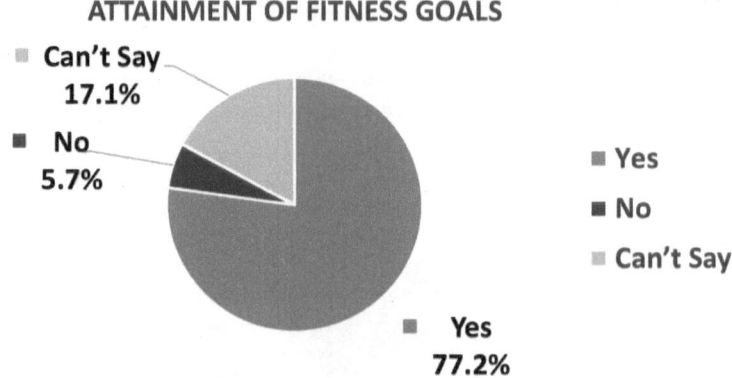

Figure 9: Attainment of Fitness Goals

Source: Primary Data

Out of the respondents who have used fitness apps, 77.2% of the respondents observed that these apps have actually helped to attain their fitness goal during pandemic as respondents could continue with their routine fitness activity with the help of these apps whereas 5.7% of the respondents felt that the app is not helpful in attaining fitness goal. Nearly 17.1% of respondents can't comment on the usefulness of the apps at this stage.

- **If Yes, rank your usage preference related to your preferred applications?**

16. If Yes, Rank your usage preference related to your preferred applications ? (1: Not Satisfied, 2:Neutral, 3: Satisfied)

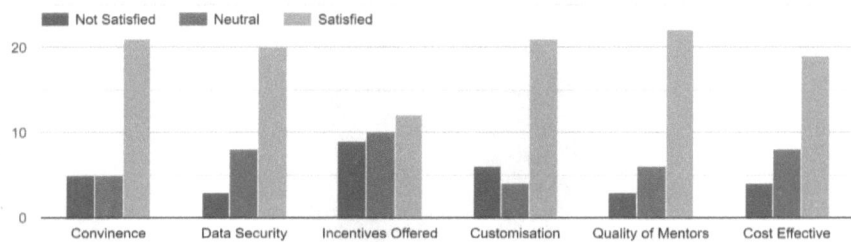

Figure 10: Usage preference of Fitness/ Mindfulness Apps

Source: Primary Data

The above chart shows that the majority of the respondents are satisfied with the fitness apps they are using with respect to the convenience level, data security, customisation, quality of mentors and cost effectiveness. Only a few respondents are not satisfied with the apps with respect to the lack of incentives offered by them.

- **Will you continue to use these Fitness/ Mindfulness Applications post pandemic?**

Table 14. Willingness to use Fitness/ Mindfulness Applications post pandemic

	Number of Respondent	Percentage (%)
Yes	26	74.29
No	9	25.71
Total	**35**	**100**

Source: Primary Data

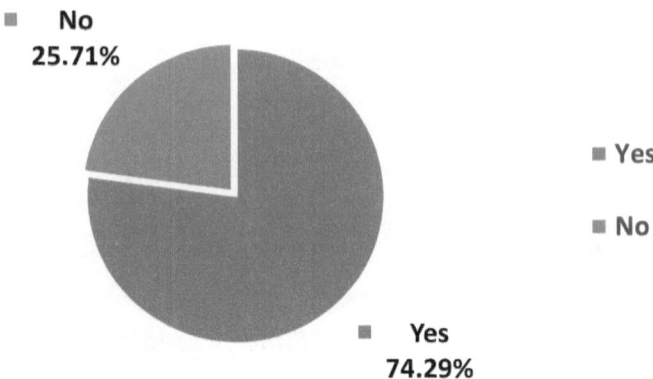

Figure 11: Willingness to use Fitness/ Mindfulness Applications post pandemic

Source: Primary Data

With respect to using the app in future, most of the respondent (74.29%) showed positive attitude and are willing to use the app post pandemic as well. Some of the respondents are keen on having hybrid system rather than completely shifting on either side.

FINDINGS OF THE STUDY

The present study reveals that there is a sharp increase in the use of fitness/mindfulness apps amongst the young generation. There are multiple fitness apps available in the market. One can select the app suitable as per their needs and requirements. Social media plays a vital role in the marketing and advertisement of these apps.

Almost every fitness app software has the same goal of encouraging users to move more and eat less. Consumers are urged to keep track of their food intake and physical activity. But at the same time, when it comes to lifestyle changes like adopting a healthier diet or becoming fit, a lack of community support from family or friends is a significant disadvantage.

It was discovered that most of the Fitness Apps use game-like incentives to encourage consumers to engage in specific activities, such as calorie counting or regular exercise. These kind of incentives really motivates the consumers to engage in fitness activities on a regular basis

It was observed that few online fitness apps permit the mentor to see mentees, check their form, and offer alterations or improvements based on their performance. This results in the users, especially beginners or those recovering from injuries inadvertently performing exercises incorrectly, or even unsafely, without knowing it. Also, the present fitness applications lack automated tools that would allow users to enter the essential data much more quickly. That's why so many people give up on fitness apps after a month or two. They simply don't have the patience to keep track of their daily activities.

Many consumers experience their smart phone battery drained after regular use of these fitness and mindfulness apps. Due to continuous tracking of activity the consumers experienced their smartphone to heat up as well.

Fitness apps exposed to data security and privacy protection issues. If the hacker receives access to the consumer device, it is possible to attack a social engineering attack based on the user's habits, and the hacker can also access confidential information such as credit card or debit card number.

SUGGESTIONS

- ❖ **Suggestion to Fitness App Industries:**

    - **Trial Week:** Fitness apps could provide a one-week trial period. During this trial week coaches can mentor the user. Since many premium options are available only after purchasing the app membership, thus a trial week can be a good insight into the app features for the consumer.

- **Encryption & decryption:** Fitness app companies can integrate end-to-end data encryption to prevent unauthorized people from accessing consumer data. Consumers can also attach the decryption key to the app's lock code along with the app's password. Consumers can avoid sharing sensitive data with the fitness applications for example Aadhaar Number, PAN number, Bank Account Details etc

- **Optimized Calorie Calculation:** New users to the app should be provided insights to how to accurately track and calculate calories. There might also be a section where the customer can enter their medical history so that diet and exercise routines can be determined accordingly. The app should employ systems that would assist users in their food choices instead of counting calories.

- **Better App Integration:** The Fitness apps can employ Artificial Intelligence and Machine Learning to allow users to enter the essential data much more quickly and efficiently. Fitness apps can improve their integration with smart watches and fitness bands of various brands. This will cut down manual intervention of the user in inputting the data.

❖ Suggestions to Consumer:

Consumers can initiate whatsapp or facebook groups to foster community support in their Fitness/ Mindfulness Journey. In order to avoid unauthorized user access, the administrators of the group may establish two factor authentication. Further consumers using similar fitness apps can team up to track their fitness progress. Members can rate the app or they can share their feedback/experience about the app which will help the new entrant to take an informed decision. Consumers can set their phone on Battery Optimization. The consumer can disable background running permission to the apps. This will help consumers to save and conserve battery.

CONCLUSION

India, as a developing country, has a variety of health challenges affecting its citizens. Many individuals in India are unable to determine their own lifestyles. In this pandemic, everyone has given importance to fitness and mental health like never before across the world. Indians were consuming home-cooked food, were exercising regularly, were going for consistent health checkups, and were upgrading their fitness regimes using advanced apps and devices. Pandemic has massive transformation in the Fitness industries in India There has been a rapid adoption of tele-health services and health or fitness apps at this time providing an alternative for health counselling at their doorstep. As a result, healthcare app development and fitness application development are creating a buzz. Fitness metaverse supported by apps are making consumers' fitness journeys more immersive and interesting. Overall it can be said that transition has begun in the Fitness Industry and the change will sustain in the form of hybrid mode in the coming years.

REFERENCES

Brad Millington (2014). Smartphone Apps and the Mobile Privatization of Health and Fitness. Critical Studies in Media Communication, 31(5), 479-493. doi:10.1080/15295036.2014.973429

H. Erin Lee and Jaehee Cho (2017). What Motivates Users to Continue Using Diet and Fitness Apps? Application of the Uses and Gratifications Approach. Health Communication, 32(12), 1445-1453. doi:10.1080/10410236.2016.1167998

Joshua H. West, P. Cougar Hall, Carl L. Hanson, Michael D. Barnes, Christophe Giraud-Carrier, James Barrett (2012). There's an App for That: Content Analysis of Paid Health and Fitness Apps. J Med Internet Res 2012, 14(3):e72.doi:10.2196/jmir.1977

Juliana Chen, Janet E. Cade, and Margaret Allman-Farinelli (2015). The Most Popular Smartphone Apps for Weight Loss: A Quality Assessment. JMIR mHealth uHealth 2015, 3(4):e104. doi:10.2196/mhealth.4334

Lynn Katherine Herrmann and Jinsook Kim (2017). The Fitness of apps: a theory-based examination of mobile fitness app usage over 5 months. Mhealth 2017, 3(2). doi:10.21037/mhealth.2017.01.03

Website:

www.skyhook.com
www.hackernoon.com
www.ncbi.nlm.nih.gov
www.rubygarage.org

4.2 MASK: A Protective Measure or A Potential Hazard?

[1]Pallavi Anant Gurav, [2]Shreya Ravi Agrawal, [3]Priyanka Dinanath Koli, [4]Aditi Umesh Patwardhan

ABSTRACT

Aim *To carry out survey in Indian urban population and to understand the physiological and psychological effects of respirator's extensive mask usage and understand its unwanted effects.*

Method: *A web-based survey questionnaire was circulated amongst the age group of 16-60 years of individuals and the data was interpreted graphically and analysed statistically.*

Participated: *160 respondents from which 117 were students and 43 were professional workers (Teachers, Heath care workers, Tour manager, Photographers, etc)*

Result obtained: *As per the survey conducted majority of the participants were aware that wearing mask & sanitization is necessary as an integral part of hygiene & preventive measure. The overall health implications of Mask Induced Fatigue Syndrome (MIFS) (like uneasiness, headache, difficulty breathing, etc) was observed as per the study conducted.*

After analysis of data, it was observed that 64.4% participants often leave home for work and other activities among 87.5% of people always wear a mask out of which 33.1% of participants have worn a mask for a period of 2 to 4 hours. Considering the extensive usage of mask by the population, headache, difficult breathing, skin breakdown, acne and impaired cognition were all recognized as common adverse effects and statistically analysed.

Conclusion*: In the majority of individuals questioned, prolonged usage of masks during COVID-19 resulted in undesirable consequences such as*

headaches, rash, acne, skin breakdown, and reduced cognition. It is important to discover strategies to manage these negative consequences in preparation for future pandemics. For future treatment of undesirable effects connected to extended mask usage, frequent breaks, enhanced hydration and relaxation, skin care, and maybe newly developed comfortable masks are recommended.

Keywords: COVID-19, Respiratory Protective Equipment (RPE), Community spread, Pandemic, mask, Physical distancing, Mask Induced Fatigue Syndrome (MIFS)

INTRODUCTION

In recent years, with an increasing incidence of infections, especially with a frequent incidence of respiratory infections, people tend to be in the high-risk group of respiratory infections. Wearing a mask is the main way to stop the new coronavirus, especially in the current outbreak of COVID-19, as the main transmission route is droplet infection. [2-5]

After wearing the mask, people suffocate and feel uncomfortable even when sitting still. Also, people wearing masks directly reduces the amount of oxygen that the body inhales, resulting in a lack of oxygen in the brain, which can even harm the health of the body. People feel uncomfortable wearing masks, especially with the arrival of summer, but the COVID-19 epidemic is not over yet and people need to continue wearing masks with. Due to lack of mask resources, people are wearing masks made of various materials. However, different types of masks have different effects on people's health and well-being. Therefore, the scientific and rational selection of suitable masks has become a hot topic in current research [8-11]. Based on this, in this paper, we conducted survey study on the effects of wearing various masks on human comfort and health in warm environments from the three perspectives of subjective evaluation, physiological tests, and thermal imaging tests. We want to provide people with an accurate foundation for selection of appropriate mask.

REVIEW OF LITERATURE

While the virus' high-activity phase has passed, many cities in India and other nations have lately voted to make wearing a mask mandatory both inside and outside public venues.

Before the present situation, articles focusing on the usefulness of wearing a mask were published. It is widely agreed that it is beneficial in potentially infectious areas, such as hospitals. Patients in high-viral-pressure environments, such as hospitals and other health-care institutions, but in other instances remained cautious, arguing a lack of evidence [1].

The World Health Organization (WHO) suggested mask usage exclusively for symptomatic, unwell patients and health care professionals in April 2020, but not for the general public. They amended their suggestion in June 2020 to support the wearing of masks in all situations, including as crowded areas. Wearing masks provided no obvious, scientifically understandable benefit of moderate or strong evidence in a meta-analysis research commissioned by the WHO (evidence level Ia). While maintaining a distance of at least one metre revealed significant evidence for the transmission of SARS-CoV-2, masks alone in everyday use showed only minimal evidence at best (non-medical setting). In the same year, another meta-analysis revealed the lack of scientific support for masks. As a result, the WHO did not promote the broad or uncritical use of masks for the general public, and it quickly enlarged its risk and danger list.

While the April 2020 guideline focused on the risks of self-contamination, possible breathing difficulties, and a false sense of security, the June 2020 guideline discovered additional potential negative effects such as headache, the development of facial skin lesions, irritant dermatitis, acne, and an increased risk of contamination in public spaces due to improper mask disposal [8][19].

While in the current pandemic scenario, people are very susceptible to most respiratory infections. Especially for COVID 19, droplets that travel through air (expelled during coughing, exhaling, sneezing, etc) are the main transmission route. The mask acts as a blocking pathway for transmission, but wearing the mask causes malaise, uneasiness, direct blood gas transfer, hypoxia (decreased O2), hypercapnia (increased CO2). Deterioration of quality of life due to reduced cardiopulmonary capacity, in the body's brain and other tissues not only while movement and locomotion but also when body is at rest, has been observed. It also depends on the material of the mask we wear. The pandemic is not over yet, hence we continue to wear masks [11] [7] [15] [13] [8].

Microdroplets and fomites have been linked to the risk of infection, but how do microdroplets behave in the air, given their large size/weight ratio? They'll go through a quick desiccation process that shrinks them down to the size of the virus. Because inert particles or viruses of the same size have equal penetrating powers, there is no reason to consider sizes other than the virus's size when determining the virus's stopping power by a mask or a respirator. As a result, the issue of the mask/respirator is extremely unique. In the workplace, at the absolute least, the FFP3 (N99) mask is advised to defend against viruses; however, current guidelines for COVID-19 protection do not prescribe the FFP3 respirator, but rather the FFP2, or even a surgical mask, which presents an evident consistency problem [4][10[11].

It is also important to note that, based on the type of mask material used, nanoparticulated coronavirus cannot be blocked by the mesh of this mask with pore size in micrometres and hence, being tiny enough it penetrates and aggregates within the mesh. A handmade cloth mask containing a drop of saliva or other droplets will absorb and retain more moisture, warm your breathing and collect most nanoparticles, providing a perfect medium for pathogen to survive or even multiply within the mask, eventually attacking the wearer. The virus can survive efficiently in moist environments and can infect carriers and the people around them. Not cleaning the mask properly can add on to the danger. [2] [3] [16].

Mask reuse and long-term usage are also frequent in many regions of the world, especially during epidemics and pandemics. Respiratory infections can be found on the layers of worn masks, causing illness in the wearer. These infections may be created in hospital settings by patients breathing, coughing, or sneezing, or during aerosol-generating medical operations. According to studies, influenza virus can stay airborne for up to three hours after a patient has passed through an emergency room. These bacteria can cause illness by hand or skin contamination, ingestion, or mucus membrane contact when wearing masks for lengthy periods of time. The presence of respiratory infections on the surface of PPE and other fomites in hospital settings is currently unknown. Influenza and respiratory syncytial virus (RSV) have been found to persist on the outer surface of PPE in previous tests [1-3].

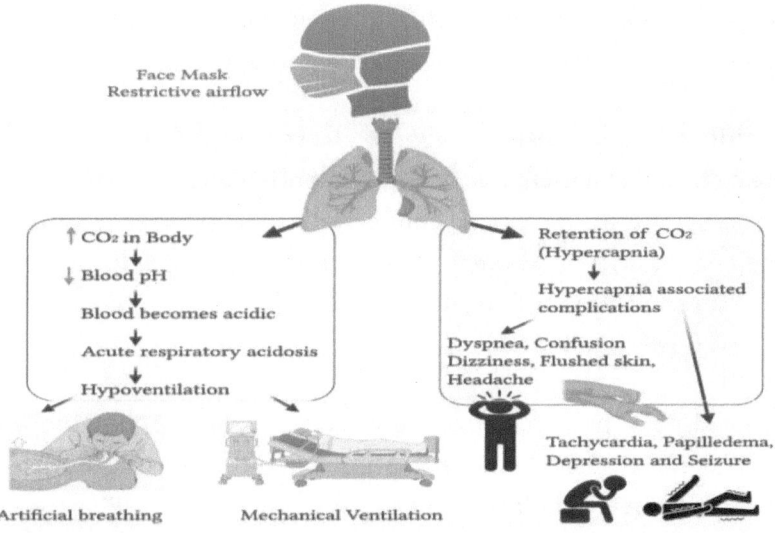

Figure 1: Restrictive airflow due to face mask may lead to hypercapnia and associated secondary complications including+ tachycardia, dyspnea, confusion, flushed skin, dizziness and headache, and severe hypercapnia can lead to respiratory failure with symptoms of depression, papilledema and seizure. [1]

Respiratory Protective Equipment (RPE) also causes harmful skin reactions such as acne, contact dermatitis, itchy face and skin rashes, as reported in the study. Experiments have proved that long-term use of masks increases skin dehydration, redness, pH, and sebum secretion. The recommended N95

mask was significantly associated with these mask-induced skin reactions [5]. Several studies have found that increased humidity causes sweating, which causes swelling of epidermal keratinocytes, which ultimately leads to acute obstruction and exacerbation of acne [9]. Literature studies have shown that both healthy and sick people can suffer from mask-induced fatigue syndrome (MIFS). However, to fully understand the potential effects of RPE on the wearer, the physiological and psychological effects of respirator's extensive mask usage should be evaluated. Like every coin has two sides RPE has its downfalls too, for example they can: disturb the state of thermal equilibrium; communication (straining of the voice box); field of vision; psychomotor skills; personal habits such as eating; unconscious distraction; cognitive ability and other aspects [6][7].

Conditions like halitosis, gingivitis, ulcers, and cavities are becoming more common in patients, according to dentists all around the world. All of these symptoms have been connected to the incorrect and excessive usage of a mask. The wearer's rapidly degrading dental health is one of the most recently identified adverse effects. This phenomenon is known by a new term called "Mask Mouth" [14].

In general, the personal practice of wearing or not wearing a mask depends on the individual's perception and interpretation of the risk of infection, as well as cultural and social considerations. There is a need to understand the current attitude of the citizens towards proper health measures and analyse the patterns and point out the faults which will help us rectify and design more effective and accurate health strategy, awareness and education sources for COVID-19 pandemic and other global disasters expected to arise in the future [12].

RESEARCH METHODOLOGY

1. Web-based survey questionnaire to collect information using google forms was conducted.
2. Since web-survey questionnaires have several advantages over traditional paper questionnaires and face-to-face interviews.
3. Web-surveys can be easily distributed to more people. Also, under the circumstances of COVID19, web-survey did not require person-to-person interaction, eliminating the risk of contamination during the inspection.
4. The questionnaire contains five broad sections:
    i. **Personal information**; this section provides the basic information of the respondents such as their ages and occupation.
    ii. **Mask-wearing habits and changing frequency correlated to lifestyle and work;**
    iii. **Types of mask use and mask cleaning and reuse**; the second and third sections analyses the fundamental mask-using habits, mask change, and reuse habits of people.
    iv. **Symptoms observed after prolonged use of mask**; this section provide information on prolonged use of masks affecting people who might already be struggling with other health issues as well as people who are completely healthy.
    v. **Spreading awareness** among the people **about how maintaining mask hygiene** is important; through this section we are trying to spreading awareness among the people about how to maintain mask hygiene.
5. Multiple types of questions were designed to obtain the information, including multiple-choice questions, single-choice questions, etc.
6. The questionnaire survey was sent out through WhatsApp, the most popular mobile social application in India and the other apps.
7. The surveys questionnaires were designed in English. The complete questionnaires was automatically stored in a database. The data then will be classified and analysed based on the above- mentioned sections.

RESULTS AND DISCUSSIONS

Section 1: Personal Informatio

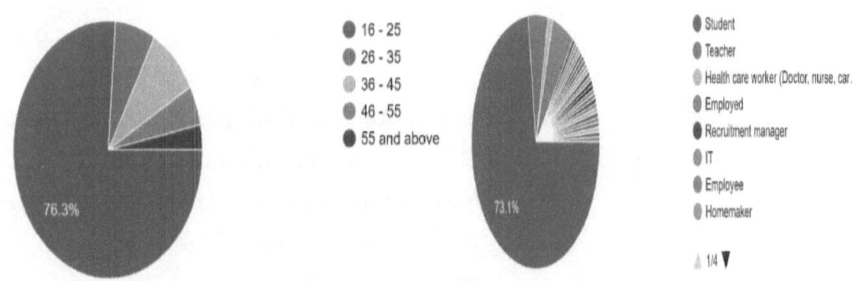

Figure 2: Age groups of participants *Figure 3: Age groups of participants*

(Graphical representation, Source: Google Form)

No specific population was targeted as mask is being used universally by all. The majority of participants belong to the category of 16 – 25 i.e. the young population consisting 122 participants (76.3%). Remaining population belongs to the rest of the age groups. Considering this, the participants are mainly unemployed i.e. belong to students category. Rest was counted under various types of profession. A wide range of population belonging to different professions participated. Majority of participants i.e. 96.9% seen were under healthy state. Out of which 5 participants were having chronic stress, hypertension, asthma etc.

Section 2: Are you aware?

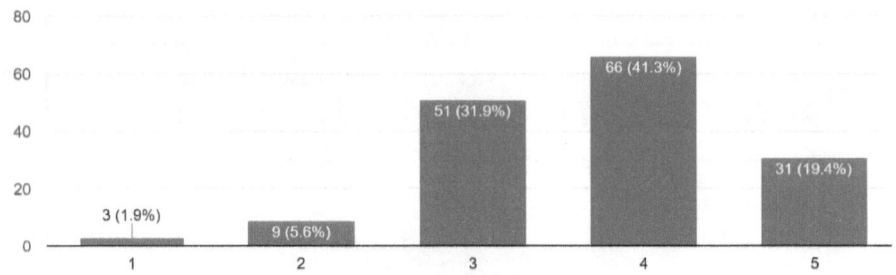

Figure 4: Knowledge rating on WHO Guidelines

(Graphical representation, Source: Google Form)

The above table represents the knowledge level rating of participants on WHO guidelines. This shows that 41.3% of participants rate themselves for 4, which means more people are being aware of guidelines as the threat of being infected increases.

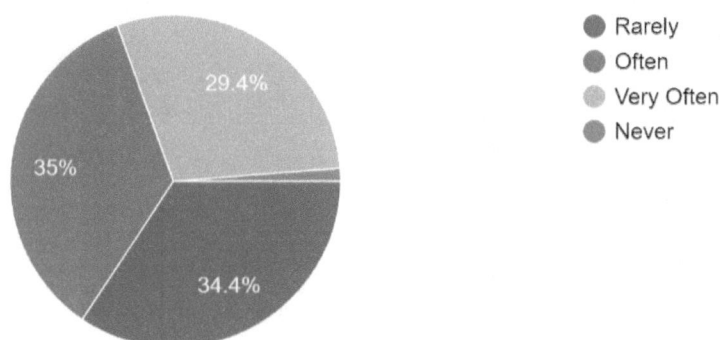

Figure 5: Frequency of participants leave home for work or other activities

(Graphical representation, Source: Google Form)

The above table represents how often does people leave home for work and other activities. Majority of participants responded often (35%) since due to their daily job, college etc. and rarely 34.4%, due to work from home policy.

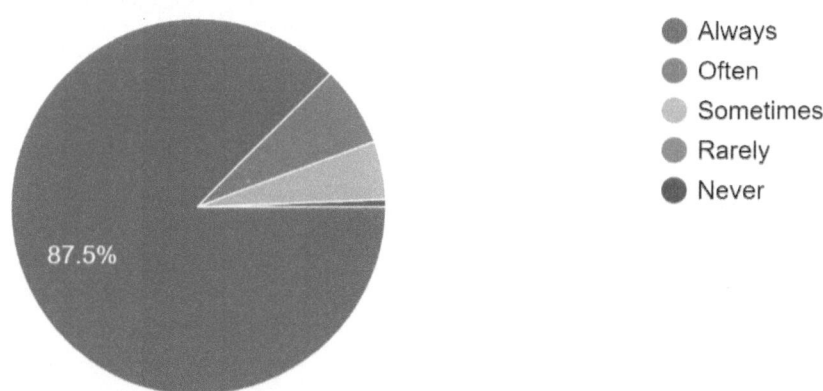

Figure 6: Frequency of participants wearing mask while going out

(Graphical representation, Source: Google Form)

The above pie chart represents majority of participants always wear a mask while going out. Majority of the participants (87.5%) ALWAYS wear mask while stepping out of their house. It is clear by the above data that percentage of people not wearing mask out of home is a very small percentage and hence negligible.

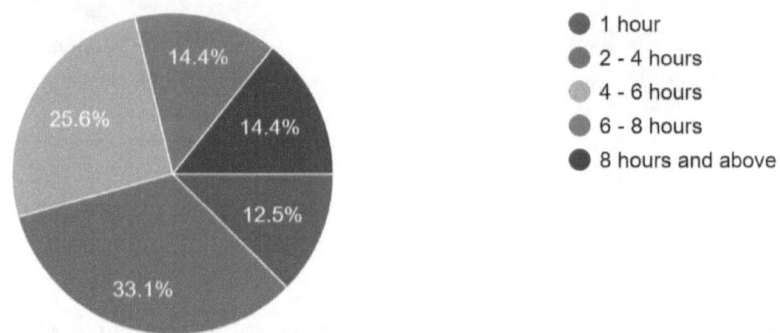

Figure 7: Duration of wearing a mask continuously

(Graphical representation, Source: Google Form)

The data given above depicts a very important aspect of this study. What is the longest duration for which you have worn a mask continuously? The results are diverse yet we can notice that majority of participants have worn a mask for a period of 2 to 4 hours. There is a considerable percentage of participants who have worn mask for a staggering period of time that is 8 hours and above.

Section 3: Types of face mask and maintenance

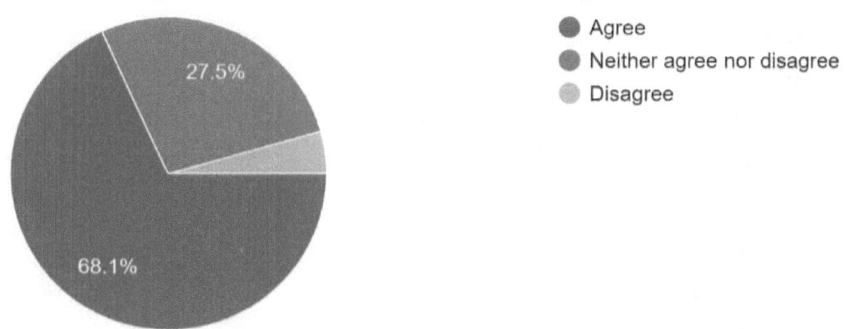

Figure 8: Does wearing a mask help to reduce the spread of the coronavirus?

(Graphical representation, Source: Google Form)

The pie chart given above indicates how many participants think that wearing a mask actually makes a difference and blocks the spread of deadly corona virus. As clearly portrayed by the huge blue section in the pie chart it seems that most participants are quite convinced that wearing a mask will definitely stop the spread of virus. However, a small yet considerable percentage of people do disagree with the notion.

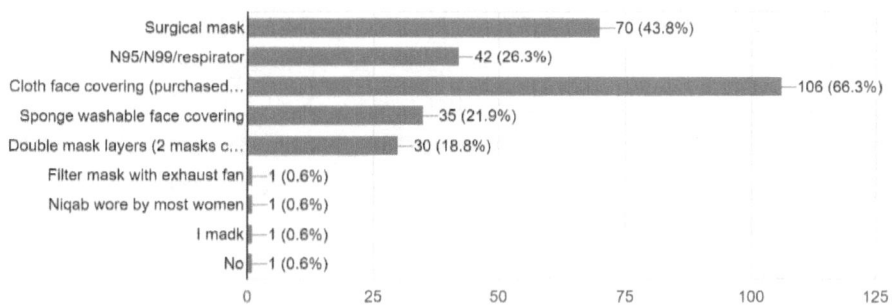

Figure 9: Type of mask used by participants

(Graphical representation, Source: Google Form)

What type of face mask do you wear usually? Select all that apply.

The responses we got for these questions focuses on some remarkable results and hidden truths of what is actually going on in this ruckus of pandemic. N95 was declared as the ideal mask for such a virus infested pandemic situation, yet it is shockingly clear that majority of the participants opt for CLOTH face covering mask instead of the WHO recommended RPE. The reasons being, cloth masks are more comfortable and cheaper.

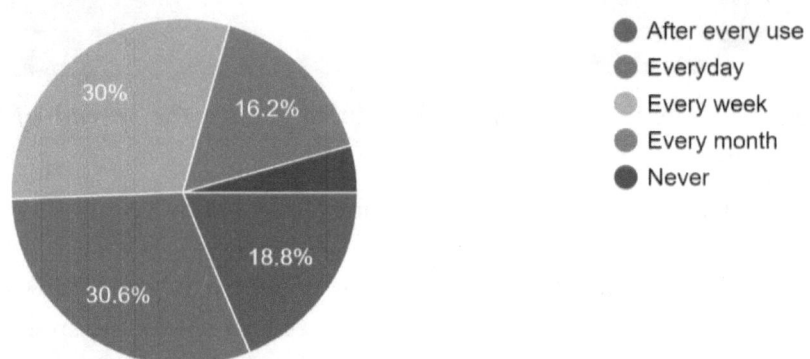

Figure 10: Mask changing habits

(Graphical representation, Source: Google Form)

The data above is very critical as it indicates how serious participants are about mask reusability and mask maintenance. As clearly shown by the pie chart majority of the participants prefer replacing used mask with a new one EVERYDAY. As recommended by WHO, a mask should be replaced with new one 8 hours after use. The above data proves that most participants understand the importance of that guideline and follow it by avoiding mask reusability.

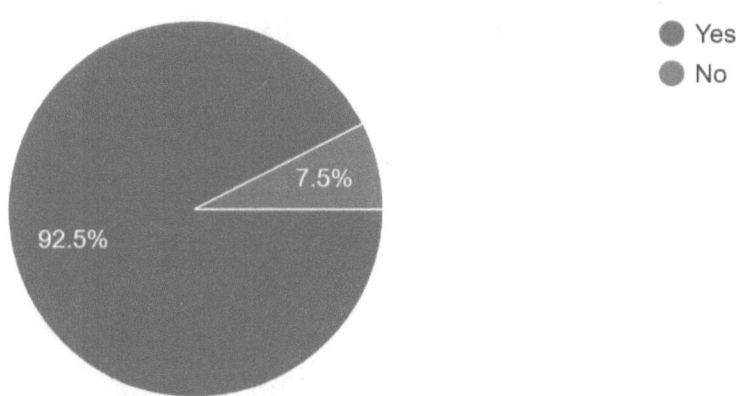

Figure 11: Mask cleaning habits, do you prefer to clean your mask?

(Graphical representation, Source: Google Form)

The data above is a result of a question that was added to the survey aiming to find out how many people prefer cleaning their masks, which is an important aspect of mask maintenance as washing the mask removes the pathogens and dust that might have accumulated over repetitive usage of same mask by the individual. As clearly shown by the pie chart, majority of the participants (92.5%) prefer cleaning (washing) the mask after multiple uses.

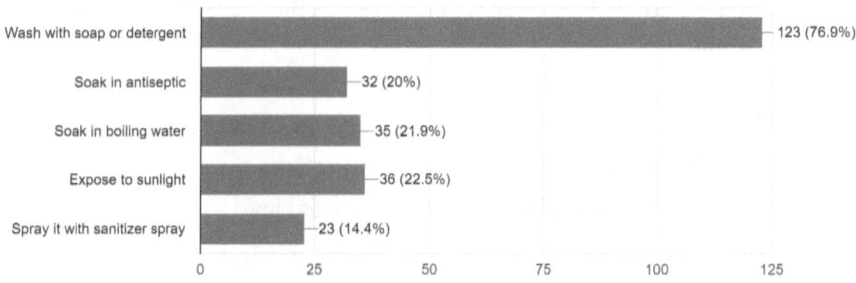

Figure 12: Mask cleaning habits, If yes, then how do you clean your mask?

(Graphical representation, Source: Google Form)

The above chart depicts the methods participants use to clean and maintain their masks. Majorly, participants prefer washing the mask with soap and detergent. Whereas the least participants prefer using sanitizer to disinfect their masks. Around same percentage of people also believe that strict exposure sunlight (Natural UV radiation) or soaking in boiling water might also do the job.

Section 4: Face mask and health

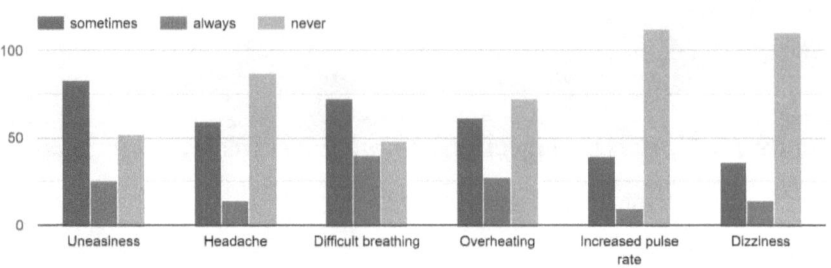

Figure 13: Assessing Mask-Induced Fatigue Syndrome (MIFS)

(Graphical representation, Source: Google Form)

The data above represents the following:

- A large portion of the population suffered difficulty in breathing as the highest response for Always can be clearly observed in this category.

- Next in line for highest response in Always is overheating which proves that sweat accumulation and improper cross ventilation through thick mask material lead to unusual increase in the temperature of the body. Competing with overheating is uneasiness with almost the same number of responses for always.

- Large numbers of people have reported to be experiencing all the symptoms sometimes.

- Looking at the data increases pulse rate and dizziness are the symptoms most participants almost never experienced.

Effects on EMOTIONAL HEALTH...

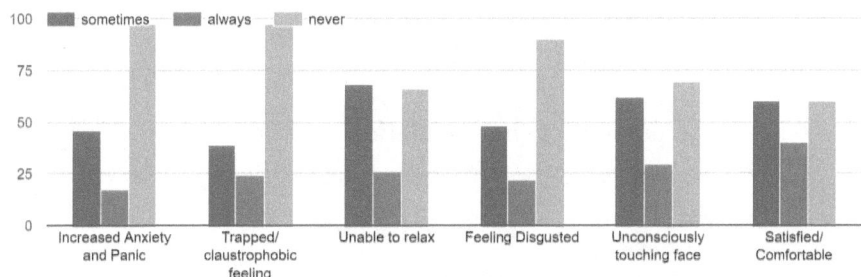

Figure 14: Assessing Mask-Induced Psychological Effects

(Graphical representation, Source: Google Form)

The data above represents the following:

- A large portion of the population seems to be fixating on the categories 'unconsciously touching face' and 'unable to relax' as the highest response for Always can be clearly observed in these categories.

- Next in line for highest response in Always is claustrophobic feeling which is the feeling of being caged as the mask is tight and might not be giving enough room for gas exchange.

- Large numbers of people have reported to be experiencing all the symptoms sometimes, especially the category 'unable to relax'.

Effects on ORAL HEALTH AND HYGEINE....

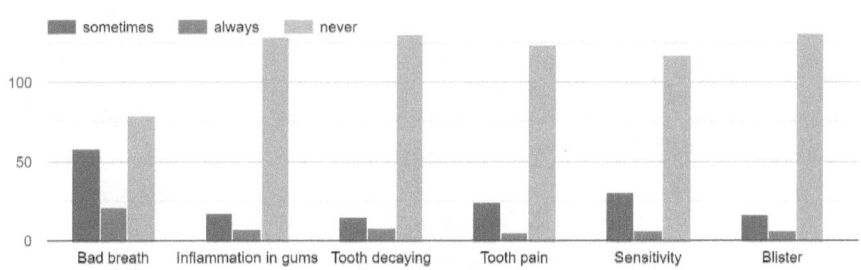

Figure 15: Assessing Oral Health

(Graphical representation, Source: Google Form)

The data above represents the following:

- A large portion of the population suffered from bad breath as the highest response for Always can be clearly observed in this category.

- Large numbers of people have reported to be experiencing all the symptoms sometimes.

- However majorly the population does not seem to be suffering from any oral health problems which is why the numbers for Never response look high in the data.

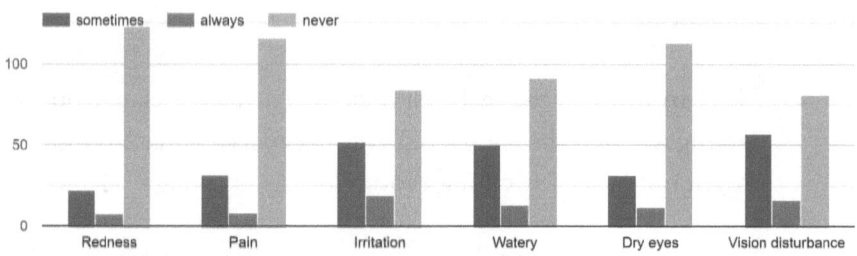

Figure 16: Assessing Effects on Eyes and Vision

(Graphical representation, Source: Google Form)

The data above represents the following:

- A large portion of the population suffered from eye irritation and vision disturbance as the highest response for Always can be clearly observed in this category.

- Next in line for highest response in Always is watery, as the sides of mask that has been sitting on the face collecting dust all day enters the eyes and causes the eyes to become watery as a response to remove that dust.

- Large numbers of people have reported to be experiencing all the symptoms sometimes.

- Looking at the data pain and dry eyes are the symptoms most participants almost never experienced.

Section 5: Be aware!!

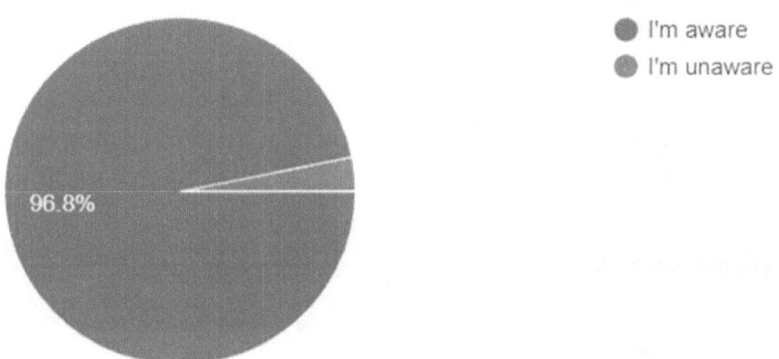

Figure 17: Wearing a face mask is necessary regardless of the condition of the individual (symptomatic/asymptomatic).

(Graphical representation, Source: Google Form)

This section in particular was to find out how awareness level has progressed with the pandemic. As clearly shown by the pie chart result above, it is safe to say that majority of the participants (96.8%) were aware of the fact that wearing mask has been made necessary by the government regardless of the condition of the individual.

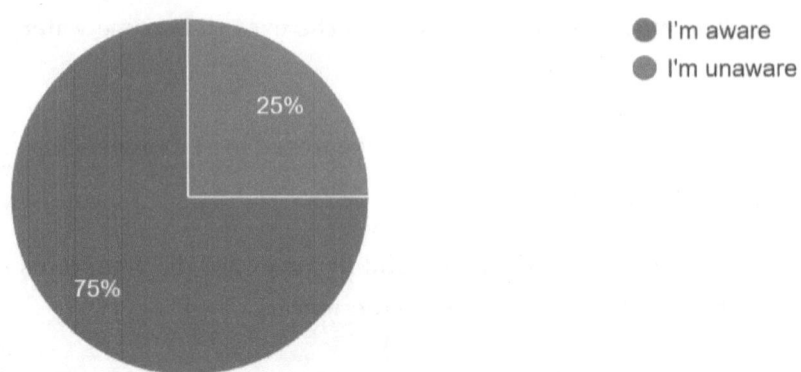

Figure 18: The mask should be discarded/cleaned after 8 hours of its use.

(Graphical representation, Source: Google Form)

The data above shows that although majority of the participants are aware of the fact that masks should be discarded 8 hours after use, however a considerable percentage of people were unaware of such an important fact, which again circles back to the concern of mask reusability *and mask maintenance.*

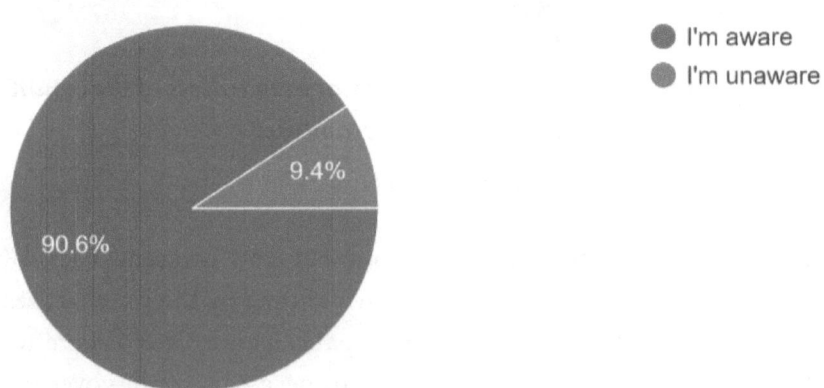

Figure 19: Sanitizing your hand before and after wearing a facemask is important.

(Graphical representation, Source: Google Form)

Constant sanitization of the hands was considered as an integral step in the strategy against the covid attack. Hence it was important to find out whether participants knew that sanitizing hands after touching the mask is also important. Through the data represented above in a pie chart it can be clarified that majority of the participants were aware of the fact that sanitizing hands not just anytime but especially after handling the mask was of great importance. It can be seen that a small percentage of people were also unaware of this important fact which might help us to educate this into the population unfamiliar with this concept.

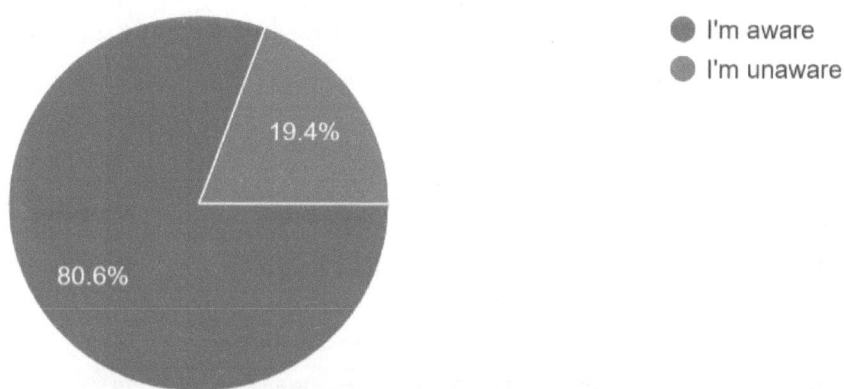

Figure 20: Leaving the mask on your neck while eating or talking, causes transfer of dirt and pathogens collected in the sweat on the skin of your neck to your eyes, nose or mouth, eventually.

(Graphical representation, Source: Google Form)

The data above sheds light on a very important point that many people unconsciously ignore and fall in the trap of pathogen attacks. Since the concept of 'mask beard' (the act of wearing the mask on your neck instead of your mouth) was catching some popularity during the pandemic, the above given pie chart shows that with the progression of pandemic and especially towards the end of it majority of the participants were able to identify the wrong method of wearing a mask and hopefully have made improvement already.

CONCLUSION

Wearing a mask or a respirator offers greater protection from high risk of respiratory infection and/or coronavirus, as being the main route of droplet infection. Altogether wearing mask make individuals susceptible to MIFS (mask induced fatigue syndromes) that occurs due to its prolonged usage. According to the demographic data more than 60% are aware of WHO guidelines for safety measures and therefore majority of the population (87.5%) ALWAYS wear mask while stepping out of their house.

Table 1. Summary

Question	Highest Responses	Number
Effect on overall health	Difficulty in breathing & Overheating	67
Effect on skin	Acne and Itchiness & Redness	59
Effect on emotional health	Unconsciously touching face, Unable to relax & Claustrophobic feeling	79
Effect on oral health and hygiene	Bad breath	21
Effect on eyes and vision	Eye irritation, Vision disturbance & Watery eyes	48

(Table representation, Source: Google Form)

On the basis of face mask and overall health, the following data was represented by large portion of the population

It was observed according to the data majority of the population suffered from MIFS (mask induced fatigue syndromes).

Moreover, the above survey made the population aware of differing risk and health problems that can endure due to prolonged usage of mask. Therefore, the highest percentage was observed based on the effect of emotional health i.e. 49.38% and next in line based on effect on overall heath i.e. 41.88%.

Overall results projected from the survey can be concluded that the Indian urban population are aware of the hygiene, sanitization & identification of wrong method of wearing mask however 20 % of the respondents are still unaware of the above conditions. This awareness can be spread by capitalizing the power of social media, so as to make aware of the merits and demerits of the usage of mask.

Some suggestions for future research include: The crucial need to analyse the pattern & current attitude of citizens, rectifying the faults that will help to design an effective and accurate health strategy for any other global disasters expected to arise in near future.

REFERENCES

1. **Ahmad, M. F., Wahab, S., Ahmad, F. A., Alam, M. I., Ather, H., Siddiqua, A., ... & Beg, R. A. (2021).** A novel perspective approach to explore pros and cons of face mask in prevention the spread of SARS-CoV-2 and other pathogens. *Saudi Pharmaceutical Journal, 29*(2), 121-133.

2. **Bean, B., Moore, B. M., Sterner, B., Peterson, L. R., Gerding, D. N., & Balfour Jr, H. H. (1982).** Survival of influenza viruses on environmental surfaces. *Journal of Infectious Diseases, 146*(1), 47-51.

3. **Chughtai, A. A., Stelzer-Braid, S., Rawlinson, W., Pontivivo, G., Wang, Q., Pan, Y., ... & MacIntyre, C. R. (2019).** Contamination by respiratory viruses on outer surface of medical masks used by hospital healthcare workers. *BMC infectious diseases, 19*(1), 1-8.

4. **De Brouwer, C. (2020).** Wearing a Mask, a Universal Solution Against COVID-19 or an Additional Health Risk? *Available at SSRN 3676885.*

5. **De Silva, A. P., Niriella, M. A., & de Silva, H. J. (2021).** Masks in COVID-19: let's unmask the evidence. *Expert review of respiratory medicine, 15*(3), 293-299.

6. **Hua, W., Zuo, Y., Wan, R., Xiong, L., Tang, J., Zou, L., ... & Li, L. (2020).** Short-term skin reactions following use of N95 respirators and medical masks. *Contact Dermatitis, 83*(2), 115-121.

7. **Johnson, A. T. (2016).** Respirator masks protect health but impact performance: a review. *Journal of biological engineering, 10*(1), 1-12.

8. **Kisielinski, K., Giboni, P., Prescher, A., Klosterhalfen, B., Graessel, D., Funken, S., ... & Hirsch, O. (2021).** Is a Mask That Covers the Mouth and Nose Free from Undesirable Side Effects in Everyday Use and Free of Potential Hazards?. *International journal of environmental research and public health, 18*(8), 4344.

9. **Klimek, L., Huppertz, T., Alali, A., Spielhaupter, M., Hörmann, K., Matthias, C., & Hagemann, J. (2020).** A new form of irritant rhinitis to filtering facepiece particle (FFP) masks (FFP2/N95/KN95 respirators) during COVID-19 pandemic. *World Allergy Organization Journal, 13*(10), 100474.

10. **Kosasih, L. P. (2020).** MASKNE: Mask-Induced Acne Flare During Coronavirus Disease-19. What is it and How to Manage it? *Open Access Macedonian Journal of Medical Sciences, 8*(T1), 411-415.

11. **Lansiaux, E., Tchagaspanian, N., Arnaud, J., Durand, P., Changizi, M., & Forget, J. (2021).** Side-effects of public health policies against Covid-19: the story of an over-reaction. *Frontiers in Public Health,* 792.

12. **Liu, C., Li, G., He, Y., Zhang, Z., & Ding, Y. (2020).** Effects of wearing masks on human health and comfort during the COVID-19

pandemic. In *IOP Conference Series: Earth and Environmental Science* (Vol. 531, No. 1, p. 012034). IOP Publishing.

13. **Martinelli, L., Kopilaš, V., Vidmar, M., Heavin, C., Machado, H., Todorović, Z., ... & Gajović, S. (2021).** Face masks during the COVID-19 pandemic: a simple protection tool with many meanings. *Frontiers in Public Health*, 947.

14. **Matuschek, C., Moll, F., Fangerau, H., Fischer, J. C., Zänker, K., van Griensven, M., ... & Haussmann, J. (2020).** Face masks: benefits and risks during the COVID-19 crisis. *European journal of medical research*, 25(1), 1-8.

15. **Muley, P. (2020).** Mask Mouth. *a Novel Threat to Oral Health in the COVID Era–Dr Pooja Muley. Dental Tribune South Asia.*

16. **Scarano, A., Inchingolo, F., & Lorusso, F. (2020).** Facial skin temperature and discomfort when wearing protective face masks: thermal infrared imaging evaluation and hands moving the mask. *International Journal of Environmental Research and Public Health*, 17(13), 4624.

17. **Srinivasa-Rao, A. S., & Krantz, S. G. (2021).** Well-Designed Studies are Needed to Assess Adverse Effects on Healthy Lung Function after Long-Term Face Masks Usage. *Microbes, Infection and Chemotherapy*, 1, e1222-e1222.

18. **Thatiparthi, A., Liu, J., Martin, A., & Wu, J. J. (2021).** Adverse Effects of COVID-19 and Face Masks: A Systematic Review. *The Journal of clinical and aesthetic dermatology*, 14(9 Suppl 1), S39–S45.

19. **World Health Organization. (2020).** *Advice on the use of masks in the context of COVID-19: interim guidance, 5 June 2020* (No. WHO/2019-nCoV/IPC_Masks/2020.4). World Health Organization.

4.3 Maintaining Corporate Culture with Special Reference to Remote Working in Covid-19 Crisis: Issues and Challenges

Ishrat Shaheen

ABSTRACT

Covid-19 epidemic affected employees at all levels of the business, putting a strain on their abilities and posing new problems for supervisors. It remains to be seen how scholars have dealt with the topic in academic papers. As the epidemic continues to rage, this paper offers a systematic assessment to examine the effect on work and employees of all vocations while keeping corporate culture unscathed while identifying research gaps. More than 50 publications from the Web of Science and Scopus databases were used to compile this review. Workers and workplaces throughout the world have felt the full brunt of COVID-19's effects. Work and organisational psychology and allied subjects are examined to understand the consequences for people, teams, and work organisations. Emergent transformations in work practises, such as working from home, telework, and their economic and socio-psychological implications are the emphasis of our review and overview of pertinent literatures (e.g., unemployment, mental well-being). The conceivable moderating influences of age, race and ethnicity; gender; family situation; personality; and cultural variations are also examined in this study. COVID-19's ramifications for work and organisations are examined using a wide-ranging, comprehensive approach that emphasises the advantages of joint cooperation while retaining the competent corporate culture with full fire and enthusiasm.

Keywords *Telework, organization, calamity, personality, remote-working, assessment, employees.*

INTRODUCTION

The Covid-19 epidemic is wreaking havoc on a wide range of sectors all around the world. As a consequence of the shutdown, the economy has collapsed, shaking the whole corporate sector. This present situation necessitates stronger guidelines from the organization in order to preserve current workers and minimise the effect on pay policies to prevent wage cuts or terminations. Patience and obeying governmental standards are the only ways to get through this circumstance unscathed.

Now that we're back in the actual world, it's safe to say that modest workplaces in your house/home will be the standard in the post-Covid era. Work from home spaces will soon be commonplace in the homes of the future, thanks to mini-offices or work-from-home areas. Organizations may try to set up rules that encourage workers to work from home in anticipation of such a work culture. Reduce the quantity of leaves in a year, and you'll be more productive and able to concentrate on your goals. Large corporate homes or branches may save the firm money in the long run. The administrative costs at WFH's office will be reduced (electricity, phone, and infrastructure maintenance). Since they are working in virtual space, the workforce will be more attentive to interact with the whole team, resulting in an increase in efficiency. To keep its workforce happy, companies won't need a tonne of parking lots or cafeterias. The country's economy would be boosted and pollution and traffic accidents will be reduced as a result of this culture. It is possible to create and execute such a culture, but it would need the enthusiastic and dedicated participation of workers in order to be successful. This ambition may be realised thanks to the power of information technology. A win-win scenario for all partners in the corporate environment may be achieved if adequate rules, instructions for work from office and home, rotational requirements of the employee in the office or home, etc. are implemented. We are about to enter a new era in the history of the workplace, and it is time for us to get on board with it.

New research from Quartz and Qualtrics, a company that assists firms in managing employee engagement, reveals the effect on corporate cultures throughout the globe hasn't been as bad as previously believed. Many more employees believed their workplace culture had improved than worsened as a result of the epidemic, but the folks who felt most positively about it had some unusual characteristics. Study participants reported a 37 percent improvement in workplace culture after the outbreak, while only 15 percent reported a decrease in morale. Most people didn't notice much of a difference. Only the gender gap seemed to be an issue when it came to cultural shift views in the study. Covid-19 may be a complicated and messy experience to go through. In a world where the future is more unpredictable than ever, we all find it difficult to figure out what we can or should do. It seems that in many situations, the epidemic has been illuminating and strengthening what individuals previously believed and felt about their workplace. Pre-crisis employees who felt their firm had a strong culture were more inclined to claim it had strengthened when the crisis struck. It was more probable for those who felt their culture was already poor to claim it has become worse since the survey was conducted. Companies that have strong cultures can weather the storms, whereas those that don't have a strong culture are severely damaged by adversity. It's hardly rocket science, but it serves as a good example for businesses of the need of promoting values like justice and compassion.

OBJECTIVES OF THE STUDY

This article, therefore, has the subsequent objectives:

- To conduct a review of the speculative literature on the impact of Covid 19 on work and workers, detecting research gaps and managerial challenges;
- To support organisations in comprehending the post-Covid19 corporate culture, as well as practises and recommendations for adapting work while remaining competitive. To accomplish the aims, we performed a systematic study of the literature using scientific databases.

REVIEW OF LITERATURE

COVID-19 is a public health emergency as well as a monetary peril for the world economies. Keeping companies and industries shut down throughout the world in order to stop the virus's spread has fashioned a variety of new and difficult problems for both workers and employers. Workers obstructed by the closure were transmuted overnight into either "work from home" employees, "essential" or "life-sustaining" workers (such as emergency room doctors and grocery workers), or "furloughed" or laid-off workers seeking the nation-specific corresponding of joblessness reimbursements. Some sectors are expected to be fundamentally altered by the economic shutdowns and accompanying government actions, while others are likely to be accelerated and new industries are likely to develop, as is frequently the case during times of war and natural catastrophe (e.g., Sine & David, 2003). Psychology at work must use the most recent findings in the area in order to make sense of the COVID-19 shock and assist people and organisations in managing risk while also generating and implementing solutions. Several nations have responded to this by implementing policies aimed at improving workers' health and working circumstances. These policies include widespread health care (as in Europe) and insurance provided by employers (US)(Van Vugt, Hogan, & Kaiser, 2008).

Focused on COVID-19-related hazards and alterations for employees, workplaces, work cultures, and work practises — we do not discriminate between COVID-19's direct health concerns and its economic implications in this area of the study. We give a review of critical literature and an evidence-based screening of vicissitudes that we anticipate to occur as a result of COVID-19 in research and practise by organising our involvements as scholars in a broad range of subject ranges. This review is broken down into three categories to help us understand how the epidemic is affecting the workplace:

- Emerging transformations in work patterns necessitated by the pandemic, such as required working from home, typically in virtual environments, on unparalleled proportions;
- Aftereffects of COVID-19 on the economy and social psychology, such as joblessness, mental disease, and substance abuse; and,
- Age, ethnicity, gender, personality, familial situation and culture are only a few examples of mitigating variables that may have a disproportionate influence on the results of the COVID-19 test.

Impact of Covid-19 On Corporate Culture with Special Reference to Remote Working and Associated Repercussions

Employees, both those who have lost their jobs and those who have kept them, will certainly bear a variety of social and economic penalties as well as the acute effects of COVID-19 on a variety of employment practices and procedures.

- **Joblessness and Downsizings:** A large number of individuals in the United States submitted fresh jobless claims in early 2020 as a result of COVID-19 shutting down whole businesses including travel, hospitality, sports, and entertainment. People who are out of work are likely to suffer from a variety of stress-related conditions, notably melancholy and anxiety, as well as physical problems (Wanberg, 2012). According to Jahoda's (1982) latent impoverishment model, employment has both apparent (e.g., money) and latent advantages (e.g., time scheduling, social interaction, holding of similar objectives, prestige, and engagement), which contributes in clarifying the detrimental consequences of unemployment on psychological well-being. Financial hardship may lead to a cycle of misfortune that affects the whole family, which can be extremely painful (McKee-Ryan & Maitoza, 2018).

- **Presenteeism:** (i.e., going to work while sick) is anticipated to rise as a result of individuals continually working after COVID-19

(Johns, 2010). According to Miko et al. (2020) around 20% of those detected with the flu did not take sick leave in Poland and Australia. It has been shown that employees who join workplace while they are sick are either obliged to do so owing to significant job demands such as exorbitant workloads, staff shortages, and needed overtime, or are devoted to their organisation and/or highly involved in their job. (Miraglia & Johns 2016) It is possible to better recognize organisational "hotspots" where the spread of COVID-19 or any other pathogen is more likely to occur with the support of earlier study. Despite the fact that most developed nations require employees to have entitled to paid sick leave, the fact that it is optional in certain states in the United States calls for further investigation (e.g., Pichler & Ziebarth, 2017). According to Dietz, Zacher, Scheel, Otto, and Rigotti (2020), the amount of presenteeism demonstrated by work team members tends to be mimicked by their superiors. A look at remuneration practises may assist guarantee that co-workers don't push one other into working while being unwell (Kessler, 2017).

- **Economic Inequality:** Many experts believe that disparity would worsen as a result of COVID-19, as it did in the upshot of other recent shocks like the financial crisis of 2008 (Wisman, 2013). A history of economic upheavals shows that these discrepancies give people with a wide range of options, but they also exacerbate disparities in wages and benefits (Bapuji, Ertug & Shaw, 2020). According to previous research, there are serious concerns that a rise in inequality following COVID-19 would lead to a downward cycle of bad tendencies at work, including decreasing work relevance, increased exhaustion, absenteeism, aberrant behaviours and bullying as well as higher turnover (Bapuji et al., 2020). COVID-19's impact on low-wage employees' risk-taking and presenteeism is anticipated to enhance public health hazards for the disease's continued spread, as well. To avoid a downward cycle, higher organisational efforts in reducing inequality are recommended.

- **Social Distancing and Isolation:** It is less evident that COVID-19 will have an influence on social ties, but we know from studies that elevated interpersonal contacts – even casual discussions among co-workers – are vital for mental and physical well-being. Schroeder et al., 2019 show that shaking hands are an important social action, but they can no longer be used. Accordingly, it is anticipated that a combination of WFH requirements and plans to de-dense workplaces in favour of physical distance would probably have undesirable penalties on people's psychological and corporeal well-being (Brooks et al., 2020). When individuals believe that their personal and social needs are not being addressed, they experience loneliness, which is more intense than the loss of social ties and was already deemed "an epidemic" erstwhile to COVID-19 (Murthy, 2017). Anxiety, affiliative behaviour, and performance have all been shown to be negatively linked to loneliness in the workplace (Ozcelik & Barsade, 2018). The lack of non-verbal indicators in virtual contacts increases the likelihood of ambiguities, which may lead to feelings of rejection and loneliness among workers (Cacioppo et al., 2006).

- **Trauma and Tension:** Since of the obscurity and vagueness created by COVID-19, businesses have had to take action to safeguard the health and safety of their workers. By examining how COVID-19 has impacted mutually the weights on and the facilities linked with certain jobs, we may draw the conclusion that employment arrangements have degraded for the mainstream of personnel, possibly particularly for healthcare frontline workers (Bakker & Demerouti, 2017). In persuit of these burdens, COVID-19 has significantly increased the probability of workers suffering work exhaustion that comprises obstinate weariness and a disconnected insolence toward work. Continuous revelation to COVID-19 news also inspires rumination, a mental process in which a person ponders, passively but repeatedly, the reasons and implications of various unpleasant feelings (Nolen-Hoeksema et al., 2008).

- **Virtual teams:** 'Virtual teams are rising in frequency and prominence,' Mak and Kozlowski (2019) distinguished beforehand the epidemic. As a substitute of pretentious consistency in cybernetic squad traits, it is imperative to recognise that "team virtuality" is a multi-faceted notion that encapsulates numerous aspects, such as the geological dispersion of teammates and the comparative quantities of (a)synchronous electronic communication (Hoch & Kozlowski, 2014). Because teams may be virtual or face-to-face, a more sophisticated understanding of virtuality has previously been created (Mak & Kozlowski, 2019), which will be useful to subsequent academics trying to define the many types of virtual cooperation imposed on employees by COVID-19. The depth of communication accessible to face-to-face teams is often lacking in virtual cooperation (Martins, Gilson, and Maynard, 2004), and classic teamwork issues like disagreement and synchronization may rapidly increase in virtual teams (Mortensen & Hinds, 2001). The heightened virtuality of teams as a consequence of the COVID-19 may potentially effect assisting and prosocial behaviour. this page. When it comes to asking for help, we know that individuals are more ready to help and deliver better-quality assistance than we normally think (Flynn & Lake, 2008; Newark, Bohns, & Fleming, 2017), maybe even more so during times of crisis (Fleming et al. 2017). In order to overcome the psychological barriers that prevent people from seeking help, "best practises" in helping can be used to maintain personal privacy (Cleavenger & Munyon, 2017), reduce stigmatisation (Ben-Porath, 2002), and inculcate hope that things will improve once help is obtained (Bohns & Flyn, 2010). (McDermott, et al., 2017). Researchers will benefit from keeping an eye on developments in virtual team technology as COVID-19 accelerates the growth of these teams. Research on specific performance has shown that remote-interacting teammates seem so to skip the imaginative perks that can circulate from prevalent in person conversations. (Allen, Golden, & Shockley, 2015). Because of the growing rise of virtual teams, new topics and treatments to assist enhance cooperation in virtual settings may be examined and developed; and in this endeavor, particular emphasis must be given to several dimensions in which remote teams' virtuality differs (Mak & Kozlowski, 2019).

- **Addiction:** Workplace alienation has been allied to a lessening in alcohol abuse because of a shift away from workplace standards of drinking (Bamberger & Bacharach, 2014). Stress-reducing assistance from work colleagues and superiors (which is often missing when people work from home) helps reduce the use of alcohol in times of crisis, according to research. There are also internet-based concise initiatives that incorporate personalised prevailing opinion and have also verified effectiveness for tackling alcohol-based self-medication (Brendryen et al., 2017).

- **Age:** It's clear from the preliminary COVID-19 assessments that the mortality rate for older persons is much higher than that of younger ones. COVID-19 and Workplace 20 are experiencing an ageing workforce as an outcome of falling fertility rates and rising life anticipation over the previous generation. For empathetic age at work and the ageing workforce, COVID-19 provides several issues. After COVID we may see a less varied workforce because of the health risks encountered by older workers as well as the early retirement incentives that firms contending with financial limitations are expected to give. On the other hand, if COVID-related losses in fixed contributing pension plans force older workers to postpone retirement and prolong functioning, we may by-product in a rise in workplace age variety as a consequence of this predicament. "Return to work" programmes and cross-generational mentorship and expertise activities have been recommended by past research (Brooke & Taylor, 2005) to "build up" human capital and boost the internal labour markets.

- **Race and Ethnicity:** Death rates from COVID-19 infection vary extensively by race (e.g., within the United States), and it has been speculated that these ethnic variances indicate inequalities in pre-existing health issues, poverty, and congested dwelling circumstances under the surface. 20 percent of nurses and midwives in the United Kingdom are from BAME groups; nevertheless, 70% of healthcare workers who have perished from the virus belong to these same communities (Cook et al., 2020). COVID-19's detrimental consequences can only be understood and mitigated via research on employee engagement. Furthermore, studies on prejudice and prejudice in the workplace have shown that employees from racial and ethnic groups are more subjected to hazardous employment settings and to get less supervisory assistance (Paustian Underdahl et al., 2017). No one has looked at whether these tactics are as beneficial in times of economic instability, when minority of colour are more susceptible to job losses (Elvira & Zatzick, 2002). Scholars who are legitimately willing to accumulate data on race and ethnicity must proceed to do so during and after. It is possible that COVID-19 influences gender in a number of ways. The fact that males are more likely to die from an infection suggests that male employees may need more physical safeguards against the virus. However, there are both financial and cognitive grounds to believe that women are more exposed to occupational hazards.

- **Personality:** COVID-19-related work dispositions and behaviours may be predicted by the Big Five personality characteristics, particularly resilience, employment harmony, and emotional well-being (Connor-Smith & Flachsbart, 2007). (Anglim et al., 2020). Extraversion and social competence are especially crucial in effective adjustment, according to second-order statistical evaluation of more than 50 meta-analyses. When it comes to adjusting to new situations, Extraversion promotes more prevalent perspectives of high associated with positive feelings as well as a more diverse set of interpersonal skills (Wilmot et al., 2019), while Agreeableness encourages dedication and persistence toward more formulaic, long-term career objectives and targets (Wilmot et al., 2019). (Wilmot & Ones, 2019). Both attributes are expected to play important but separate roles in the workplace's response to the epidemic. Considering that COVID-19 may be seen as a "strong scenario" that limits the usual expression of personality, it may serve as a parameter for a trait's conventional prognostic implications (Meyer et al., 2010).

DISCUSSION AND CONCLUSION

In order to understand COVID-19's for topics relevant to work and organisational psychology, we formed a big, diversified virtual team. When it comes to COVID-19, the advantages of cooperation amongst researchers are clear since numerous people accomplish light work and many brains are superior than a handful, as has been shown in past study (Kniffin & Hanks, 2018). In spite of this, we can be sure that our vision is restricted and that predefined tendencies or events that subsequently turn out to be important may have slipped our radar screen. We don't yet know how terrible the worldwide economic condition will be harmed and how fast it will rebound from the present economic crisis. Even if there is a vaccination, we don't know when and how broadly or fast it will be made accessible. Notwithstanding the uncertainties, it is certain that COVID-19 will be hailed for primarily altering the way we do business changed the related with working outside of co-located workplaces were expedited by COVID-19. In light of the recognised health implications with customary open offices, virtual work practises are beginning to transmit as organisations realise the cost savings from framing labour with very few comprehensive staff and more contractors linked terms of technology. Individuals who want to work in this fashion will face several problems, not the least of which is the need to adapt to working styles that are vastly different from those of older eras. COVID-19 shows us how susceptible we are both as workers and employers. Due to the contagion, many initiatives throughout the globe will have to be reformed. In order to meet the requirements of workers who fall into one of many susceptible groups, professionals need to have a firm grasp of how these sudden shifts occur. More severe or demanding bosses may have distinct professional development requirements than more participatory and empathetic bosses in influencing their employees in virtual settings. Research is likewise beset by a slew of difficulties. It is possible that our predictions of issues that may become relevant may be applicable beyond the COVID-19 pandemic since "extreme occurrences" typically reveal processes that are crucial but not always obvious in regular situations. We don't yet tell how communal remoteness and corporeal distance procedures will affect workers in the extended course. What impact will it have on employee well-being and output? WFH that is mandated for the whole population is a quite different animal than the voluntary WFH that has been the subject of much of the research too far. In order to better understand the long-term impacts of epidemics and pandemics, organisational researchers may want to look back at how they were addressed in the past. As a global health hazard, COVID-19 necessitates a distinct set of measures than other strains. Philosophy advancement is thus desirable to understand how various types of universal intimidations and calamities affect businesses in distinct manners. A recurrent feature of human development is the spread of infectious illnesses, which have had an unexpected but predicted impact on our psyche, conduct, and society. In today's interconnected world, infectious illness risks such as COVID-19 must be taken into consideration. We need to create better and safer methods to operate collaboratively if we are enduring to enjoy the rewards of global collaboration.

REFERENCES

Allen, T. D., Cho, E., & Meier, L. L. (2014). Work–family boundary dynamics. Annual Review of Organizational Psychology and Organizational Behavior, 1(1), 99-121.

Allen, T. D., Golden, T. D., & Shockley, K. M. (2015). How effective is telecommuting? Assessing the status of our scientific findings. Psychological Science in the Public Interest, 16(2), 40-68.

Alon, T. M., Doepke, M., Olmstead-Rumsey, J., & Tertilt, M. (2020). The Impact of covid-19 on gender equality. National Bureau of Economic Research.

Anglim, J., Horwood, S., Smillie, L. D., Marrero, R. J., & Wood, J. K. (2020). Predicting psychological and subjective well-being from personality: A meta-analysis. Psychological Bulletin, 146(4), 279–323.

Antonakis, J., & Day, D. V. (2017). Leadership: Past, present, and future. In J. Antonakis & D. Day (Eds.), The nature of leadership (3rd ed.), p. 56-81. Thousand Oaks: Sage Publications.

Antonakis, J., & Atwater, L. (2002). Leader distance: A review and a proposed theory. The Leadership Quarterly, 13(6), 673-704.

Antonakis, J., Bastardoz, N., Jacquart, P., & Shamir, B. (2016). Charisma: An ill-defined and ill measured gift. Annual Review of Organizational Psychology and Organizational Behavior, 3, 293-319.

Ashford, S. J., Caza, B. B., & Reid, E. M. (2018). From surviving to thriving in the gig economy: A research agenda for individuals in the new world of work. Research in Organizational Behavior, 38, 23-41.

Bacharach, S. B., Bamberger, P. A., & Sonnenstuhl, W.J. (2002). Driven to drink: Managerial control, work-related risk factors, and employee problem drinking. Academy of Management Journal, 45(4), 637-658.

Bakker, A.B., & Demerouti, E. (2017). Job Demands–Resources theory: Taking stock and looking forward. Journal of Occupational Health Psychology, 22, 273-285.

Bamberger, P., & Bacharach, S. B. (2014). Retirement and the Hidden Epidemic: The Complex Link Between Aging, Work Disengagement, and Substance Misuse – and what to Do about it. Oxford University Press.

Bapuji, H., Ertug, G., & Shaw, J. D. (2020). Organizations and societal economic inequality: a review and way forward. Academy of Management Annals, 14(1), 60-91

Baumeister, R. F., & Leary, M. R. (1997). Writing narrative literature reviews. Review of General Psychology, 1(3), 311-320.

Bhagat, R. S. (1983). Effects of stressful life events on individual performance effectiveness and work adjustment processes within organizational settings: A research model. Academy of Management Review, 8(4), 660-671.

Bhave, D.P., Teo, L.H., & Dalal, R.S. (2020). Privacy at work: A review and a research agenda for a contested terrain. Journal of Management, 46, 127-164.

Ben-Porath, D. D. (2002). Stigmazation of individuals who receive psychotherapy: An interaction between help-seeking behavior and the presence of depression. Journal of Social and Clinical Psychology, 21(4), 400-413.

Blair-Loy, M. (2009). Competing devotions: Career and family among women executives. Harvard University Press. Bloise, S. M., & Johnson, M. K. (2007). Memory for emotional and neutral information: Gender and individual differences in emotional sensitivity. Memory, 15(2), 192-204.

Bohns, V. & Flynn, F. (2010). "Why didn't you ask?" Overestimating the willingness to seek help and underestimating discomfort in help-seeking. Journal of Experimental Social Psychology, 46, 402-409.

Brendryen, H., Johansen, A., Duckert, F., & Nesvåg, S. (2017). A pilot randomized controlled trial of an internet-based alcohol intervention in a workplace setting. International Journal of Behavioral Medicine, 24(5), 768-777.

Brooke, L., & Taylor, P. (2005). Older workers and employment: managing age relations. Ageing & Society, 25(3), 415-429. doi: 10.1017/S0144686X05003466

Brooks, S. K., Webster, R. K., Smith, L. E., Woodland, L., Wessely, S., Greenberg, N., & Rubin, G. J. (2020). The psychological impact of quarantine and how to reduce it: Rapid review of the evidence. Lancet, 395, 912–920.

Cacioppo, J. T., Hawkley, L. C., Ernst, J. M., Burleson, M., Berntson, G. G., Nouriani, B., & Spiegel, D. (2006). Loneliness within a nomological net: An evolutionary perspective. Journal of Research in Personality, 40, 1054–1085.

Campbell, A. (2013). A mind of her own: The evolutionary psychology of women. Oxford University Press.

Cleavenger, D., & Munyon, T. (2015). Overcoming the help-seeker's dilemma: How computermediated systems encourage employee help-seeking initiation. Organization Studies, 36(2), 221-240.

Combe, I. A., & Carrington, D. J. (2015). Leaders' sensemaking under crises: Emerging cognitive consensus over time within management teams. The Leadership Quarterly, 26, 307-322.

Connor-Smith, J. K., & Flachsbart, C. (2007). Relations between personality and coping: A meta-analysis. Journal of Personality and Social Psychology, 93(6), 1080–1107.

Cook, T., Kursumovic, E., & Lennane, S. (2020). Exclusive: deaths of NHS staff from covid-19 analysed. Health Service Journal. Last accessed May 8, 2020.

Creary, S. J., Caza, B. B., & Roberts, L. M. (2015). Out of the box? How managing a subordinate's multiple identities affects the quality of a manager-subordinate relationship. Academy of Management Review, 40(4), 538-562.

Demerouti, E., Mostert, K., & Bakker, A. B. (2010). Burnout and work engagement: a thorough investigation of the independency of both constructs. Journal of Occupational Health Psychology, 15(3), 209-222.

DeRosa, D. M., Smith, C. L., & Hantula, D. A. (2007). The medium matters: Mining the long-promised merit of group interaction in creative idea generation tasks in a meta-analysis of the electronic group brainstorming literature. Computers in Human Behavior, 23(3), 1549- 1581.

Diamond, J. M. (1998). Guns, Germs, and Steel: A short history of everybody for the last 13,000 years. Random House. Dietz, C., Zacher, H., Scheel, T., Otto, K. & Rigotti, T. (2020). Leaders as role models: Effects of leader presenteeism on employee presenteeism and sick leave. Work & Stress. In Press.

Dunbar, R. I. (2018). The anatomy of friendship. Trends in Cognitive Sciences, 22(1), 32-51. Eckel, C. C., & Grossman, P. J. (2008). Men, women and risk aversion: Experimental evidence. In C. Plott & V. Smith (Eds.), Handbook of Experimental Economics Results (Vol. 1, pp. 1061-1073). Elsevier.

Eisenberg, N., & Lennon, R. (1983). Sex differences in empathy and related capacities. Psychological Bulletin, 94(1), 100-131 Elvira, M. M., & Zatzick, C. D. (2002). Who's displaced first? The role of race in layoff decisions. Industrial Relations: A Journal of Economy and Society, 41(2), 329-361.

Flynn, F. J., & Lake, V. K. (2008). If you need help, just ask: Underestimating compliance with direct requests for help. Journal of Personality and Social Psychology, 95(1), 128-143.

Flynn, J., Slovic, P., & Mertz, C. K. (1994). Gender, race, and perception of environmental health risks. Risk Analysis, 14(6), 1101-1108.

Grabo, A., Spisak, B. R., & van Vugt, M. (2017). Charisma as signal: An evolutionary perspective on charismatic leadership. The Leadership Quarterly, 28(4), 473-485.

Grant, B. F., Chou, S. P., & Saha, T. D., Pickering, R. P., Kerridge, B. T., Huang, B., Jung, J., Zhang, H., Fan, A., & Hasin, D. S. (2017). Prevalence of 12-month alcohol use, high-risk drinking, and DSM-IV alcohol use disorder in the United States, 2001-2002 to 2012-2013: Results from the National Epidemiologic Survey on alcohol and related conditions. JAMA Psychiatry, 74(9), 911-923.

Harrington, J. R., & Gelfand, M. J. (2014). Tightness–looseness across the 50 united states. Proceedings of the National Academy of Sciences, 111(22), 7990-7995.

Hirsh, C. E., & Kornrich, S. (2008). The context of discrimination: Workplace conditions, institutional environments, and sex and race discrimination charges. American Journal of Sociology, 113(5), 1394-1432.

Hoch, J. E., & Kozlowski, S. W. (2014). Leading virtual teams: Hierarchical leadership, structural supports, and shared team leadership. Journal of Applied Psychology, 99(3), 390-403.

Hofstede, G. (1984). Culture's Consequences: International differences in work-related values (Vol. 5). New York, NY: Sage.

Huang, W. W., Wei, K. K., Watson, R. T., & Tan, B. C. Y. (2002). Supporting virtual teambuilding with a GSS: An empirical investigation. Decision Support Systems, 34, 359–367.

Kniffin, K. M., & Hanks, A. S. (2018). The trade-offs of teamwork among STEM doctoral graduates. American Psychologist, 73(4), 420-432.

Martins, L. L., Gilson, L. L., & Maynard, M. T. (2004). Virtual teams: What do we know and where do we go from here?. Journal of Management, 30(6), 805-835.

McCabe, K. O., & Fleeson, W. (2012). What is extraversion for? Integrating trait and motivational perspectives and identifying the purpose of extraversion. Psychological Science, 23(12), 1498–1505.

McDermott, R., Cheng, H., Wong, J., Booth, N., Jones, Z., & Sevig, T. (2017). Hope for helpseeking: A positive psychology perspective of psychological help-seeking intentions. The Counseling Psychologist, 1-29.

Meyer, R. D., Dalal, R. S., & Hermida, R. (2010). A review and synthesis of situational strength in the organizational sciences. Journal of Management, 36(1), 121–140.

Michel, J. S., Kotrba, L. M., Mitchelson, J. K., Clark, M. A., & Baltes, B. B. (2011). Antecedents of work–family conflict: A meta-analytic review. Journal of Organizational Behavior, 32(5), 689–725.

Mikos, M., Juszczyk, G., Czerw, A., Strzępek, Ł., Banaś, T., Cipora, E., Deptała, A., & Badowska-Kozakiewicz, A. (2020). Refusal to take sick leave after being diagnosed with a communicable disease as an estimate of the phenomenon of presenteeism in Poland. Medical Principles and Practice, 29, 134-141.

Miraglia, M., & Johns, G. (2016). Going to work ill: A meta-analysis of the correlates of presenteeism and a dual-path model. Journal of Occupational Health Psychology, 21, 261- 283.

Mogilner, C., Whillans, A., & Norton, M. I. (2018). Time, money, and subjective wellbeing. In E. Diener, S. Oishi, & L. Tay (Eds.), Handbook of Well-Being. Noba Scholar Handbook series: Subjective well-being. DEF publishers.

Mortensen, M., & Hinds, P. J. (2001). Conflict and shared identity in geographically distributed teams. International Journal of Conflict Management, 12, 212–238.

Murthy, V. (2017). Work and the loneliness epidemic: reducing isolation at work is good business. Harvard Business Review. Retrieved from https://hbr.org/coverstory/2017/09/work-and-the-loneliness-epidemic.

Newark, D., Bohns, V., & Flynn, F. (2017). A helping hand is hard at work: Underestimating help quality. Organizational Behavior and Human Decision Processes, 139, 223-226.

Nkomo, S., & Hoobler, J. M. (2014). A historical perspective on diversity ideologies in the United States: Reflections on human resource management research and practice. Human Resource Management Review, 24(3), 245-257.

Nolen-Hoeksema, S., Wisco, B. E., & Lyubomirsky, S. (2008). Rethinking rumination. Perspectives on Psychological Science, 3, 400–424.

Obradovich, N., Migliorini, R., Paulus, M. P., & Rahwan, I. (2018). Empirical evidence of mental health risks posed by climate change. Proceedings of the National Academy of Sciences, 115(43), 10953-10958.

Oprea, B. T., Barzin, L., Vîrgă, D., Iliescu, D., & Rusu, A. (2019). Effectiveness of job crafting interventions: a meta-analysis and utility analysis. European Journal of Work and Organizational Psychology, 28(6), 723-741.

Ozcelik, H., and Barsade, S. (2018). No employee an island: Workplace loneliness and employee performance. Academy of Management Journal, 61(6), 2343-2366.

Park, T. Y., & Shaw, J. D. (2013). Turnover rates and organizational performance: A metaanalysis. Journal of Applied Psychology, 98, 268-309.

Paustian-Underdahl, S. C., King, E. B., Rogelberg, S. G., Kulich, C., & Gentry, W. A. (2017). Perceptions of supervisor support: Resolving paradoxical patterns across gender and race. Journal of Occupational and Organizational Psychology, 90, 436-457.

Pejtersen, J. H., Feveile, H., Christensen, K. B., & Burr, H. (2011). Sickness absence associated with shared and open-plan offices—a national cross sectional questionnaire survey. Scandinavian Journal of Work, Environment & Health, 37, 376-382.

Petriglieri, G., Ashford, S. J., & Wrzesniewski, A. (2019). Agony and ecstasy in the gig economy: Cultivating holding environments for precarious and personalized work identities. Administrative Science Quarterly, 64(1), 124-170.

Petriglieri, J. L. (2019). Couples That Work: How dual-career couples can thrive in love and work. Harvard Business Review Press. Petriglieri, J. L., & Obodaru, O. (2019). Secure-base relationships as drivers of professional identity development in dual-career couples. Administrative Science Quarterly, 64(3), 694- 736.

Pichler, S., & Ziebarth, N.R. (2017). The pros and cons of sick pay schemes: Testing for contagious presenteeism and noncontagious absenteeism behavior. Journal of Public Economics, 156, 14-33.

Popovici, I., & French, M. T. (2013). Does unemployment lead to greater alcohol consumption? Industrial Relations: A Journal of Economy and Society, 52(2), 444-466.

Pritchard, R. D., Harrell, M. M., DiazGranados, D., & Guzman, M. J. (2008). The productivity measurement and enhancement system: a meta-analysis. Journal of Applied Psychology, 93(3), 540.

Ramarajan, L., & Reid, E. (2013). Shattering the myth of separate worlds: Negotiating nonwork identities at work. Academy of Management Review, 38(4), 621-644.

Roberts, L. M., Mayo, A. J., & Thomas, D. A. (2019). Race, Work, and Leadership. Harvard Business Review Press: Boston. Rothbard, N. P., Phillips, K. W., & Dumas, T. L. (2005). Managing multiple roles: Work-family policies and individuals' desires for segmentation. Organization Science, 16(3), 243-258.

Rudolph, C. W., Marcus, J., & Zacher, H. (2018). Global issues in work, aging and retirement. In K. Schultz & G. Adams (Eds.), Aging and work in the 21st century (2nd ed), p. 292-324.

Rudolph, C. W., & Zacher, H. (2020). "The COVID-19 generation": A cautionary note. Work, Aging & Retirement. doi: 10.1093/workar/waaa009

Schaller, M., & Murray, D. R. (2008). Pathogens, personality, and culture: Disease prevalence predicts worldwide variability in sociosexuality, extraversion, and openness to experience. Journal of Personality and Social Psychology, 95(1), 212-221.

Schmitt, D. P., Realo, A., Voracek, M., & Allik, J. (2008). Why can't a man be more like a woman? Sex differences in Big Five personality traits across 55 cultures. Journal of Personality and Social Psychology, 94(1), 168-182.

Schroeder, J., Risen, J. L., Gino, F., & Norton, M. I. (2019). Handshaking promotes deal-making by signaling cooperative intent. Journal of Personality and Social Psychology, 116(5), 743-768.

Sine, W. D., & David, R. J. (2003). Environmental jolts, institutional change, and the creation of entrepreneurial opportunity in the US electric power industry. Research Policy, 32(2), 185- 207.

Sirola, N., & Pitesa, M. (2017). Economic downturns undermine workplace helping by promoting a zero-sum construal of success. Academy of Management Journal, 60(4), 1339- 1359.

Smith, A. N., Watkins, M. B., Ladge, J. J., & Carlton, P. (2019). Making the Invisible Visible: Paradoxical Effects of Intersectional Invisibility on the Career Experiences of Executive Black Women. Academy of Management Journal, 62(6), 1705-1734.

Spicer, R. S., & Miller, T. R. (2005). Impact of a workplace peer-focused substance abuse prevention and early intervention program. Alcoholism: Clinical and Experimental Research, 29(4), 609-611.

Stoker, J. I., Garretsen, H., & Soudis, D. (2019). Tightening the leash after a threat: A multi-level event study on leadership behavior following the financial crisis. The Leadership Quarterly, 30(2), 199-214.

Van Solinge, H., & Henkens, K. (2014). Work-related factors as predictors in the retirement decision-making process of older workers in the Netherlands. Ageing & Society, 34(9), 1551-1574.

Van Vugt, M., Hogan, R., & Kaiser, R. B. (2008). Leadership, followership, and evolution: Some lessons from the past. American Psychologist, 63(3), 182-196.

Vlahov, D, Galea, S, Resnick, H, Ahern, J, Boscarino, J., Bucuvalas, M, Gold, J. & Kilpatrick, D. (2002). Increased use of cigarettes, alcohol, and marijuana among Manhattan, New York, residents after the September 11th terrorist attacks. American Journal of Epidemiology, 155(11), 988–996.

Wanberg, C. R. (2012). The individual experience of unemployment. Annual Review of Psychology, 63, 369-396.

Wanberg, C.R., Ali, A., & Csillag, B. (2020). The process and experience of looking for a job. Annual Review of Organizational Psychology and Organizational Behavior, 7, 315-337.

Williams, A. L., Parks, A. C., Cormier, G., Stafford, J., & Whillans, A. (2018). Improving resilience among employees high in depression, anxiety, and workplace distress. International Journal of Research in Management, 9(1-2), 4-22.

Wilmot, M. P., & Ones, D. S. (2019). A century of research on conscientiousness at work. PNAS Proceedings of the National Academy of Sciences of the United States of America, 116(46), 23004–23010.

Wilmot, M. P., Wanberg, C. R., Kammeyer-Mueller, J. D., & Ones, D. S. (2019). Extraversion advantages at work: A quantitative review and synthesis of the meta-analytic evidence. Journal of Applied Psychology, 104(12), 1447–1470.

Wisman, J. D. (2013). Wage stagnation, rising inequality and the financial crisis of 2008. Cambridge Journal of Economics, 37(4), 921-945

4.4 Leading through the Crisis of 2020

Dr Rahul Mirchandani

ABSTRACT

The year 2020 has been a year that challenged every leader to the core. While the world was in lockdown, the ways of the world changed forever. Leadership needed to be rewired and old principles and rule books seemed redundant. It was during this time that 100 leaders convened from across 21 cities of India and struck deep conversations on how each of them is dealing with the crises posed by the Pandemic. A set of curated readings (listed as 'References') were used as anchors for these conversations. This paper is a summary of discussions with four separate cohorts spread over the period May 2020 to January 2021. Using specific words, interjections and anecdotes of the leaders, this is an attempt to capture the voices of this diverse group and comprehend how the mind of leaders of different ages and from different backgrounds got reset during this unprecedented crisis. The paper also provides frameworks with which the cohort learnt to balance the ideological perfect and the achievable good. New mental models, moral codes, fresh sets of realities and challenges and a completely renewed definition of risk have evolved. This paper documents these and suggests ways to build back better and lead effectively in a whole new world.

Keywords: *pandemic, crisis, lockdown*

Circa March 2020: **World War-C** is upon us. Our world as we know it is on an **indefinite pause**. We have moved into the seemingly safer cocoons of our homes. Work has come to a standstill. The unseen enemy has slammed sudden brakes on all our lives. Nothing is certain anymore. Rulebooks appear like they were written in a parallel universe. A nervous peek into our bank accounts reveal we have cash for just over a month. Bills to pay, staff to sustain, a home to run and family to support. Several billion citizens of the world in an identical tizzy, and no leader who was taught how to deal with such an existential crisis.

Here began the time of our lives – a time to discover, a time to create, a time to heal. This was the perfect time to relearn the fine art of leadership. A month into what later became one of the longest lockdowns on the planet, a first cohort of leaders I knew came together to question, introspect and learn. As more cohorts* assembled in the weeks and months that followed, we moved from demystifying chaos to a new set of certainties, from angst to agility, from the great pause to robust resilience. Through this paper, I hope to chart the journey of the mind of a diverse set of almost a 100 leaders*, in the hope that we regain some clarity and find some urgent answers.

Regaining Balance

The best place to begin was to ask ourselves how we feel. Each of us had our own crises and had made mental models to redefine our priorities. As we moved into the months that followed, there was a **distinct shift in our minds.**

In month one, leaders seemed confused and uncertain. However, they were thankful for their inner strength to draw courage to deal with the new realities. Three months later, patience and realism had taken over. Leaders had grown supercharged. Their intuitive nature and inventiveness had started finding solutions. Hope had dawned. Determination and patience had challenged the crisis. Introspection had found specific solutions. Some leaders had even drawn on their sense of adventure and many had made peace with the new norms. Grit, determination and the fighting spirit raged while leaders regained some sense of balance.

Surprisingly, a few more months later, **two very distinct clusters of leaders emerged.** One group had evolved into a set of hopeful, calm, focussed, upbeat, optimistic, energetic, determined and rewired leaders. Whereas on another extreme, a set of leaders was overwhelmed and stressed beyond belief. Too much had drained their souls and minds that they had lost their sense of balance.

Table 1: Frame of Mind of Leaders in the middle of the Crisis of 2020

		Young leaders	Mid-career leaders	Mature age leaders
Optimistic		Thankful	Hopeful	Thankful
			Joyful	Proud
Constructive		Excited	Rediscovering	Strong
		Opportunities	Solution finder	
		Curious	Reinventing	
			Challenged	
Negative		Confused		
		Uncertain		

Note: These were specific words used by the cohort of leaders[8] during their discussions with the Author

Checking on the Kids

While we dealt with the immediate and coped to survive, a profound question needed to be asked that challenged our newfound, **fragile sense of equilibrium.** How are our children coping with this suddenly unknown world? Whom are they leaning on? Have they discovered new, unique ways to start living their lives or are they feeling burdened and overwhelmed? If the children are truly doing well, perhaps this is a good measure to test if the world is doing fine too.

---

[8] *Cohort Profile:* This paper draws on the in depth conversations with four cohorts of over 100 leaders who came together during 2020. This diverse group of leaders (60% Male, 40% Female) were from 21 cities and towns across 12 states and 2 Union Territories of India. *Age Profile:* The average age of the cohort was 33 years, with the youngest member of the cohort being 18 years of age, and the eldest being 57 years old. **Professional Experience:** 33% of the cohort were business owners, 20% were first generation entrepreneurs, 7% each were from junior, mid and senior management positions (totalling 21% professionals), 14% were students and 12% were faculty members. **Educational Backgrounds:** 38% of the cohort had Masters' degrees, 36% had Bachelor's degrees, 10% had Doctoral degrees and 7% were Charter members (CA/CFA/CS).

The fluidity of this new world presents us with a unique opportunity. It offers a time to adapt and build back better. Suddenly, kids are allowed to fail and falter, and they have discovered that their elders know as little or as much as they do. The pandemic has served as a great leveller of previously lofty expectations. New, specific solutions are an immediate need.

At the Gates of Hope

Leadership can get lonely. **Defiance is confused with arrogance. Poise intersects with apathy.** However, standing at the gates, looking towards a new way of life, we stared at Hope as a mysterious unknown, with a sense of wonderment. The future awaited us at the other end of a labyrinth - for everyone the challenges looked uncertain, ambiguous and bumpy. The long uphill, uncharted maze was certainly exciting and adventurous, but patience, innovation, vigilance and persistence had become essential skills.

We had all become acutely aware of the infinite possibilities of today. However, the togetherness of cooperation is the succour we crave and even the fiercest of competitors are learning to shelve the ego of the 'I-know-best' and the futile 'I told you so'. Such is the **gift of this audacity of hope** that we are enticed to grab our own blank sheets of paper to **restart, reimagine and renew.**

As leaders we also tend to grab the benefit of hindsight. However, our assumptions, our postulates, our frameworks have all proved a **Grand Illusion.** 'I know exactly how to do this' can perhaps not be repeated for a fairly long time. The acceptance of being hopelessly ignorant is perhaps the beginning of learning a brand new way. Self-righteousness has no place in our New world. But, what compromises will we need to make while choosing between the **ideological perfect** and the **achievable good**?

Making Crucial Trade-offs

When it is decision time, as leaders the choices we make are rarely perfect. They are necessary, given our unique new circumstances. The first compromise we all made was to trade-off personal face to face interactions with online platforms. What was until yesterday considered inappropriate and impersonal became acceptable and efficient. However, with every additional task that we managed to do online, demands of work further eroded personal time and space. Experiential learning took place in a very different virtual dimension and engaging teams needed very different methods.

Having teams close by versus working remotely, invasion of private space with work tasks, travelling versus discovering new experiences online, giving up street food for home cooked meals, home schooling our children, sustaining long distance relationships, human touch versus health concerns, retaining quality clients while worrying about quarterly results are some of the trade-offs many of us dealt with. These choices had consequences on money, time, accountability, trust, predictability, health, perfection, nature, celebrations and efficiency.

Data to decide on which trade-offs to make was scarce and incomplete. There were **no rules and precedents** to cite. Our **moral compass was in disarray**. As leaders, we introspected on what guides us and our decision making styles. Circumstances created brand new constraints and imperatives. However, they could not be allowed to become crutches for excuses and inaction.

What did we all lose?

When leaders were asked what we had collectively lost during the Pandemic and consequent disruptions, a very humbling discussion ensued. The biggest toll was on our **illusions** and our **innocence**. Freedom and Balance, Faith and peace of mind, Identity and pride were all challenged. There was growing **outrage** in how leaders were dealing with the crisis in many instances. Reputation and legacy needed to be preserved. New allies extended their hand of friendship and support. The power of persuasion, individual generosity and imagination was recognized. Restoring human decency and cultural values became an obsession to regain stability in our social structures.

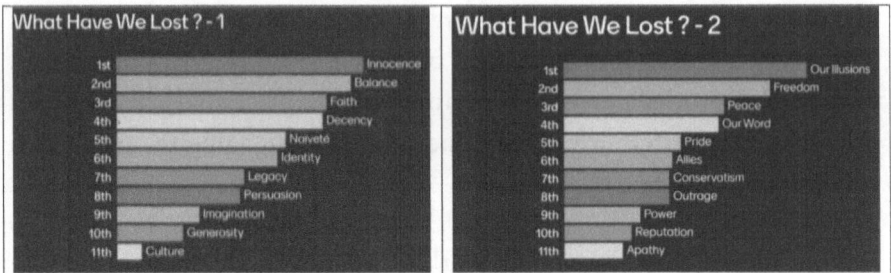

Figure 1: Taking stock of what we have lost during the crisis of 2020

Note: The cohort of leaders was asked to rank two sets of words (above) and state, in their opinion, which of these elements of their personal and professional lives have been sacrificed or lost during the year 2020. The graphs above are the consolidated rankings of members of the cohort.

Making a new Set of Choices

Over the past 6 months, we have become more aware and have learnt to listen to each other's perspectives. Clarity, Vigilance, Adaptability, Empathy, being non-judgemental have become more common. We have also engaged in developing new products and services after deep reflection, introspection and more informed decision making. Many of us also ensure we communicate better and engage in some philanthropy.

Our discussions showed that we have **paused the capitalistic treadmill** and **satisfaction has won over greed**. Wants have been realistically aligned and we have questioned the burden of expectations from 'others', including the 'older US'.

A clear realisation amongst leaders has emerged that we have zero control over outcomes. Leadership has pivoted and new skills need leaders to be calm, reasonable and positive. Leaders need to learn to deal with 'no constants', have tremendous foresight and be okay with unpredictability.

We do believe **detachment from established norms** is a key. Having no rules should be the main rule in dealing with teams and they must realise that it is ok to make errors, as no one has been trained in the new ways. It is however scary that we have lost our innocence and our illusions.

While building back better, we have to create a solid foundation of the **'new truths'**. Individual accountability, faith in humanity, learning from our rich histories, removing the veils of fake causes, removing divisions and divisiveness, and having collective faith and confidence in people and institutions is crucial.

Creating Our Own Moral Codes

Our minds and sense of morality has gotten rewired through this crisis. **What is just and fair** has to be decided using a brand new lens. For the Virus, we were all equal. It did not discriminate on the basis of demographic variables; however, the impact of the consequent lockdowns was disproportionately more detrimental to some sections of society. Hence, it was essential to provide unequal better treatment to those less fortunate. Doing more for those most disadvantaged by the virus raised questions on the **'equality principle'**. It became important for leaders to take calls that benefitted some more than others. This needed exceptional integrity in taking seemingly 'unequal decisions' in the interest of 'fair' final outcomes.

Providing **greatest good to the greatest number** of people impacted by a decision became a metric to evaluate decisions with the payoff being maximizing net total utility. In the process, the sacrificing of those left out or disadvantaged was the consequent collateral damage.

In the uncharted territories we found ourselves in, offering complete **freedom** to teams needed to be sacrificed and leadership found itself becoming more prescriptive. Regimented discipline needed to be enforced, at times to the detriment of individual liberties. Individual rights did count, but not more than institutional rules which were strictly enforced. When mandatory contact tracing was introduced, it became mandatory to provide information about one's whereabouts and personal interactions even outside of working hours. Many teams lived on site for several days in a bubble created within organisation's factory or office premises, sacrificing even their right to go home, in the interest of protecting themselves and for ensuring business continuity.

These circumstances and the moral codes with which decisions were made wrote an entirely **new chapter in situational ethics** and new leadership styles evolved. At different stages of the lockdown, it was also interesting to see how leaders rewired their minds. When asked which decision making style adequately described their methods, leaders explained themselves as follows:

Table 2: Frame of Mind of Leaders in the middle of the Crisis of 2020

Phase of 2020	Following the Equality principle (Rawlsians)**	Providing greatest good to the greatest number (Utilitarians)**	Giving full freedom to their teams to take all decisions (Libertarians)**	Enforcing institutional rules, even while reducing individual freedom (Communitarians)**
Early lockdown	30%	25%	0%	45%
Mid of Lockdown	0%	40%	30%	30%
End of lockdown	20%	0%	35%	45%

* These were philosophies described (as in the table) in Authers, John (2020) and used as an anchor to a detailed conversation with the cohort. Leaders were then asked to select the one moral philosophy that they seem to align with the most and that guides their decision *making process. The percentages of leaders who selected each philosophical construct are summarised in the table.*

This analysis captured the rollercoaster that every leader faced in the year that was. In the beginning of the lockdown, **liberty and individual freedom** were completely sacrificed to enforce order using **community norms**. It was also felt that all must be taken care of equally and no one should be left behind or sacrificed. Later, as the lockdown proceeded, the reality and enormity of the crisis became evident and **utilitarianism** took over, where it was considered necessary to evaluate the net total benefit of each decision, and complete equality was set aside in the hope that greatest good for as many as possible could be achieved, and in the interest of this greatest good some would need to be left out. Then while the lockdowns eased, the pendulum swung back and demands for equality and reinstating individual freedoms started getting stronger, while respecting the new frameworks of institutional and changed societal rules (like mask wearing, social distancing, restrictions on public gathering and celebrations, etc.)

Throughout these phases, leaders had to constantly evaluate the ideological perfect versus the achievable good. **Compromises were made and choices had to be enforced, even if they were inconvenient.** Leaders seemed stretched and could not clearly identify with one moral philosophy without feeling compromised. And that was part of the moral dilemma we all faced. A new hybrid style was emerging and we as leaders had to build our own unique ideology. No cookie cutter approach or established paradigms remained relevant.

Leaders reconciled to giving up equality (if it ever existed) and freedom (a cherished right) to create a new social order (since it was certain that our old grand illusion had completely shattered).

Contours of the New World

2020 had changed the world. While we were locked in, the external forces that drive the way we live were in a state of flux. A whole new set of urgent personal and organisational challenges emerged and there was an **overwhelming feeling of losing control** of our lives.

Personal goals were reset to what really matters. Materialism lost to realism. Being alive was indeed the biggest blessing, even at the cost of losing on opportunities.

Table 3: Identifying the new World's realities and challenges

External Realities	Personal Challenges	Organisational Challenges
Unemployment	Liquidity	Liquidity
Information overload	Family pressures	Debt
Growing inequality	Peer pressure	Infrastructure
Mass migration	Illness & Physical handicap	Business Failures
Changing consumption trends	Stress, Anxiety	Reputation
Autocratic governance	Mental ill health	Disruption
	Need for new skills	

Note: These were specific words used by the cohort of leaders during their discussions with the Author

We let go of the burden of expectations, especially those that were externally imposed. As leaders in the new world, we had the opportunity of freeing ourselves from the handcuffs of our old identity and stereotypes. We had the privilege of rewriting the ways in which we choose to reciprocate and reward those within our spheres of influence. Since the **ways of the world were renewed**, we needed to rely on **instinct** to make these choices, rather than precedents. As leaders, we were set free from the past.

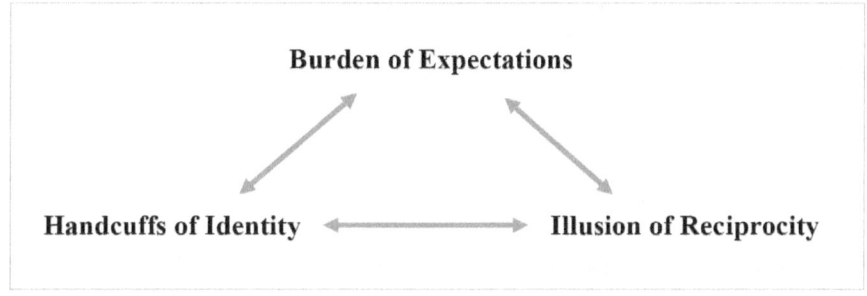

Figure 2: Leaders in the new World need to break free of this Restrictive Trinity

Redefining Risk

An assessment of the set of risk factors affecting 'Generation Lockdown' is important. Who would have thought that in the perennially connected, information overloaded smart phone world, leaders would still be largely ignorant on how to deal with a health crisis. Leaders who asked people to resume work, were now taking responsibility for a life, and not just of work tasks. Every scenario, pessimistic or optimistic, was rendered irrelevant and the nature and sources of risk needed a complete rethink. Even thinking one year ahead seemed like a distant long term.

The following emerged as the dominant set of risk factors that will occupy leaders for the imaginable future.

Table 4: Rewriting the definitions of Risk

New Personal Risks	New Organisational Risks
Basic Human face-to-face interaction	Access to market for offline businesses
Mental capacity and intellect	Stockpiling and hoarding essentials
Patience and Tolerance	Systems and Organisational processes
Reskilling priorities	Cybercrime and data security
Self-confidence and belief	Unknown Demand drivers

Resetting life in a slow motion	Long term capital expenditure
	Contingency funds and expenditure buffers
	Competition from 'Pay-as-you-Go' businesses

This has necessitated trade-offs to balance the risk and keep things moving. In the virtual work mode, traditionally perfected work environments were sacrificed for efficient virtual workspaces. Human touch and travel were sacrificed for health. Spontaneity to travel anywhere to discover and work was curtailed. Spaces at home needed to be repurposed and reimagined to deal with the blurry lines between work and personal time. Large office campuses lost their significance in work life and borders disappeared with co-workers connecting from anywhere to collaborate and perform on the job. The need for urbanisation was challenged and quality of life for those who worked remotely from their rural and semi-urban towns improved. Many who have adapted well do not feel the need to return to the expensive and crowded cities, when they can continue to deliver virtually on their tasks, and believe that their jobs are secure even with remote working.

The era of 'Conscious money' has dawned, with every expense being questioned and allocations being made out of concern for others, beyond the immediate and extended families. Even when inconvenient, genuine desire to assist communities has **rekindled some of the lost human decency**.

Repaying a Debt of Gratitude

We realised that the roles of many were taken for granted. Once we left behind our daily clutter, the shadows lifted on those who never stopped working and doing their duty, despite immense personal risk to their own lives. Without the security guards, our property in the locked down offices and factories would have been at massive risk. Without the healthcare workers and doctors, no one would have got medical attention to overcome the Pandemic. Imagine what would have happened if the internet services went offline, if the food delivery and restaurant take away kitchen staff stopped coming on duty, if grocery store owners had shut shop, if the milkman and dairy farms had closed, if the electricity and sanitation workers stayed home and most importantly, if farmers had stopped tilling the land and harvesting fresh food that continued to feed billions who were indoors.

So many **sacrificed for the benefit of others**, most of the times benefitting anonymous and unseen beneficiaries of their actions. They did their duty, and the world survived. This was a War against an unseen enemy, that was fought without firing a single bullet. Humanity overcame this crisis with the power of coming together with their minds and hearts and what triumphed was the indomitable human spirit and strong collective will.

Leading in the Future

We have all had to overcome serious obstacles to survive 2020. Initially, in the confusion and chaos of the sudden pause, we came face to face with many who lacked empathy and had so much selfishness. Human interactions and peer connect reduced, unreliable and dishonest information was everywhere. There was so much fear of the unknown, with the economy falling and sudden lack of livelihood. Mental health took a massive toll due to fear, self-doubt and inhibitions. Festivities reduced, friendships were lost as were business opportunities. Many lost loved ones. It was only human to rethink and question even the obvious.

It is now time to rebuild. We must have the courage to face the unexpected, to be fearless and optimistic. The excitement of unlimited opportunities awaits us. Agility however, is the key. We must be open to explore and experiment while we hustle and act. The skill of dealing with adversity while always radiating positivity must be learnt on the go.

As responsible leaders, let us now start dreaming of a more empathetic, values-based, sensitive, recession-proof, accommodating, understanding, cleaner, responsible, agile, resilient and healthy world. We now hold the crucible of hope. We must rise above the ordinary and renew our pledge to lead.

The new reality is intimidating. But it is also inspiring. Suddenly everything is up for grabs and this is our new world to shape. What a time to be alive!

Note on Methodology:
The cohort of 100 leaders, in four groups of 25, met five times every alternate evening for 90-100 minutes, and had a moderated conversation with the author. The 4 groups met in May 2020, June 2020, September 2020 and January 2021. The deep dive 'Huddles' involved text anchored dialogues within a circle of trust. The leaders were encouraged to share personal anecdotes and experiences within a safe space, with a singular outcome of peer learning. The key words and first-person stories shared by the cohort were recorded using extensive notes and assimilated to curate this reflective essay. No names and references to specific organisations and people have been made in this paper, to maintain confidentiality and to refrain from revealing the identity of the members of the cohort. The partner organisations who encouraged the participants to join the cohort were the Aries Agro Knowledge Centre, Confederation of Indian Industry's Young Indians and ITM Business School.

REFERENCES

The following are the set of curated readings used as anchors for the conversation with each of the four cohorts of leaders. The same set of readings was discussed with all the cohorts in a similar sequence.

Authers, John (2020). *How Corona Virus Is Shaking Up the Moral Universe. The Pandemic is putting profound philosophical questions to the test.* The Economic Times, March 30, 2020. Available at: https://economictimes.indiatimes.com/news/international/

world-news/how-coronavirus-is-shaking-up-the-moral-universe/
articleshow/74888344.cms?from=mdr

Daniels, Mitch (2018). *We Won't Know how foolish we look until a long time from now.* The Washington Post, April 21, 2018. Available at: ttps://www.washingtonpost.com/opinions/we-wont-know-how-foolish-we-look-until-a-long-time-from-now/2018/04/20/8b0f2dbe-4315-11e8-bba2-0976a82b05a2_story.html

Mawdsley, Craig (2020). *The World has changed forever. Are you ready?* Campaign, 30 March 2020. Available at: https://www.campaignlive.co.uk/article/world-changed-forever-ready/1678192

Obama, Barack (2020). *Full Transcript of Obama's High School Commencement Speech.* The New York Times, May 16, 2020. Available at: https://www.nytimes.com/2020/05/16/us/obama-graduation-speech-transcript.html

Oliver, Mary (1963). *The Journey (Poem).* No Voyage and Other Poems, Houghton Mifflin. Available at: http://www.phys.unm.edu/~tw/fas/yits/archive/oliver_thejourney.html

O'Neill, Patrick T. Rev. (n.d.). *And How are the Children?* Unitarian Universalist Association. Available at: https://www.uua.org/worship/words/reading/and-how-are-the-children

Safford, Victoria (2002). *The Small Work in the Great Work,* Birmingham Lecture: Living Our Mission (p.p. 4-5) Available at: https://cdn.ymaws.com/www.uuma.org/resource/collection/20FCD5D4-D494-4817-93F4-D4264C5B8ACD/BirminghamLecture4.4.pdf

Shanghvi, Siddharth Dhanvant (2020). *They're not fleeing the pandemic; they're fleeing us: What Covid says about India's privilege divide.* Daily O, 12 May 2020. Available at: https://www.dailyo.in/variety/coronavirus-pandemic-migrant-labourers-india-aurangabad-train-accident-lockdown/story/1/32884.html

Wade, Cleo (2018). *Tired.* (Poem) Heart Talk: Poetic Wisdom for a Better Life, Atria Books

'As published in International Journal of Business Insights and Transformation', 2021

4.5 Re-engineering of Hybrid Workplace System for Management Education: An Empirical Analysis

Dr. Mehraj Ud Din Shah

ABSTRACT

A hybrid workplace system is a distinctive techno-driven work model that overwhelmingly was rolled out by industrial houses around the globe on the outbreak of the covid-19 pandemic. Nevertheless, it was operational limited scale only in advanced European countries. It is an unusual work mechanism where under employees enjoy flexibility and freedom to work either exclusively from home or in the office or a combination of both. The system facilitates employees to work according to their choice, will, and schedule. However, it is essential that they have to stay equally productive and effective as they are in a non-hybrid work system. Understandably, the system has proved highly beneficial for both employers and employees on many counts for the majority of business organizations, including higher education. Nevertheless, higher education has witnessed some inherent backend technological and human skill-centric bottlenecks while using hybrid workplace systems. It is in this background that the present study has been undertaken to examine whether the hybrid work system is equally applicable, effective, and productive in business education as in a non-hybrid workplace system. Therefore, the study on the basis of the primary data revealed that the hybrid model is well fit to all the domains of business education barring some exceptions provided the system is welded and supported with robust technology, skilled human capital coupled with uninterrupted internet connectivity and backend institutional policy support. Accordingly, the study opines that a hybrid work system would be a future reality in higher education and physical higher educational institutions would rarely exist and would be overwhelmingly replaced by hybrid institutions where faculty engaged in the teaching-learning process would be working borderless across the nations and survival of fittest would be the rule.

Keywords: *Hybrid work system, effective, productive, technocratic skills, work model, business education*

INTRODUCTION

A hybrid workplace system conceptually is a dual work model engaging employees to work from home and at the office depending upon the organization's needs. The hybrid model has been in force in many industries across the world right since 2016's (Savic 2020). Consistent with this O'Sullivan et al. (2002) say that a hybrid workplace integrates remote work and office work. Accordingly, it is largely seen as a blend of two work schedules: one work from home and the other work in the office. In this context, Hussein and Rolstadas (2002) hint that primarily a hybrid workplace is a move that intends to work out a mechanism wherein employees are given a choice to work either closely or distantly for their organizations and be equally productive. Supporting the argument, Richard (2000) opines that a hybrid workplace is a model that allows freedom to its employees and it would be the workplace of the future. He recommended the solution to be used to deliver education for an organization with a large number of people that are distributed over a large geographic area. Similarly, Hussein and Rolstadas (2002) believe that a hybrid workplace in education supports in wide delivery of education at the doorsteps of a learner and facilitates excess leisure for the participants. The hybrid work model synchronized with technological innovations has been also supported by the vast number of researchers for execution in the business education sector (Albrecht & Sack, 2000; Ives & Jarvenpaa, 1996; Lenzner & Johnson, 1997). The research of Chong, (1997) hints that a hybrid work system delivers a competitive advantage to business schools and can help them to transform and improve their educational process. Nevertheless, a hybrid workplace demands that educational institutions need to invest heavily in communication technology to allow the system to work effectively besides making some key HR work-centric changes, including training and handholding on some relevant software applications, tech operations, and their executions hints Kathleen

(2020). Globally, business education overwhelmingly is transacted in the traditional model. The business school usually engages students in the physical classroom environment and transacts knowledge dissemination in a face-to-face model. However, the technological innovations coupled with contagious and health hazards effects of Covid-19 pandemic gave an overwhelming fillip to the hybrid workplace model in the education sector all over the globe. Under the mechanism, the teachers work from home and engage students in the teaching-learning process through an online platform. The model has worked effectively for the program. However, the direct teaching-learning engagement process in certain cases and courses becomes significantly unavoidable. Therefore, the study entitled re-engineering of Hybrid Work Place of Management Education: An Empirical Analysis has been undertaken to study how far the hybrid workplace in management education is needed?

REVIEW OF LITERATURE

The hybrid workplace is a work operation model combining remote work with office work. Rightly, it is an amalgamation of a virtual and physical office. In view of the advancement in information technology coupled with existing fearful situations unleashed by pandemics, the hybrid workplace model is an emerging new reality. Longqi et al (2021) report that before the pandemic about 50 percent of American workers were working from home for at least three days a week. However, in post-covid-19, it turned wide reality. Accordingly, Hussein and Rolstadås (2002) hint that hybrid workplace discourse is receiving wide recognition in the corporate sector across the globe The companies are attempting to leverage cost-cutting benefits through the emerging model of hybrid workplace mechanism. Consistent with this, Hunt et al. (2004) say that digital business offers a radical new way of operation and the factor of 'speed to customer delight' challenges industry executives to incorporate many new approaches and activities, as it involves advanced use of information and communication technology in every link of the supply chain while simultaneously reducing cost and lead times and increasing profit. The target group for a hybrid solution is characterized by having a diverse social, cultural and academic background. Therefore, the model must address multiple learning styles. Multimedia and technology are used increasingly to accomplish this challenge. Multimedia uses text, graphics, animation, pictures, video, and sound to present information. All of the above can now be integrated using a computer and delivered over the World Wide Web. Accordingly, Hussein and Rolstadas (2002) views that the hybrid model has the following properties:

- It offers an environment for learning that address multiple learning styles
- It allows active participation
- It enables the learners to build personal social networks
- It allows the use of ICT for designing the content in order to enrich the learning experience
- It limits the need for on-campus delivery
- Hybrid learning involves a mix of plenary and virtual sessions.

According to McKinsey (2021) organizations are clear that post-pandemic working will be hybrid. The preliminary research has shown that it is game a changer approach for both the employers and employees and leads to a win-win situation for all the stakeholders. Therefore, it is on the agenda of almost all the major companies to work out some suitable mechanism for broader introduction and execution of hybrid workplace model. A study by Boston Consulting Group revealed that 75 percent of employees who have transitioned to or remained remote during COVID-19, are at least as productive in performing their tasks as were before the pandemic struck. And about half report that they are at least as productive on collaborative tasks that normally would be performed in conference rooms. Consistent with this, various studies have investigated the impact of remote work on productivity, numerous of which reported that remote work has a positive impact on productivity (Vitterso 2003; Collins 2005; Bloom et al. 2013). Coenen and Kok (2014) discovered that remote work has a positive influence on the performance of innovative product development through facilitating cross-functional cooperation, inter-organizational participation, and knowledge sharing. Kazekami (2020) discovered that appropriate remote work hours increase productivity, however, when remote work hours are too extensive, productivity will decrease. Similarly, Microsoft is contemplating giving an option to its majority of employees to work from home only, says Bhatia (2020). Over the past few weeks, Microsoft announced that it plans to let more workers work from home post-pandemic. The Redmond, Washington-based company unveiled plans to adopt a "hybrid workplace" environment as it copes with the coronavirus crisis. The company said part of its strategy is to offer employees greater flexibility once the outbreak subsides permanently. The approach fosters work-life balance and flexibility, says Kathleen (2020) in a blog post as "flexibility can mean different things to each of us, and we recognize there is no one-size-fits-all solution given the variety of roles, work requirements, and business needs we have" Therefore, the company plans to provide guidance to employees to make informed decisions around scenarios that could include changes to their worksite, work location, and/or work hours once offices are open without any COVID-19 restrictions." The scenario is somewhat similar in other companies as well. San Francisco-based Twitter and Square have said more of their workforce can work from home permanently. In May, Facebook would eventually begin allowing most of its employees to request a permanent change in their jobs to let them work remotely. Similar to companies, the individual employees are demanding work settings and job positions that offer greater flexibility, freedom, and work-life balance say Kaloya (2020). This was factually impossible in the distant past. Nevertheless, the continuous development in technology, robust internet, etc has made it easier to operate this model, and it is going to be a widespread reality in the future. The other side of hybrid research has shown that hybrid leads to weak connections among employees, restrains the knowledge transfer (in which experiences from one set of people within an organization are transferred to and used by another set of people within that same organization) which otherwise forms a cornerstone of employee learning, growth, and organizational development. A similar experience is also felt by the companies.

In the context of Management Education, a hybrid workplace model can be well executed and can work effectively with the active backend technology and intranet support. Hybrid learning involves a mix of plenary and virtual sessions. A plenary session comprises of traditional teaching methods such as lectures, assignments, and group work. At the same time, a virtual session is based on material that enables the course participant to select a time and place for learning within certain limitations (Hussein and Rolstadås, 2002). Supporting the debate, Chu et al. (2010) opine that communities (i.e students) excessively learn from information technology including social networks faster and more conveniently than formal classroom or office work hours. They share and understand knowledge for the application and execution of decisions. Consistent with this, the research of Rolstadas (2011) has shown that training based on a combination of on-campus and Web-based is an effective approach. This concept may be significantly more effective than traditional programs with plenary sessions only or with virtual content only. Similarly, Mears et al. (2009) hint that engineering of the curriculum through hybrid technological interventions brings phenomenal improvement in project management education. Alike to this Chu et al. (2010) have developed a model to understand the organizational culture with four business strategies: innovation, responsiveness, core competency, and efficiency and subscribes to the view that a hybrid workplace can foster competition, competency and can become a game-changer for all the concerned. Supporting the debate, the IMS (2020) research also showed a need for personalized and ubiquitous learning (Vigtil et al. 2010). This is a strong argument for more focus on e-learning—a view that is shared by O'Sullivan et al. (2009). They say that education has a significant role to play in the success of manufacturing organizations and that there are two sides to learning: creating courses and finding effective ways to deliver the content of the courses. Favoring the debate O'Sullivan et al. (2009) hints that hybrid workplace learnings outcomes are exceptionally productive and unveil a wide range of benefits for students, faculties, and the other stakeholders including convenience, freedom, and work-life balance. This would only happen when the target group of the hybrid solution is learners with high competence in their field of expertise, tutors, instructors, and facilitators must bring this experience into focus when designing the content says Rolstadas (2011). Moreover, the business schools can engage distantly most profound and expert faculties who can reach to students depending upon the availability and flexibility. The GEM project developed a framework for a curriculum in manufacturing strategy (Rolstadås 2007). Simultaneously, it can unfold huge opportunities for business schools to enhance their quality of education, image, and returns having on its faculty board distinguished experts in domains of their concern. Therefore, it is undoubtedly to conclude that the future work model in management education would be a hybrid workplace and the same needs to be properly re-engineered that suit it. Hussein and Rolstadås (2002), the target group for a hybrid solution is characterized by having a diverse social, cultural and academic background. Therefore, it is fundamentally important that the model addresses multiple learning styles. Accordingly, the present work is a modest effort that examined how the hybrid workplace model evolved and can be applied to management education, as yet no such study is available on the domain in the region under study.

OBJECTIVES

The study has been undertaken to attain the following objectives

- To examine whether or not management education needs a hybrid work place.
- To study the areas and courses where the hybrid work place in management education is required
- To study the perception of key stakeholder-the Faculty about the efficacy of hybrid workplace model in management education.
- To study the level of satisfaction and dissatisfaction of stakeholders- Faculty about their hybrid workplace based on their past experience of Covid-19 pandemic.
- To suggest the appropriate policy guidelines and measures for an effective hybrid workplace model for management education

SCOPE OF THE STUDY

The scope of the study is confined to management education in three prominent management institutions in the Kashmir Division of the state.

NATURE OF THE STUDY

The study is exploratory by nature

Hypotheses:
$H0_1$: Hybrid workplace model has significant objectivity for business education

$H0_2$: Hybrid workplace model receives huge strategic support for business education

$H0_3$: Hybrid workplace model leads to work-life balance for faculty engaged in management education

$H0_4$: Hybrid workplace model is significantly supported with adequate backend technology support

$H0_5$: Hybrid workplace model would emerge future workplace model in management education

$H0_6$: Hybrid workplace system model is significantly effective and productive for management education

RESEARCH METHODOLOGY

The study is exploratory by nature and is based exclusively upon empirical data which was culled out from the main stakeholder of management education - faculty by administrating a well-designed pre-tested questionnaire randomly to the faculty members of the selected colleges of the state of Jammu and Kashmir. In this context, three colleges were selected from the Kashmir Division on the basis of their brand, status, age, and location. From these selected sample colleges around **99** faculty members were selected for the purposes of the study, comprising **27** from College I, 36 from college II and 33 from college III by using a systematic sampling approach. The data collected were tabulated and put into various parametric and nonparametric statistical operations to derive meaningful inferences by using the undermentioned scale scores:

Strongly Disagree =1
Disagree =2
Natural =3
Agree =4
Strongly Agree =5

Where the mean score of the variable or statement would range between the two extremes 1to 5. The highest extreme mean score of 5 would indicate that the hybrid work model is very good while as, the lowest extreme mean score of 1 would refer that the hybrid model is very bad. Further, the mean score of 4 would hint that the hybrid work model is good but still needs somewhat added policy measures to make the same very good and the mean score of 2 would refer that the hybrid workplace model is not good and needs complete attention of the management to make the same better or discontinue the same. The Mean score of 3 hints at the indecisive situation indicating that the hybrid work model is somewhat neither good nor bad.

The given scale for the purposes of the study has been developed by the researcher in accordance with the requisite research needs at various levels. Primarily on the basis of the literature review, 67 items or variables pertaining to the domain were identified. Most of the items identified were already incorporated by the earlier researchers for their research studies. The items identified were put to the item selection and deletion process at stage second through the active involvement and support of experts relevant to the field. Thereafter, 20 items or variables were chosen. These items were clubbed into six dimensions. Finally, the items or variables selected were incorporated into the questionnaire for the pilot study for which about 32 sample respondents were chosen. The reliability of the items of a questionnaire for the given sample was conducted on a pilot run with the help of Cronbach's Alpha (1951) which worked our

0.78 and 0.82 respectively indicating both the instrument and scale is valid and reliable to use.

Profile of the Sample Respondents

The profile of sample respondents (faculty members) hints that an overwhelming percentage of sample respondents have sufficient experience of more than ten years (80%), PhD qualification (55%), adequate awareness and knowledge of using IT-enabled technology (70%), stable internet connection (90%), and are working from home mainly (90%) as can be seen in the table given below 1.1.

Table No 1.1: Profile of the sample Respondents (figures in Percentage)

S.No	Profile Indicator	Percentage
1	Experience: 10 years and above / < 10 years but > 5 years and < 2 years but > 0 years	79 (80%)/ 15 (16%) / 4 (4%)
2	Qualification: PG/MPhil/PhD	39 (40%) / 5 (5%) / 55 (55%)
3	Awareness and Knowledge of using IT enable Technology: Adequate Awareness and Knowledge / Inadequate awareness and knowledge/ No Awareness and Knowledge	70 (71%)/ 20 (20%) /9 (09%)
4	Availability of Stable Internet Connection at home: Available/ Un stable Available/ not available at all	90 (90%) / 9 (10%) / nil
5	Working from: Office only/ Both office and home/ home only	7 (07%) / 2(02%)/ 90 (91%)
6.	Gender: Male/ Female	69 (70%) /30 (30%)

ANALYSIS AND DISCUSSION

Although, the hybrid workplace system was somewhat used at a limited scale in many countries in the world, with the eruption of covid-19 pandemic and following the consistent lockdown of business establishments and educational institutions, etc the concept of the hybrid workplace system gained wide adaptability globally in a majority of business houses and service providers. This was equally extended to the education sector all around the world including in India, where educational leaders and institutions decided to disseminate education through online transmission mode all across the courses and domains so as not to prolong the duration of courses and help the students to complete their degrees well on time. Accordingly, the faculty engaged in the teaching-learning process of various domains had no option but to get abrased themselves to a greater extent about the latest technological interventions required for online delivery of education from their home. Nevertheless, for certain courses, the online mode of education worked quite well and for some, it didn't yield productive results. Therefore, the success of hybrid workplace mechanisms or work from home approaches emerged a question of debate and discussion at various forums and for researchers as well. It is accordingly, the present study is the outcome of a modest effort that examined empirically different aspects of hybrid workplace mechanism and the put the same to rigorous statistical operations and analysis using descriptive and parametric statistics to understand the overall efficacy of the same as under.

Objectivity

Objectivity means the quality of being able to make a decision or judgment in a fair way and is not influenced by personal feelings or beliefs. More specifically, the dimension objectivity refers to measuring a domain based on facts and grounded reality rather than viewing a domain unfairly or ambiguously. Therefore, the dimension intends to judge how far the hybrid workplace system has a role and utility in the delivery of education through virtual mode and to what extent it upholds the purposes for which it has been executed in the education system, especially in the management education system. Accordingly, in this dimension, four variables were incorporated to record the objectivity of the hybrid work mechanism. They include management education needs a hybrid workplace approach for the future as well, all the subjects or areas of management education can be effectively taught and learned under a hybrid workplace mechanism, only non-technical subjects can be effectively taught and learned through a hybrid workplace mechanism and hybrid workplace in management education is equally productive as the traditional form of education. The descriptive and parametric statistics of the dimension are presented in the given table 1.2

Table No 1.2: Descriptive and Parametric Statistics of Dimension Objectivity

S.No	Statement	Mean	St.Dev	Z value	Sig	Hypothesis Status
1	Management education needs Hybrid workplace approach for the future as well	3.153	0.925	4.999	0.000	H_0 Accepted
2	All the subjects or areas of management education can be effectively taught and learned under a hybrid workplace mechanism	2.281	1.051	-8.599	0.000	H_0 Accepted
3	Only non-technical subjects can be effectively taught and learned through a hybrid workplace mechanism	3.305	0.965	7.4003	0.000	H_0 Accepted
4	Hybrid workplace in Management education is equally productive as the traditional form of education	2.593	0.8119	-3.792	0.000	H_0 Accepted
	Overall	2.76	0.932	4.21	0.000	H_0 Accepted

From table 1.2 it is evidently clear that the overall mean score of the dimension objectivity has not exceeded 2.76 indicating that the objectivity of the hybrid work mechanism is somewhat questionable. This hints that the hybrid workplace system is not absolutely computable for management education, as the variable that hybrid workplace in management education is equally productive as the traditional form of education has recorded the lowest mean score of 2.59 indicating that the hybrid workplace system is not fully well fit teaching-learning of management education in true sense. This seems predominantly due to the fact, that the course is welded with many technical subjects which become somewhat difficult to teach through online mode. The mean score of the variable has exceeded 3.03 implying that some critical and calculous-based courses can't be learned effectively through hybrid workplace mechanisms and only non-technical courses can be taught through online transmission. The parametric statistical operations of the data also unfold that the hybrid work mechanism is not absolutely productive for all across the course as the overall z value at 5% level of significance is 4.21 with p-value of 0.000 implying that the null hypothesis is rejected in favor of the alternative hypothesis. The parametric statistical findings are almost uniform for all the individual variables leading to conclude that the hybrid workplace mechanism significantly lacks objectivity in management education. The finding is not in tune with the earlier research observations of Roca & Gagne, (2008); Shroff, Deneen & Ng, (2011); Edmunds, Thorpe & Conole, (2012) which reveals that online teaching learning process in many ways is objective centric and can replace the face to face teaching learning process in higher education including in business education.

Strategic Support Facilities

Strategic Support facilities refer to a long-run and long-lasting institutional strategic administrative backup, and human capabilities available for the effective execution of hybrid workplace system. Under the educational set up strategic support facilities system depends upon the institutional policies, awareness, knowledge, and commitment of institutional management besides the faculty capability, competence, skills, and student's willingness to execute the system for the benefit of each stakeholder. More specifically, strategic support facilities are a broad spectrum of cantors which however around three main stakeholders of education (Administrators, Faculty and Student). Administrators are the individuals who run and formulate the administrative strategic discourses and policies for the execution of a hybrid work system having long-run efficacy. This surely would include the administrative attitude in terms of favourable policies, and the role of administrators towards the hybrid system vis-a-vis facilitating the physical and financial resources for effective delivery of online education. While as, faculty refers to individuals who are trained and capable to operate the teaching-learning gadgets and systems in an effective way for the online delivery of knowledge. Similarly, the students are the learners who are desirous to gain knowledge and understanding through online platforms. Therefore, the dimension intends to search whether higher educational institutions have or not the requisite strategic facilities in place for the management of a hybrid education system. Although, there are various aspects that fall in the domain of strategic support system facilities. Nevertheless, the dimension is measured through the three main variables namely- hybrid workplace in management education has the full support of institutional administration, the hybrid workplace has the full support of institutional faculty and the hybrid workplace mechanism is demanded by the students. The descriptive and parametric statistics of the dimension are presented in the given table 1.3.

Table No 1.3: Descriptive and Parametric Statistics of Dimension Strategic Support System

S.No	Statement	Mean	St.Dev	Z value	Sig
1	Hybrid work place in Management education has a full support of institutional administration	3.612	0.9100	-2.539	0.000

2	Hybrid work place has a full support of institutional faculty	3.949	0.991	1.579	0.111
3	Hybrid work place mechanism demanded by the students	3.893	0.9412	0.961	0.334
4	Overall	3.781	0.910	0.097	0.222

The descriptive statistics depicted in the table 1.3 shows that the overall mean score of the dimension has not exceeded 3.781 indicating that strategic support system for execution of hybrid work place system is appropriate and effective. This indicates that strategic support system is up to the mark in sample higher education institutions under reference and drives stakeholders to deliver requisite academic service as desired by student stakeholders. This profoundly is visible due to commendable support of the institutional faculty and students coupled with institutional management. The means score of these three variables has not pegged down 3.62 and moved beyond 3.94 implying that the support system facilities are somewhat not bad but adequate and satisfactory. Accordingly, the parametric statistics depicted in the table supports the fact that the stakeholders lend sufficient support to the hybrid work mechanism in sample higher education institutions as the overall Z value 0.97 at 5% level of significance with p value 0.222 of the dimension reveals that alternative hypothesis is rejected in favour of null hypothesis implying that the institutional administrative role policies, faculty and students to hybrid work place system or line teaching learning process is significantly visible and present. This in other sense hints that institutional administrative backup and strategies coupled with faculty's skills in terms of soft and technical skills including student seriousness and willingness to learn are vividly visible and present under hybrid work place system. This seems specifically due to the fact that during the existing pandemic there was not any other alternative left for the academic administrators, faculty and of course for students to execute education only the through the hybrid mechanism. This was the only maiden option for them to stay relevant to attain their short and long term goals, otherwise they could have lost their time and resources. The finding is well in tune with earlier research of and the basic fundamentals of Technology Acceptance Model (TAM) theoretical framework (Davis 1989) which hints that there are two main factors which influence an individual's and institutions to use technology: perceived ease of use and perceived usefulness. The research has shown that a serval multidisciplinary studies have used TAM either in its original form or in the extended model (Venkatesh and Davis, 2000). Arbug (200); Davis and Wong (2007) found ATM helped the students and had moderate effect on student learning.

Technological Support and knowhow

Technological support and knowhow includes all types of technical service available in the form of technical equipment's and expert human resources which help in the hassle-free execution of the hybrid work system. Rightly, the hybrid work system requires organizational backend work service support loaded with adequate technical service personals having great deal of experts in the field of IT and its related domains. Technological support is one of the most essential input for the successful operation of hybrid work system. In fact, this input is fundamental backend support for hybrid work system. The research on hybrid work mechanism in major IT business centric houses have shown that technological support has remained the primary factor for cost effective and productive execution of hybrid workplace system. While as, it has badly doomed many organization which do not have a required technological support. In the context of higher education, the technological support for hybrid work place system is somewhat at a lowest ebb due to low government funding and frenzy initiatives of institutional leadership. The adequate technological support seldom all forms of failures of hybrid work place mechanism and ensure perpetual successful of the domain mainly in education sector. This is because, the technological support is blend of the multiple inputs including equipment, internet, technical knowhow and above all the management support. Therefore, to map the extent of technological support and knowhow adequacy in higher educational institutions using hybrid work system, three variables have been co-opted. They include institutions have requisite technological support in place for smooth execution of hybrid work place approach, hybrid work place in management education in UT J&K suffers due to the lack of backend internet support and hybrid work place in management education suffers due to lack technical skills in faculty. The descriptive statistics of the dimension is presented in the table 1.4 below

Table No 1.4: Descriptive and Parametric Statistics of Dimension Technological Support and Knowhow

S.No	Statement	Mean	St.Dev	Z value	Sig
1	Institutions have requisite technological support in place for smooth execution of hybrid work place approach	1.864	0.706	-18.97	0.0000
2	Hybrid work place in management education in UT J&K suffers due to the lack of backend internet support	4.491	0.6531	-17.79	0.0000
3	Hybrid work place in management education suffers due to lack technical skills in faculty	3.305	1.262	1.1866	0.2352
4	Overall	3.230	0.862	-16.15	0.000

The descriptive statistics depicted in the table 1.4 shows that overall mean score of the dimension technological support and knowhow has not exceeded 3.230 implying that the overall technical support and knowhow is not somewhat attractive in the sample institutions under study. This hints that the technical support system and technical knowhow needs potential improvement to execute hybrid work system effective for all the stakeholders especially for the ultimate end user -the student. This is because, the descriptive statistics more closely unfolds sample institutions significantly have negligible technological backend support available to operate hybrid work system systematically and effectively as the mean score the variable institutions have requisite technological support in place for smooth execution of hybrid work place approach has pegged around 1.86 indicating that somewhat abysmal technological support is in place in sample institutions under study. The similar picture has also been revealed by parametric statistics as the overall Z value - 16.15 at 5% level of significance with p value 0.000 of the dimension reveals that null hypothesis is rejected in favour of the alternative hypothesis implying that the technological support and technical knowhow is largely invisible in higher education institutions to run hybrid work system successfully. The finding is in tune with the research of Deepeka (2020) which has found that online education quality has remained significantly poor in higher education due to lack of technological backend support and skills in faculty. The research findings of her study showed that the negative aspects of online education were poor connectivity, power cuts, broadband issue, poor audio and video quality as reported by her majority of sample respondents around 64.24%.

Work Life Balance

Work life balance is the level of parity or imbalance between the personal and official life of an employee. Work life balance of employees often remains a matter of concern for all employees. Therefore, securing a reasonable level of work life balance is a daunting challenge for all employees irrespective of their occupational level and work setting. The past research has shown that appropriate work life balance improves employees all round performance, productivity and organizational growth. While poor work life balance derails employee's efficiency, effectiveness and organizational image. Work life balance of employees usually is causality in most of the organizations due to high work overload, long working hours, ill-defined work role, absence of freedom and leisure during work. In the context of higher education, work life balance is overwhelmingly viewed a most demanding feature of the work by employees especially the teaching faculty, researchers and students. Therefore, to map the level and status of work life balance of faculty members under hybrid education system, three variables have incorporated in the dimension which include hybrid work place helps the faculty to save their time, money and enjoy leisure, hybrid work place approach gives freedom to faculty, hybrid work place has led work life balance in faculty and hybrid work place approach contributed to delight faculty and reduced their job stress. The descriptive statistics of the dimension is presented in the table 1.5 below

Table No 1.5: Descriptive and Parametric Statistics of Dimension Work Life Balance

S.No	Statement	Mean	St.Dev	Z value	Sig
1	Hybrid work place helps the faculty to save their time, money and enjoy leasiure	3.864	0.996	2.9156	0.031
2	Hybrid work place approach gives freedom to faculty	3.728	1.095	0.838	0.1091
3	Hybrid work place has led work life balance in faculty	3.474	0.816	-3.029	0.0024
4	Hybrid work place approach contributed to delight faculty and reduced their job stress	3.672	1.0811	0.7090	0.478
	Overall	3.722	0.91	0.672	0.015

The descriptive statistics shown in the table No: 1.5 reveals that the overall mean score of the dimension has not remained below 3.72 indicating that quality of work life of employees is somewhat good and up to the desired level of employees working under hybrid work mechanism. This in other sense unfolds that hybrid work mechanism adds to the delight of employees in the sample institutions under study as the variable hybrid work place helps the faculty to save their time, money and enjoy leisure has got the highest mean score 3.86. The similar facts have also been revealed by the parametric statistics as the overall Z value 0.67 at 5% level of significance with p value 0.015 of the dimension reveals that alternative hypothesis is rejected in favour of the null hypothesis implying that the employees enjoy better quality of work life due to hybrid work system. The finding is in tune with the earlier research of (Dhawan; 2020) which has unfolded that easy work schedules and work from home arrangement has contributed in the work life balance of employees in the

IT sector of employees. Therefore, it would be somewhat appropriate to conclude that hybrid work mechanism is making work more attractive, rewarding, delightful for employees provided they are equally productive as in normal offline working mechanism.

Futuristic Work Model

Although, the hybrid work place model was in use in many countries, but predominantly emerged globally due the compulsions of pandemic. Under the mechanism, employees in organizations were given option to work from home without coming formally to office regularly to avoid the spread of covid-19 infections and to help organizations to continue their operations. The employees initially reacted it with some pessimism and perplexity, as they were largely unaware about how to work remotely to stay effective and productive. Nevertheless, with the support of information technology and Wifi connectivity majority of the employees in all most all the organizations learned to work distantly and were equally productive as in normal offline work setting. These positive outcomes of hybrid work place phenomenon motivated employers to redesign the future work policy mechanism for employees and shifted overwhelmingly towards hybrid work place system. Consistent to this, the hybrid work system was given wide fillip in education sector all over the world. Rightly, it was viewed well sacrosanct in the higher education sector, where online education brought classroom and teacher into the house of every student and he/she learned in the same ways as he/she did in her normal offline class. Here, the argument raised is that whether the hybrid work system would sustain in future or it will die down with the death of pandemic? The theoretical research on the domain have unfolded that hybrid work place is a future reality and its roots will get more strengthened with every progressive improvement in the information technology, rising growth of artificial intelligence and machine learning system coupled with handholding skills secured by employees. Accordingly, to understand on the basis of empirical research whether the hybrid work system would sustain in higher education sector and to what extent it can replace the normal traditional classroom system, three variables have been incorporated in this dimension. They include hybrid work place approach was a temporary approach for teaching learning in covid-19, hybrid work place would emerge a preferred style of teaching learning process, hybrid work place in teaching learning process would be used in combination with traditional teaching system. The descriptive statistics of the dimension is given in the table No 1.6

Table No 1.6: Descriptive and Parametric Statistics of Dimension Futuristic

S.No	Statement	Mean	St.Dev	Z value	Sig
1	Hybrid work place approach was a temporary approach for teaching learning in covid-19	3.898	1.189	-4.514	0.000
2	Hybrid work place would emerge a preferred style of teaching learning process	3.796	1.103	0.4100	0.6183
3	Hybrid work place in teaching learning process would be used in combination with traditional teaching system	4.107	0.941	4.104	0.004
4	Overall	3.933.	0.981	3.461	0.205

The descriptive statistics presented in the table 1.4 reveals that the overall mean score of the dimension is 3.933 indicating that the future of the hybrid work system is not somewhat dismal in the education sector, as almost all the variables of the dimension have recorded mean score 3.5 above unfolding that hybrid work place system in higher education sector though temporary for the time being has potential to emerge a parallel teaching learning process provided seamless infusion of technology in the system is pushed uninterruptedly. The argument is supported by the fact as the variable that the hybrid work place would emerge a preferred style of teaching learning process has recorded the mean score of 3.79 hinting that a considerable number of sample respondents opine that hybrid work system holds merit to do away many fallacies of conventional education system and overwhelmingly institutions in the immediate future may have to upskill its people with enabling technology and transact knowledge dissemination through virtual mode only. Nevertheless, it would be a wonderful discourse and significantly beneficial for all the stakeholders in the higher education sector if they resort to blend model in teaching learning processive combining conventional offline and online mechanism together, as the mean score 4.17 of the variable has remained highest among the other variables of the dimension. The parametric statistics of the dimension has also revealed somewhat similar outcomes as the overall Z value 3.46 at 5% level of significance with p value 0.205 of the dimension reveals that alternative hypothesis is rejected in favour of the null hypothesis implying that the future of the hybrid work place system is quiet bright and with the advent of new technological gadgets and upskilling of the teachers and availability of hassle-free internet and WIFI connectivity surely will pave the ways for hybrid work system in higher education sector including in business education. The finding is in tune with the past research of Fortune and Pangelinan (2011); Tratnik (2017) and Deepika (2020) which have reported that hybrid work model is highly relevant to higher education in view of its distinguishing features and benefits for all the stakeholders. However, its future largely depends upon quality of backend equipment support, quality of teachers, the skills of teachers and student's willingness

Effectiveness

Effectiveness is an overwhelming merit in the shape of minimum cost, effort and resources by which an individual or an organization or a specific system attains its objectives, stays productive and yields desired results. A scientific mapping of effectiveness for a domain unfolds how far an underlying subject is sacrosanct for continuation or discontinuation in view of its set objectives and resources. In the context of hybrid work system consistent to higher education, the term effectiveness is not altogether unelusive. However, it needs to be seen, viewed and mapped through prism of its multiple stakeholders including institution, teachers, students and teaching learning process outcomes. Therefore, effectiveness is a multifarious domain when evaluated under higher education vis-à-vis hybrid work system. Here, a successful and effective hybrid work approach necessarily has to unfold a win-win situation for all the stakeholders to yield desired results, otherwise its partial success would gloom the other stakeholders with negativity and dissatisfaction i.e., if it please one or two groups and displeases the other. Accordingly, the domain was mapped to underline its effectiveness for management, students and faculty. Therefore, rightly under the dimension three main variable have been incorporated including hybrid work place approach saves various costs to management institutions, hybrid work place contributes to the quality of management education, hybrid work place contributes to job satisfaction of faculty. A descriptive statistic relating to these variables is presented in the table No 1.7below

Table No 1.7: Descriptive and Parametric Statistics of Dimension Effectiveness

S.No	Statement	Mean	St.Dev	Z value	Sig
1	Hybrid work place approach saves various costs to management institutions	3.593	1.219	-4.514	0.426
2	Hybrid work place contributes to the quality of management education	3.271	1.310	-2.692	0.007
3	Hybrid work place contributes to job satisfaction of faculty	3.694	1.070	1.896	0.597
	Overall	3.521	1.150	-3.451	0.372

The descriptive statistics presented in the table No 1.7 shows that the mean score of the dimension has not remained less than 3.521 indicating that the hybrid work system is somewhat moderately effective in higher education sector. This in other sense hints that the new work order system has unleashed favourable advantage for all the stakeholders including institutional management, students and faculty. With regard to the institutional management, the descriptive statistics hints that the new work system has successfully diminished the overall administrative institutional costs. The mechanism surely would help the institutional management to perform better and provide adequate institutional support to other stakeholders, as the mean score of the variable has remained 3.59 implying that hybrid workplace has placed institutional management on progressive turf and they would be more inclined to push the new work order for overwhelming execution in the future. Similarly, the descriptive statistics shows that the other key stakeholder- students have enjoyed and experienced a good quality of education through online mode. It has helped them to save their time, resources, life and above all gain knowledge and wisdom to learn with unconventional mechanism, as the mean score of the variable - hybrid work place contributes to the quality of management education has not pegged below 3.27 indicating that students are equally benefitted and delighted with the hybrid work system. Consistent to this, faculty are experiencing the overwhelming job satisfaction and delight due to hybrid work system. The mean score of the variable, hybrid work place contributes to the quality of management education, hybrid work place contributes to job satisfaction of faculty. The mean score of the variable has however around 3.69 implying that hybrid work has raised the job satisfaction level of faculty in higher education. The parametric statistics of the dimension have also revealed somewhat similar outcomes as the overall Z value -3.451 at 5% level of significance with a p-value 0.372 of the dimension reveals that the alternative hypothesis is rejected in favor of the null hypothesis. This hints that a hybrid work system has the merit to emerge as a new model for the dissemination of knowledge in the higher education sector. However, it needs to be seen whether this reality prevails for a long or may disappear with time and subsequent technological developments, academic demands, and societal developments. Consistent with this, the research of Dhawan (2020) hints that natural disasters can stimulate our motivation for the adoption of highly innovative communication technology and e-learning tools (Tull et al., 2017). To make e-learning effective in such difficult times, we need to focus on the use of technology more efficiently, that is, the usage of that technology that has minimum procurement and maintenance costs but can effectively facilitate educational processes.

MAIN FINDINGS

The study unfolded that the hybrid workplace model is equally effective and productive in business education for all domains except the technical subjects involving multilevel complicated accounting and mathematical calculations. Further the all the stakeholders of academics including faculty and students are somewhat delighted with the hybrid workplace model. However, it seldom team-based learning within groups and limits normal direct face-to-face interaction between teacher and students.

SUGGESTIONS

Against the backdrop of the above discussion and analysis, the following suggestions are put forth for the effective operation and execution of a hybrid work system in business education.

- The institutional management should frame a comprehensive policy approach for the execution of a hybrid workplace system. The policy document should spell objectives and strategies for adopting the hybrid workplace system. It should demonstrate the institutional role for strengthening and operating a hybrid work system. Moreover, the policy document must explain the process to be adopted for a hybrid workplace system.

- The institutional management should design appropriate strategies which lead to the successful operation of the hybrid workplace model. The strategies should be in tune with the overall policies of the institution. The strategies should include discourses relating to the installation of backend support systems, development of infrastructure, creation of a favourable culture for the smooth operation of hybrid workplace systems, upskilling and training of stakeholders, and establishing a monitoring mechanism to evaluate the outcome of the hybrid workplace system.

- The business schools should put in place robust and advanced backend technology along with uninterrupted internet connectivity for all stakeholders for the induction of a hybrid workplace system. The backend technology includes the advanced web server, computers, etc. staffed with competent human resources. The technological equipment and human expertise act as drivers/catalysts for the seamless operation of hybrid workplace systems.

- The business schools should upskill their faculty and students about the use of technological equipment for the effective execution of a hybrid workplace system. For this purpose, the institutions should arrange special training programmes for the faculty and students so that the hybrid workplace model in business education works smoothly and effectively. The upskill training course be designed by IT professionals preferably that would help the stakeholders to benefit from hybrid workplace approach.

- The business schools should create a culture that supports the environment of the hybrid workplace approach. The culture should be groomed through the education and involvement of all stakeholders. The hybrid culture be gradually infused from minuscule areas to all areas of education. Initially, the hybrid workplace in education be introduced for conducting group discussions, classroom presentations, mock tests, assignment and subsequently extended to the other areas of education till all the aspects of education are transacted effectively.

LIMITATIONS OF THE STUDY

The study is somewhat limited in scope in the state of Jammu and Kashmir. Moreover, it is confined to a minuscule percentage of sample respondents in three higher education institutions. Further, the study divulges upon the perception of only one group of stakeholders i.e faculty and has not examined the reaction of the other stakeholder i.e student. The Study also suffers on account of lack of reliability and validity of the instrument used for collection of data for the study. Nonetheless, the study is a modest effort to put forth the realistic information based on founded facts and professional understanding and knowledge of the subject.

CONCLUSION

The future of hybrid workplace is a viewed reality in business education. however, it success largely depends upon the availability of backend strategic and technological support.

REFERENCES

Bloom, N., Liang, J., Roberts, J., Ying, Z-J. N. (2013). Does Working from Home Work? Evidence from a Chinese Experiment, Quarterly Journal of Economics, Volume 130, February 2015, Pages 165-218.

Chong (1997) quoted in Virtual Learning- Current Situation for Management Education and Training" Richard Walter (2000)" Chapter in Edited book by

Chu, M.-T., Khosala, R., & Nishida, T. (2010). Communities of practice driven knowledge management in multinational knowledge based enterprises. Journal of Intelligent Manufacturing. Published online November 27, 2010

Collins, M. (2005). The (not so simple) case for teleworking: A study at Lloyd's of London. New Technology, Work and Employment, 20(2), 115–132.

Deepika Nambiar(2020). The impact of online learning during COVID-19: students' and teachers' perspective The International Journal of Indian Psychology ISSN 2348-5396 (Online) | ISSN: 2349-3429 (Print) Volume 8, Issue 2, April- June, 2020

Dimple Kaloya (2020). "Hybrid workplace model is here to stay" www.google.com

Edmunds, R., Thorpe, M. & Conole, G. (2012). Student attitudes towards and use of ICT in course study, work and social activity: A technology acceptance model approach. British Journal of Educational Technology, 43(1), 71-84. http://dx.doi.org/10.1111/j.1467- 8535.2010.01142.x

Fortune M, Spielman M and Pangelinan D (2011). Students' perceptions of online or face-toface learning and social media in hospitality, recreation and tourism Journal of Online Learning and Teaching 7(1) pp 1-16

Gurpreet Bhatia (2020). "How to make Hybrid Workplace Model successful" www.google.com

Hussein, B., & Rolstadås, A. (2002). Hybrid learning in project management—potentials and challenges, PMI research conference. Seattle, USA

Ives and Jarvenpaa (1996) quoted in Virtual Learning- Current Situation for Management Education and Training" Richard Walter (2000) " Chapter in Edited book by Kathleen Hogan (2020) "Hybrid work Place- The Future work" www.google,com

Kazekami, S. (2020). Mechanisms to improve labor productivity by performing telework. Telecommunications policy, 44(2), p.101868

Lenznen and Johnson (1997). quoted in Virtual Learning- Current Situation for Management Education and Training" Richard Walter (2000)" Chapter in Edited book by Longqi yang; David Holtz; Sonia Jaffe; Siddgarth Sari' Shilpi Sinha; Jeffery Weston;Cannor Joyce; Neha Shah; Kevin Sharma; Brent Hecht; Taime Tavven (2021) "The Effects of Remote Colloberation among Information Workers (2021) https/doi.org/10.1038/s 41562-021

Mears, L., Omar, M., & Kurfess T. R. (2009). Automotive engineering curriculum development: Case study for Clemson University. Journal of Intelligent Manufacturing. Published online October 22, 2009.

O'Sullivan, D., Precuo, L. E., Duffy, P., van Dongen, S., & Guochao, X. (2002). Survey of existing manufacturing curricula. GEMEUROPE project report, Galway, Ireland.

O'Sullivan, D., Rolstadås A., & Filos, E. et al. (2009). Global education in manufacturing strategy. Journal of Intelligent Manufacturing. Published online October 15, 2009.

Richard Walter (2000). "Virtual Learning- Current Situation for Management Education and Training" Chapter in Edited book

Roca, J. C. & Gagne, M. (2008). Understanding e-learning continuance intention in the workplace: A self-determination theory perspective. Computers in Human Behavior, 24(4), 1585-1604. http://dx.doi.org/10.1016/j.chb.2007.06.001

Rolstadås, A. (2007). Global education in manufacturing. In K.-D. Thoben, M. Taisch, & M. Monotorio (Eds.), Advanced manufacturing—an ICT and systems perspective (pp. 229–238).

Savic, D. (2020). COVID-19 and Work from Home: Digital Transformation of the Workforce. 53 Grey J. (TGJ) 2020, 16, 101–104.

Shivangi Dhawan (2020). "Online Learning: A Panacea in the Time of COVID-19 Crisis" Journal of Educational Technology Systems 2020, Vol. 49(1) 5–22

Shroff, R. H., Deneen, C. & Ng, E. M. W. (2011). Analysis of the technology acceptance model in examining students' behavioral intention to use an e-portfolio system. Australasian Journal of Educational technology, 27(4), 600-618. http://www.ascilite.org.au/ajet/ajet27/shroff.htm

Tratnik A (2017). Student satisfaction with an online and a face-to-face Business English course in a higher education context Journal Innovations in Education and Teaching International 15(1) pp. 1-10

Tratnik, A., Urh, M., & Jereb, E. (2019). Student satisfaction with an online and a face to-face Business English course in a higher education context. Innovations in Education and Teaching International, 56(1), 36-45

Vigtil, A., Rolstadås, A., Fradinho, M., Carpanzano, E., & Brondi, C., et al. (2010). Methods for competence development in sustainable manufacturing. In Proceedings from conference on advances in production management, Cernobbio, Politecnico di Milano. October 11–13, 2010.

Vitterso, J., Akselsen, S., Evjemo, B., Julsrud, T., Yttri, B., Bergvik, S. (2003). Impacts of Home-Based Telework on Quality of Life for Employees and Their Partners. Quantitative and Qualitative Results from a European Survey. J. Happiness Stud. 2003,

Books

McKinsey. (2021). What executives are saying about the future of hybrid work. https://www.mckinsey.com/business-functions/organization/our-insights/what-executives-aresaying-about-the-future-of-hybrid-work#. [Accessed on 4 Jun. 2021].

Chapter 5

Entrepreneurship and Sustainability

5.1 New Indian food plate and its implications on agriculture and human health

Dr. Amruta Krishna Patil

ABSTRACT

For thousands of years India has refined its culinary art and assimilated a wide variety of vegetables fruits and animal products mostly belonging to this subcontinent. But in the last 500 years due to the influx of foreign cultures and intermediate trades, Indians were introduced to new kinds of vegetables fruits and meat products. Due to globalization and world-wide media Indians are getting attracted to "fancy food' of foreign lands, which has influenced the food habits, and agriculture industry in India. Today's food industry is a multi-million-dollar industry with various branches, branch which specialize in hybrid vegetables, plants and animals, Genetic alteration, processed foods, ready-to-cook etc. There is a whole industry producing chemicals and alternatives in food. Invariably today's generation believes in eye appeal and ease of cooking and fall easy prey to the industrial products most of the times unknowingly.

Keywords: food habits, human health, agriculture

INTRODUCTION

India a land of rivers, which had a glorious history and culture beyond the knowledge of today's historians. It has over the ages mastered the art of culinary science, as it was the first to create unique and flavourful dishes incorporating a wide variety of vegetables, pulses, cereals, meats and spices.

India developed various cuisines using locally available ingredients and blending various spices to create a totally vegetarian flair of its own. No other country in the world can boast as many dishes created in India both veg and non-veg put together.

It is very important to understand the history of the region before commenting on the present, similar is for the culinary history. Various text in ancient India shed knowledge about the recipes, vessels to be used, use of herbs and spices not only to enhance the taste and colours but help in ease of digestion. Patients were prescribed specialized diets suggesting their knowledge about the medicinal properties of items used and their effects on human body. Vedic food with a blend of spices, which was not only tasty but also healthy is an example of scientific way of preparing food. With the advent of invaders newer cuisines were added with foreign vegetables and meat preparations (potato, tomato, chilly etc.). It is during this period we have lost a lot of our ancient and ancestral text during the burning of ancient universities like Nalanda and Taxila by muslim invader Khilaji and many knowledgeable text were looted and taken out of India by the British and found in various museums in western countries.

Even with limited texts that we are left with, we still have a vast knowledge about ancient food habits, as they are practiced widely throughout the length and breadth of India.

OBJECTIVES OF THE STUDY

- To understand the implication of changing food habits.
- To understand difference between healthy traditional food and unhealthy fat rich artificial flavoured hybrid food
- To make the reader alert and responsible about what they consume.
- To encourage the reader to inculcate good eating habits.

LIMITATION OF THE STUDY

- Length of the paper in words.
- Conflicts arising from cultural food habit and today modern belief about good food.
- Availability of unbiased research.

RESEARCH METHODOLOGY

It is secondary research data collected from authentic sources like, articles, research papers, web sites, news etc. and analysed.

REVIEW OF LITERATURE

- "A randomized study of coconut oil versus sunflower oil on cardiovascular risk factors in patients with stable coronary by Maniyal Vijayakumara D.M.Vasudevanb K.R.Sundaramc Sajitha Krishnanb Kannan Vaidyanathane Sandya Nandakumard RajivC handrasekhara Navin Mathewa", this paper analysed oils consumption effects on human health.
- "Studying India's changing food culture" article by Shreya Roy Chowdhary showed the impact of changes in food culture.
- "Impact of soy consumption on human health: integrative review" this article showed the effect of soya consumption on human health.

MAJOR FINDINGS

A. Effect on human health

Before the advent of the British and Portuguese, food was prepared using local ingredients which were suitable for people living in that particular area, example oil; Most of North India consumed mustard oil, groundnut oil was prevalent in central India and coconut oil dominated the south. Mustard oil is suitable for people living in cold climate, in moderate climate groundnut oil is best and coconut oil is suitable for hot and humid climate similar was for all other food habits and ingredients.

It was only after the advent of Islamist, Portuguese, British and the French that new verities of chilies, potatoes, tomatoes and many other vegetables were added to our menu. Some of the new foreign items were assimilated into India's cuisines without any negative impact on the health of the people.

In today's times commercialization has made a huge impact on the food habits of our country. The decision making of what we consume has been taken over by the manufacturing and retail companies, which use aggressive advertising to push their products into our kitchens.

Advertisements where novice actors are shown in doctor's uniform to spread a false narrative are very common. Before we even came to senses, noodles, soft drinks, oats and cornflakes have already invaded our kitchens.

There is no proper scientific research in food materials in India therefore there is a constant state of unawareness and partial knowledge about the introduction of new kind of food products. Most of the research that is available on the net is funded by the manufacturers themselves. They are biased and only show the partial truth. Only the advantages are highlighted and disadvantages are seldom referred to as doubtful due to lack of more research, even if the research show otherwise.

Let's take a trending example of Soya Bean it is touted as the new age super food. We all know about the benefits as the same are prominently advertised. What is hidden takes a little more effort to find. Soya bean itself contains Toxins. Soy foods increase the risk of developing hypothyroidism as it inhibits the activity of an enzyme called thyroid peroxidase. It may cause Testosterone imbalance in males. It may trigger Alzheimer's Dementia. Soya foods were traditionally cooked only after fermentation thus destroying most of the anti-nutrients which affect vital systems of the body including the brain.

We require only 50grams of protein per day and can easily achieve it with our normal traditional foods. Now most of you will say, how does it affect us? We do not have soya in our daily diet. This is where our awareness is lacking, soya flour or oil is present in the bread, cake mix, farsan, Mayonnaise, chakli, Atta, fudges, bakery products, candies, pancake mixes, pickles and many more products.

Similarly, no research on long term effects on health is available on new oil products like rice bran, sunflower, soya, and palm. Refining is a chemical process. Refined sugar increases the risk of obesity, type 2 diabetes and heart disease. Refined oils are extremely harmful as it may be treated with acid or alkali or bleached then neutralized filtered and deodorized which require chemicals like hexane. Even in some cases cheaper oils are blended in to reduce costs. It's a myth that sunflower oil is the best for heart as study suggest Coconut oil even though rich in saturated fatty acids in comparison to sunflower oil when used as cooking oil media over a period of 2 years did not change the lipid-related cardiovascular risk factors and events in those receiving standard medical care.

But Doctors have no say on this, even they consume the same as no alternative is available. Cold press oil is now available but buyers are less and rates are high and this local industry cannot compete with the bigger branded giants.

In the market there is competition for all the commodities, lower material cost is the new age mantra so much that instead of cream, oil is used in some ice creams and cream is made up of some powder on your cakes. "Who cares what it is made up of?" the chemicals smell and taste better than the original.

Substandard products like noodles biscuits, chemically polished rice, pulses and sugar, hormone injected cows for milk and addition of toxic substances in the name for food enhancers and preservatives have become a new norm.

Effects of meat, milk and eggs by breeding hybrid animals those are kept in congested spaces with antibiotics, fat enriched foods and hormone injections can result in:

- Excess fat in human body lead to heart ailments.
- Chemicals and industrial fertilizers are responsible for multiple health issues.

- New age foods causes problems in- growth, digestion, sexual maturation, thyroid health, and breast cancer risk. Antibiotic resistance is also a major issue.

B. Effect on Agriculture

Coming to modern vegetables, Hybrid is the new trend, taste may be ok but they look really perfect (weight, shape and colour). We have lost almost all of the local varieties of nutritious vegetables, pulses and fruits. Injection for fast growth, colour and sweetness, excessive fertilizers, pesticides, herbicides is on the rise. Emphasis is solely on increased production and profitability. Farmers today are not self-sufficient as they no more grow for their needs and the needs of their community. Today they are more money oriented as they have taken to the city diet and require more money to ape city lifestyle. Farming itself has become a business and a tool to earn more money. Depending on the market only a single type of crop is sometimes grown by all the farmers for sale in market, and if market rates fall they face huge losses and are in debt, so much that they have nothing to feed their family.

The media is full of mouth-watering recipes, with renowned chefs from around the world educating people about new age recipes. Meat dishes being very prominent among them. Using broiler chicken has become a norm in these shows. Benefits of which are being said to be fast cooking and soft. The glamour hides the dark truth about meat and domestic animal industry. Broiler chicken was introduced in India in early 1980s, fed with high fat and protein diet and antibiotic. Kept in unhealthy conditions they are highly susceptible to ascites, heart attacks, lung collapse and leg problems. Imagine a chicken which cannot support its own weight. Consuming the same regularly leads to obesity, high blood pressure and heart problems. In some cases, Cows and buffalos are given oxytocin injections just before milking every day to increase milk production.

Exotic cross-breed vegetables and lab grown meat is an upcoming trend. Hope time will prove how beneficial they will be? These new age foods have pushed Indian masses from a balanced healthy diet to unhealthy fat rich artificial flavoured hybrid diet, leading to fast growing multi-billion-dollar healthcare and pharmaceuticals industry.

Today's diet is more of a totally foreign affair. Indians are totally influenced by the media and people have lost their instinct, to accept the new norm. Knowledge is no more a cutting edge tool of constant learning and improvement but just a source of making a living.

A variety of African cat fish was introduced in India in the 1990s in Andra Pradesh. Similar to Broiler chickens this fish also grows really fast. Today it is banned by the government as it has become a threat to the local varieties. Still it is illegally cultivated and available in the market.

Mushrooms are fat free low sodium low calorie and cholesterol free but are used in making unhealthy dishes like pizza and pasta. Cheese is great source of calcium and protein but processed cheese is harmful for human health. Similar is the story with other foreign ingredients used in Indian Sub-continent. Today in the restaurants, stalls and cookery shows a rampant use of processed oil, cheese, butter and cream is evident. The vegetables used in recipes are very limited. Working parents find readymade and easy to cook processed foods a better option. Kids now a days are more aware of American corn, mushroom, baby corn, potato fries, lady finger, burgers and fried chicken, very few have even consumed Shorgam (Jowar), Pearl millet (Bajra), Finger millet (Ragi/Nachani), White corn, Leafy vegetables like (Kardi, Bathua), dishes of which are healthier.

We can observe following overall effect on today's Indian farming.

- Single crop farming only for monetary gains became the goal. Now almost whole village grows similar crops and if the crop fails, farmers are left with huge loans and no money to buy food pushing them to suicide.

- In a land which relied on diversity and community sharing basic needs, became dependent on the market where-in industrial products are forced to the masses by way of false marketing.
- For some short term gains, farmers are investing heavily in purchase of costly hybrid seeds, fertilizers, pesticides and herbicides. It has also deteriorated the natural fertility of land.

SUGGESTIONS

Influx of new fruits and vegetable from distant lands was never a problem in India but when the local verities and the original varieties were pushed out by the hybrid ones, it led to an unhealthy diet and deteriorating ecosystem in India.

As of now situation is grim but as awareness increases, unlike foreigners Indians can look back to the vast knowledge of their ancestors and demand healthy foods for their family. A little research can make us aware before we include and new product to our diet knowing that advertisements are deceptive. The demand should be for all organic and natural food to this subcontinent, regulate food processing industry minutely, crack down on food alternative and chemical producing industry, revive natural and old crop varieties instead of genetically modified ones, educate and incentivise farmers for growing organic and attain self-sufficiency from their lands and sell the excess produce only. Support local industry at village level. Incorporate healthy alternatives like jaggery for refined sugar, cold pressed oil for refined oil, fresh milk for milk powder or soya milk etc. Introduce or import products only after proper research. (parthenium plant also called congress grass came in to India when government imported wheat from USA in the 1950s causes substantial losses to the farmers). Bridge the gap between scientific research and policies in the interest of the society. Building self-sufficient villages is the need of the hour. A proper unbiased study is required to ascertain the reason for increase in health problems due to current food habits.

CONCLUSION

It is a false notion that we all believe, "we consume what we decide as we earn enough to afford the best for our family" but contrary to this belief we still plate out an unhealthy diet for our dear ones. Today the commercial minded manufacturers push their unhealthy products on to us and we are only left to decide which brand and price of these product we choose from nothing more. We have become like the guinea pigs in a large laboratory, who don't have the choice to avoid what's being fed to them.

REFERENCES

Sushilkumr and Jay G. Varshney (2010). Parthenium infestation (congress grass) and its estimated cost management in India, National Research Centre for Weed Science, Maharajpur,

Adhartal, Jabalpur (Madhya Pradesh) http://isws.org.in/IJWSn/File/2010_42_Issue-1&2%20Supplymentary_73-77.pdf

Maniyal Vijayakumara D.M.Vasudevanb K.R.Sundaramc SajithaKrishnanb Kannan Vaidyanathane Sandya Nandakumard Rajiv Chandrasekhara Navin Mathewa. A randomized study of coconut oil versus sunflower oil on cardiovascular risk factors in patients with stable coronary heart disease. https://www.sciencedirect.com/science/article/pii/S0019483215008299#!

Bharti, Deepa Indoria, R.L. Solanki and Meena, B.S. (2017). A Comparative Impact Study of Edible Oils on Health. Int. J.Curr. Microbiol.App.Sci. 6(11): 601-612.

https://www.ijcmas.com/6-11-2017/Bharti,%20et%20al.pdf

Gil-Izquierdo, A., Penalvo, J. L., Gil, J. I., Medina, S., Horcajada, M. N., Lafay, S., Silberberg, M., Llorach, R., Zafrilla, P., Garcia-Mora, P., & Ferreres, F. (2012). Soy isoflavones and cardiovascular disease epidemiological, clinical and -omics perspectives. *Current Pharmaceutical Biotechnology, 13*(5), 624-631. PMid:22122477. http://dx.doi.org/10.2174/138920112799857585

Hamilton-Reeves, J. M., Vazquez, G., Duval, S. J., Phipps, W. R., Kurzer, M. S., & Messina, M. J. (2010). Clinical studies show no effects of soy protein or isoflavones on reproductive hormones in men: results of a meta-analysis. *Fertility and Sterility, 94*(3), 997-1007. PMid:19524224. http://dx.doi.org/10.1016/j.fertnstert.2009.04.038

The impact of junk food on health – Frontiers published on 25th April 2022

Chemicals found in food packaging an urgent health risk: report (Chemicals found in food packaging could be posing a risk to our health according to 33 scientists across the globe.) Article by- By Jessica Paige and Srivani Venna

https://eatingrules.com/assets/Cooking_Oil_Comparison_Chart_2.2.pdf

https://www.ncbi.nlm.nih.gov/pmc/articles/PMC4990724/
https://www.eatthis.com/soy-side-effects/

5.2 Entrepreneurs in Jammu and Kashmir— A Case Study of Women Entrepreneurs

Dr. Shabana Ali

ABSTRACT

Women Entrepreneurship was a neglected domain during the past but with the spread of education and awareness among the women, the picture has been changed and the women have emerged a today's most memorable and inspirational entrepreneurs. It is said that family is a chariot with wheels which are driven by both the male and female members of the family. If one of the wheels is lagging behind, the chariot i.e., the family will not be able to grow and develop. In the same way when we speak about a nation, the women play a dominant role in the economic development and makes significant contributions to the economic growth of the country. However, Jammu and Kashmir has a different picture as it is an industrially backward state where participation of women if allowed can contribute a lot in the economic development of the state. Past researches revealed that women in the state of Jammu and Kashmir participate less as compared to other states of India. In this contest, the present research is meant to investigate the influencing or inhibiting factors that come in their way of economic participation. This research is based on primary as well as secondary sources of data and the data so collected shall be analyzed and interpreted with the help of descriptive statistical tools.

BACKGROUND OF THE STUDY

There is a growing interest in nurturing entrepreneurial activities because of the rising problems of unemployment in various countries around the world. Entrepreneurs not only change their employment status from unemployed but also provide employment opportunities to hundreds of unemployed youth. The interest in entrepreneurship lies on the fact that entrepreneurship stimulates economic growth and development. Naude, 2011. According to Entrepreneurship Indicator Programme EIP, "Entrepreneurs are those persons, business owners who seek to generate value, through the creation or expansion of economic activity, by identifying and exploiting new products, processes or markets." The three essential requirements of an entrepreneur as defined by the EIP framework are enterprising human activity, value creation and innovation (Ahmad and Hoffman, 2008). The persons that have a direct control over the activities of an enterprise, by owning the totality or a significant share of the business and employ at least one other person are known as entrepreneurs. Entrepreneurs are said to have a strong influence on the sustainable development processes of both the developed and developing countries due to its role in poverty alleviation, employment creation and innovation. The role of women within the entrepreneurial environment is of significant importance. The women entrepreneurship has to be studied separately for two reasons. The first being that women entrepreneurs have emerged as an untapped source of economic growth during the last decade. They not only create jobs for themselves and others but also provide society with different solutions to management, organization and business problems as well as to the exploitation of entrepreneurial opportunities. However, they still represent a minority of all entrepreneurs as a result of which there exists a market failure discriminating against women's possibility to become successful entrepreneurs. This failure needs to be addressed by policy makers so that economic potential of this group is fully utilized. The second reason is that the topic of women entrepreneurship has been neglected both in society in general as well as in social sciences in particular. The women not only have lower rate of participation in entrepreneurial activities than men but they also choose to start and manage firms in diverse industries than man tend to do (Duchenaut,1997; Franco &Winquuvist,2002; Reynolds&White,1997).there is indication to advocate that women are key players in entrepreneurial activities and make significant contributions to the economic development of the nations around the world(Barringer &Ireland,2010;Minitti et al.,2005). due to their unique role, the field of women entrepreneurship has emerged as an important research area over the years both for the government as well as researchers in developed and developing countries giving it great deal of attention (Brush and Gate wood,2008;Carter et al;2001;Crater et al ;2007;Carter &Marlow, 2006;Mc Clelland et al;2005;Minniti et al,2004;Verheul et al,2006).

RESEARCH METHODOLOGY

The study was conducted in the state of Jammu and Kashmir using a wellstructured questionnaire. A total of 60 women entrepreneurs engaged in different sectors were selected for the study, Convenience sampling technique was used for data collection.questionaire focused on two dimensions. First dimension pertained measuring demographic variables and the second dimension focused on various parameters like challenges, hurdles, level of innovation and the factors which can foster entrepreneurial culture in the state of Jammu and Kashmir. Data so collected was analyzed using SPSS Software.

Analysis:

The findings in relation to the age of women entrepreneurs showed a varied age range, 36.67 percent were in the age group of 31-40 years followed by 20-30 as depicted in table 1.1. The findings reveal that the women in Jammu and Kashmir are likely to become entrepreneurs in the middle section of their working life. In terms of education qualification, the findings reveal that 41.67 percent of the women entrepreneurs obtained college level education and 25 percent have obtained university level education or are post-gradutaes in various disciplines as shown in table 1.1 and 1.2.

Table 1.1. General profile of women entrepreneurs

Characteristics	Frequency N=60	Percentage N=60
Age		
20-30	19	31.67
31-40	22	36.67
41-50	12	20
51-60	5	8.33
60 and above	2	3.33
Educational Qualification	9	15
Secondary level	11	18.33
Higher secondary level	25	41.67
College level	15	25
University level		
Previous experience		
Professional experience	18	30
Skilled manual	13	21.67
Unskilled	8	13.33
Unemployed	21	35

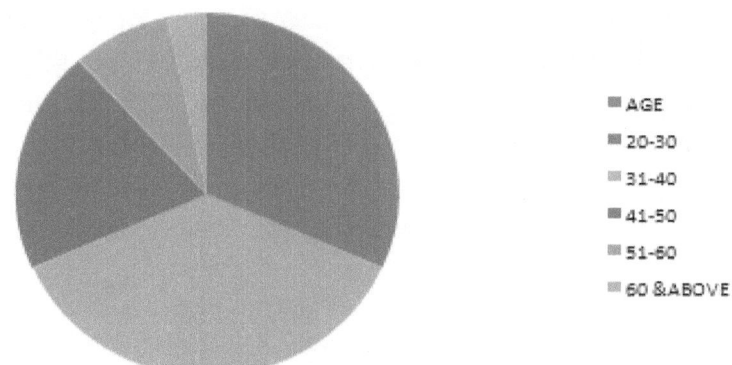

Figure 1: Profile of Women Entrepreneurs- Age

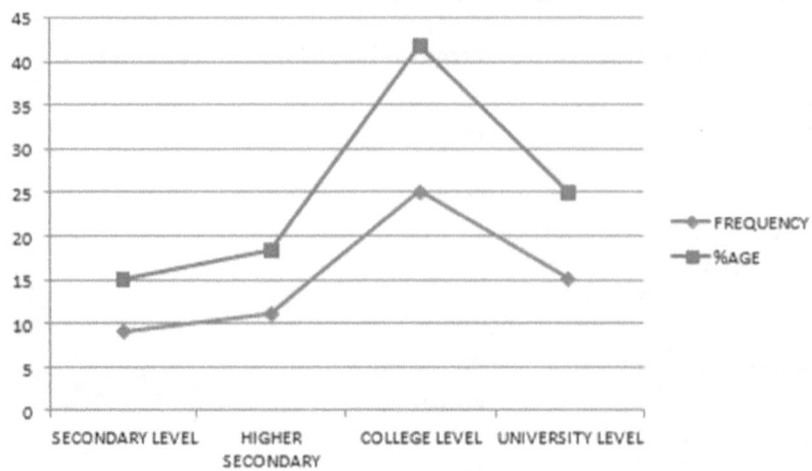

Figure 2: Profile of Women Entrepreneurs- Educational Qualification

This finding is supported by the research work of Barley et al (1994) supporting that women entrepreneurs are likely to be as educated as their male counterparts in order to find out the motivational level of women entrepreneurs, the most motivating factor for starting the ventures was the need for job satisfaction and the financial motive. Further, it was found that the women of Jammu and Kashmir also start out their own ventures in order to improve their socio-economic status and standard of living. The financial sources used to establish the business ventures reveal that 90 % of women entrepreneurs relied heavily on their own savings for starting their business or at the introductory stage. However, the other sources of finance used were Government incentives and schemes and borrowings from family and friends also proved to be another source of finance comprising total of 56.67% as shown in table 2.1.the findings reveal the government support to women entrepreneurs is an encouraging factor for initial start-ups for promoting women entrepreneurship.

Table1.2. Motivation for starting the new business venture

Motivational factor	Frequency N=60		Percentage N=60	
	Yes	No	Yes	No
Desire to be Independent	33	27	55	45
Threat of unemployment	37	23	61.67	38.33
Financial motives	42	18	70	30
Job satisfaction	46	14	76.67	23.33
Attractive life style	27	33	45	55
Help in creating employment	41	19	68.33	31.67

SUGGESTIONS AND RECOMMENDATIONS

To resolve the issues faced by women entrepreneurs various suggestions were recommended as:

- ➢ Special training programmes, mentoring sessions must be conducted to develop skills and enhance productivity among women entrepreneurs.
- ➢ Government must further strengthen their role in providing hassle free support in terms of finance for women entrepreneurs.
- ➢ Since women entrepreneurs play a dual role as family organiser and manager of women enterprises support from family is a crucial factor for women entrepreneurs in order to boost their morale.
- ➢ Incubator facilities which focus on manufacturing products without investing on infrastructure to be encouraged by providing technology and information by start –ups.

➢ Women entrepreneurs must combine creativity and innovation with social media to run successful start-ups.

REFERENCES

Dipesh,D.Uike (2012). Entrepreneurship Development Obstacles and Solutions, Himalaya Publishing House, New Delhi.

Eric Reis (2011). The lean Startup

H.Jhanji (2021). Dynamics of entrepreneurial development and management, Himalaya publishing, New Delhi.

Khanka,S.S.(2002). Entrepreneurial Development, New Delhi, Chand and Company Ltd.

NaudeW.A.(2011). Entrepreneurship and economic development. Basingstoke: Palgrave Macmillan

P. Sarvanavelu .(2020). Entrepreneurship development, Eskapee publications

Revenga,A and Sudhir,(2012). Empowereing women is smart economics.Finance and development.

Zuhaib Mustafa (2012). Prospects and challenges of women entrepreneurship.

5.3 Does gender play a role in Sustainability orientations? A Study on Sustainable entrepreneurship

Saba Nazir Reshi and Mohd Rafiq Teli

ABSTRACT

Entrepreneurship with a sole focus on economic gains is posited as a reason for social and environmental issues. This has led to increasing attention toward sustainable entrepreneurship. With its Triple bottom line, sustainable entrepreneurship is considered to be a holistic form of entrepreneurship. However, there is a dearth of literature on intentions toward sustainable entrepreneurship among students in the context of India. Given that sustainability and entrepreneurship are frequently posited to have a trade-off relationship, this study explores the role of sustainable entrepreneurial goals and Entrepreneurial Intentions in developing attitudes toward sustainability. Also, gender is posited to play a role in developing sustainability intentions. Data were collected from 149 students from universities in Jammu & Kashmir. The data were analysed using SPSS. The results show that all the three variables i.e., social entrepreneurial goal, entrepreneurial intentions, and attitude towards sustainability were present in females more than in their male counterparts. The implications are discussed.

Keywords: *Sustainability, Sustainable entrepreneurship, Attitude towards sustainability, entrepreneurial intentions*

INTRODUCTION

An increasingly important factor of economic progress is entrepreneurship. However, any kind of activity, including self-employment, without a holistic approach and unfocused towards its impact on society and the environment is unsustainable. "Entrepreneurship is a process of identifying, evaluating and pursuing opportunities through creativity, innovativeness and transformations to produce new products, processes and values that are beneficial (Maijd and Koe, 2012)." It is widely recognized as a crucial tool for socioeconomic growth, stimulating the job market and resulting in improved goods and service (Shane and Venkataraman, 2000; Koe et al., 2014). The pivotal objective of an entrepreneur is to close an existing gap or enhance the way needs are satisfied. This does not automatically imply positive socio-environmental values are being generated. Contrarily, entrepreneurial activity has been strongly (and traditionally) related to environmental degradation (Pacheco et al., 2010; Dean and McMullen, 2007) with an often related or not, negative social influence. Thus, entrepreneurship without consideration for environmental and social impact is no longer viable due to its unsustainable characteristics.

The United Nations' Brundtland report in 1987 endorsed entrepreneurship as one of the mechanisms for achieving sustainable development. Moreover, rather than being a possible source, entrepreneurship has emerged as an important catalyst for alleviating social inequalities and environmental destruction (Munoz and Cohen, 2018). This has led to the development of sustainable entrepreneurship. "Sustainable entrepreneurship (SE) has thus become a prevalent topic in the broader field of entrepreneurship (Munoz et al., 2018)", and has received much interest from governments, businesses, academia, policy-makers, and international organisations. The concept of Sustainability aims to integrate three different factors: environmental upkeep, societal development and economic gains.

"Sustainable entrepreneurship is defined as a process in which an entrepreneur realizes his or her entrepreneurial intention in building up a venture taking into account the enterprise's sustainability, by organizing this process in a way that a variety of economic, social and environmental angles are addressed (Peng, 2021)." "Sustainable entrepreneurship is focused on the preservation of nature, life support, and community in the pursuit of perceived opportunities to bring into existence future products, processes, and services for gain, where the gain is broadly construed to include economic and non-economic gains to individuals, the economy, and society (Shepherd & Patzelt, 2011)." Entrepreneurs are increasingly considering incorporating sustainability into their new enterprises due to social and environmental concerns (Peng, 2021). As entrepreneurship has traditionally been said to be motivated by economic gains, it is usually perceived as opposed to social and environmental values. Therefore, an exploration is needed to understand what drives a positive attitude towards sustainability.

THE RATIONALE OF THE STUDY

In their study, Vurio et al (2018) noted that "The extant literature on entrepreneurship has focused on five main themes: the core entrepreneurial intention models, the factors influencing entrepreneurial intentions, the entrepreneurial intention-behaviour link, including individual-level, regional, cultural and institutional variables, entrepreneurship education, and social and sustainable entrepreneurship. However, the last theme about social and sustainable entrepreneurship has developed more recently. Furthermore, of these two types of entrepreneurship streams, limited attention has been paid to entrepreneurial intentions in the context of sustainable entrepreneurship." However, intentions towards a particular behaviour are precluded by attitude towards that behaviour. Therefore, this study explores the development of attitudes towards sustainability among students. Towards this endeavour, Social entrepreneurial goals and entrepreneurial intentions are taken as their antecedents (Vurio et. al., 2018).

The role of gender:
Previous research demonstrates that gender is crucial in forming entrepreneurial attitudes and aims (Kuckertz and Wagner, 2010; Fellnhofer et al., 2016). Yet, limited attention has been paid to role of gender differences in formation of entrepreneurial intentions (Arshad

et al., 2016). For example, higher entrepreneurial intentions were found among female business students (Kuckertz and Wagner, 2010). Another study revealed female MBA students had lesser entrepreneurial intentions compared to their male counterparts (Zhao et al., 2005). In the context of sustainable behaviours and attitudes, research shows that females were likely to have greater socio-environmental entrepreneurial goals than males, while males were likely to have higher economic goals (Hechavarria et al., 2017). Also, compared with females, males tended to be less emphatic toward others (Hockerts, 2015). Thus, researchers such as Vuorio et al., have stressed the need to study gender in sustainable entrepreneurship. It is necessary to determine the extent of similarities or variations of sustainability attitudes based on gender in students. There are not many empirical studies that establish the role of gender, and there are essentially no empirical studies in the literature that focus on emerging nations, particularly India. Hence, there exists a prevalent gap in research on the influence of gender on sustainability attitudes.

Similarly, research on sustainable entrepreneurial intentions among college students remains relatively lopsided. Moreover, the entrepreneurial and environmental consciousness among today's young college-going adults ("Generation Z") is more and also, they have greater social awareness than prior generations (Hewlett et al., 2009). Therefore, it is imperative to explore the relationships between individual values and attitudes towards sustainability.

REVIEW OF LITERATURE

The concept sustainopreneurship was first introduced in 2000 (Schaltegger, 2000); further evolved and tentatively was defined in 2006 (Abrahamsson, 2006).

(Romero-Colmenares & Reyes-Rodríguez, 2022) conducted a study of sustainable entrepreneurial intentions in Colombia based on the TPB model. The study added to the TPB model by adding variables such as altruism, self-efficacy and education for entrepreneurship aspects. Survey data of 314 undergraduate students were analysed using multiple regression analysis. The results from the study revealed that were individuals' attitudes toward sustainable business, the level of perceived difficulty, and the subjective norms have an effect on sustainable entrepreneurial intentions. Furthermore, individuals' altruistic values, the belief in achieving goals, as well as sustainable entrepreneurship education positively influenced sustainable entrepreneurial intentions.

(Abdelnaeim & El-Bassiouny, 2021) empirically explored the relationships among entrepreneurial assumed behaviour and sustainability orientation among entrepreneurs. Using data from 351 respondents collected through a structured questionnaire, the findings revealed a negative relationship between entrepreneurial cognitive scripts and sustainability orientations.

(Polas et al., 2021) examined the individual-level factors i.e., individual competencies, perceived capability, and social perception impact on rural women's sustainable entrepreneurial intention. Data was collected from 297 Bangladeshi women. The results showed that there is a positive and significant association between social perception and perceived capability with intention to become a sustainable entrepreneur. However, no association was found between women's competencies and their intention to become an entrepreneur, Moreover, these relationships between individual competencies and perceived capability with intention to become an entrepreneur were mediated by perceived opportunity.

(Nuringsih et al., 2019) investigated the factors such as green value, role models, entrepreneurship education, and entrepreneurial support in the context of sustainable entrepreneurial intention among female students in Jakarta. Data from 300 female students in the Management Program who passed the basic entrepreneurship class from one of the entrepreneurial universities were analysed using multiple regression. The results showed that the perceived green value can predict sustainable entrepreneurial intention. However, entrepreneurship education, entrepreneurial support, and perceived role models were found to be insignificant.

(Yasir et al., 2021) conducted a survey on intention of sustainable entrepreneurship using the theory of planned behavior as the theoretical underpinning. The data of 520 university students in Pakistan were analysed through structural equation modelling. Along with the core dimensions of TPB, the study incorporated three additional constructs to explain the interrelationship between the antecedents of sustainable entrepreneurial intention. The results from the study showed that sustainable intentions are positively associated with attitudes, perceived behavioral control, and social norms. Moreover, an indirect influence of intrinsic and extrinsic rewards, environmental values, and consideration of future consequences on sustainable entrepreneurial intentions was found (Agu, 2021) explored intentions towards sustainability-oriented micro-entrepreneurship using the theory of planned behaviour (TPB). The study analysed the role of education for sustainable entrepreneurship between the TPB constructs and sustainable entrepreneurial intention relationship. Data from 435 business and science students were analysed using structural equation modelling. The results showed that for sustainable entrepreneurial intention attitude and subjective norms are significant and positive drivers. Further, a significant influence of education on intention was found.

DATA AND METHODOLOGY

Data collection:
Higher education has been linked to greater entrepreneurial activity therefore, the research context for this study was considered to be university students (Levie and Autio, 2008). Thus, the respondents were targeted between 18 and 35 years old. The study design was cross-sectional and correlational research. This study used convenience sampling method that is often employed in entrepreneurship research

even though the concerns of the possibility of generalisation exist. (Yasir et. al., 2021).

A sample of 149 university students from various universities in Jammu & Kashmir was selected. Frequency analysis showed that the majority of the respondents were female (57%), and in the 20-25 years age bracket (71.8%), followed by those in the 25-30 years age group (21.5%). **Table 1** shows the frequency analysis based on gender:

Table 1. Frequency Analysis based on gender

GENDER	Frequency	Percent
Male	64	43.0
Female	85	57.0
Total	149	100.0

RESULTS

Descriptive statistics

First, to summarize the observed data, means and standard deviations were calculated. These are presented in **Table 2**. The descriptive statistics exhibit that the mean of the dependent variable - Attitude towards sustainable entrepreneurship is 3.79 with a maximum of 5.00 and a minimum of 1.00. This implies that the attitude toward sustainability in general and sustainable entrepreneurship, in particular, is not yet fully developed among India's young adults. The existence of a minimum score of 1.00 implies that there are prospective entrepreneurs that completely have no idea or do not have anything regarding sustainable entrepreneurship while the existence of a maximum score of 5 means that there are prospective entrepreneurs that have realised the importance of sustainable entrepreneurship. For independent variables: Social entrepreneurial goal, the mean for SEG is 3.43 with a minimum score of 1.00 with a maximum score of 5.00. Also, the mean score for Entrepreneurial intention is 3.46 with a minimum score of 1.00 with a minimum score of 4.00. Since the standard deviations are less than the calculated means, especially in the case of the independent variables, this implies that the calculated means highly represent the data (Field, 2009; Saunders et al., 2007).

Table 2. Descriptive Statistics

Descriptive Statistics

	Minimum Statistic	Maximum Statistic	Mean Statistic	Std. Deviation Statistic	Skewness Statistic	Std. Error	Kurtosis Statistic	Std. Error
SEG	1.00	5.00	3.4340	.89540	-.143	.199	-.418	.395
EI	1.00	4.00	3.4664	.58252	-.852	.199	1.558	.395
ATTSE	1.00	5.00	3.7953	.71190	-1.225	.199	2.201	.395

Correlation Analysis:

The results reveal that there exists a negative correlation between Social entrepreneurial goals and Entrepreneurial intention (-.208*). However, Social entrepreneurial goals and Attitudes toward sustainability were positively correlated (.160). Further, Entrepreneurial intentions and Attitudes toward sustainability were negatively correlated (-.117). Moreover, there exists a positive correlation between gender and Attitude towards sustainability (.200*). **Table 3** summarises the correlational analysis.

Table 3. Correlational Analysis

Correlations			SEG	EI	ATTS	GEN
Spearman's rho	SEG	Correlation Coefficient	1.000	-.208*	.160	.191*
		Sig. (2-tailed)	.	.011	.042*	.020
		N	149	149	149	149
	EI	Correlation Coefficient	-.208*	1.000	-.117	.083
		Sig. (2-tailed)	.011	.	.154	.314
		N	149	149	149	149
	ATTS	Correlation Coefficient	.160	-.117	1.000	.200*
		Sig. (2-tailed)	.042*	.154	.	.015
		N	149	149	149	149
	GEN	Correlation Coefficient	.191*	.083	.200*	1.000
		Sig. (2-tailed)	.020	.314	.015	.
		N	149	149	149	149

*. Correlation is significant at the 0.05 level (2-tailed).

(Note: SEG= Social entrepreneurial goal; EI= Entrepreneurial intention; ATTS= Attitude towards sustainability; GEN= Gender)

Mean difference analysis based on Gender:
After checking the correlations between the study variables, the study used t-test analysis to check for variability between samples based on gender. The mean differences were checked separately. The results show

that social entrepreneurial goal was slightly higher among females (mean = 3.25) as compared to males (mean = 3.57). Entrepreneurial intentions were also higher in females (mean = 3.39) than in males (mean = 3.51). Also, attitude towards sustainability was higher in females (mean = 3.59) than in males (mean = 3.94).

Table 4. Social entrepreneurial Goal

Social entrepreneurial Goal

	GEN	N	Mean	Std. Deviation	Std. Error Mean
SEG	male	64	3.2500	.89581	.11198
	female	85	3.5725	.87493	.09490

Table 5. Independent Samples Test

Independent Samples Test

		Levene's Test for Equality of Variances		t-test for Equality of Means						
		F	Sig.	t	Df	Sig. (2-tailed)	Mean Difference	Std. Error Difference	95% Confidence Interval of the Difference	
									Lower	Upper
SEGa	Equal variances assumed	.005	.945	-2.205	147	.029	-.32255	.14629	-.61165	-.03344

Table 6. Entrepreneurial Intentions

Entrepreneurial Intentions

	GEN	N	Mean	Std. Deviation	Std. Error Mean
EI	male	64	3.3958	.72648	.09081
	female	85	3.5196	.44202	.04794

Table 7. Independent Samples Test

		Levene's Test for Equality of Variances		t-test for Equality of Means					95% Confidence Interval of the Difference	
		F	Sig.	t	Df	Sig. (2-tailed)	Mean Difference	Std. Error Difference	Lower	Upper
EIa	Equal variances assumed	8.768	.004	-1.287	147	.200	-.12377	.09619	-.31388	.06633

Table 8. Attitude towards sustainability

Attitude towards sustainability

	GEN	N	Mean	Std. Deviation	Std. Error Mean
ATTS	male	64	3.5938	.87230	.10904
	female	85	3.9471	.51768	.05615

Table 9. Independent Samples Test

		Levene's Test for Equality of Variances		t-test for Equality of Means					95% Confidence Interval of the Difference	
		F	Sig.	T	df	Sig. (2-tailed)	Mean Difference	Std. Error Difference	Lower	Upper
ATTseA	Equal variances assumed	18.555	.000	-3.084	147	.002	-.35331	.11457	-.57973	-.12689

DISCUSSION

The current study shows that there exists a negative correlation between Social entrepreneurial goals and Entrepreneurial intention (-.208*). This implies that as the goal of entrepreneurial venture is aligned with sustainability, the traditional entrepreneurial intentions, which are often related to economic gains, decrease. Sustainable entrepreneurs are often potrayed more motivated toward social and environmental issues than profit earning. Many entrepreneurs think that considering sustainability in their business may reduce economic profit. Previous research also demonstrates that it is assumed there exists a trade-off relationship between inclination towards sustainability and traditional entrepreneurial intentions (DeVito & Bohnsack, 2017). A study by Wagner & Maximilians (2012) revealed that sustainability orientation negatively effects entrepreneurial intention of business students. Similarly, research on nascent entrepreneurs reveals that they tend to view sustainability-orientated business as having a tradeoff relationship with entrepreneurship orientation (Kirzner, 1973; DiVito & Bohnsack, 2017).

The results revealed a positive correlation between entrepreneurial goals and attitudes towards sustainability. This is in line with the existing literature. E.g., Yasir et.al., (2021) found a significant positive relationship between sustainable entrepreneurial Intentions and environmental values. This relationship was moderated by attitude toward sustainability.

Entrepreneurial intentions and attitudes towards sustainability were negatively correlated. Consistent with the research on sustainable entrepreneurship, the results are maintaining the dualilty of entrepreneurship versus sustainability, suggesting that there exist trade-off relationships between the two (Sung & Park, 2018).

(Nguyen, 2018) suggested that entrepreneurial intentions are associated with socio-demographic factors such as gender. Regarding the mean differences based on gender, results show that females were highly inclined towards entrepreneurial ventures with social goals as well as having a positive attitude towards sustainability than their male counterparts. On average, a higher positive attitude toward sustainability is found among women. This is in line with the extant literature. (found that while males are more likely to have economic goals. females are more likely than males to have socio-environmental entrepreneurial objectives than males,

IMPLICATIONS

Environmental damage is posited as one of the adverse consequences of entrepreneurial behaviour. However previous research has posited entrepreneurship as a possible means of solving this problem. Consequently, entrepreneurship's role in reducing environmental challenges and pursuing economic benefits through sustainable entrepreneurship is gaining unprecedented interest from academicians, government and individuals alike. Thus, the present study adds to the sustainable entrepreneurship literature. However, these novel approaches and practices are yet to be fully grasped and accepted by many nascent entrepreneurs. One reason for this is the duality of aims between them as sustainability is often perceived to have a trade-off relationship with economic orientation. This study, in line with previous research (Yasir et. al., 2021), demonstrates that traditional entrepreneurial orientation may hinder sustainable entrepreneurship activities even with the entrepreneurial goal is aligned toward social and environmental issues. This result is consistent with the research on entrepreneurship versus sustainability, noting that there exists a trade-off relationship between the two (Sung & Park, 2018).

Since the results show a higher inclination toward sustainability in females, policies oriented towards female students should be put forward encouraging to think sustainably in their future entrepreneurial aspirations. Besides, the primary emphasis should be particularly on supporting and removing obstacles to sustainable entrepreneurship and to encourage entrepreneurial activity through public policy, (Vuorio et al., 2018). This can be a solution to address the unfavourable perception of sustainable entrepreneurship success.

LIMITATIONS AND DIRECTIONS FOR FUTURE STUDIES

The study is limited in its scope as the primary focus of the present study was on student sample. Further studies are required to further validate the findings. One way to provide more insight into the context could be to extend the research to actual entrepreneurs of India. Further, quantitative survey has its limitations in terms of choice to the respondents in expressing their views, this study. To find additional factors that may contribute to the explanation of sustainable entrepreneurship, a mixed methods design or qualitative research technique is suggested to be used.

REFERENCES

Abdelnaeim, S. M., & El-Bassiouny, N. (2020). The relationship between entrepreneurial cognitions and sustainability orientation: the case of an emerging market. *Journal of Entrepreneurship in Emerging Economies.*

Abrahamsson, A. (2006). Researching Sustainopreneurship-conditions, concepts, approaches, arenas and questions. In *Proceedings of the International Sustainable Development Research Conference.*

Agu, A. G., Kalu, O. O., Esi-Ubani, C. O., & Agu, P. C. (2021). Drivers of sustainable entrepreneurial intentions among university students: an integrated model from a developing world context. *International Journal of Sustainability in Higher Education.*

Anna Maija Vuorio, Kaisu Puumalainen, Katharina Fellnhofer, (2017). "Drivers of entrepreneurial intentions in sustainable entrepreneurship", *International Journal of Entrepreneurial Behavior & Research*

Arshad, M., Farooq, O., Sultana, N., & Farooq, M. (2016). Determinants of individuals' entrepreneurial intentions: a gender-comparative study. *Career Development International, 21*(4), 318-339.

Fellnhofer, K., Puumalainen, K., & Sjögrén, H. (2016). Entrepreneurial orientation and performance–are sexes equal? *International Journal of Entrepreneurial Behavior & Research*.Zhao et al., 2005

Hechavarría, D. M., Terjesen, S. A., Ingram, A. E., Renko, M., Justo, R., & Elam, A. (2017). Taking care of business: the impact of culture and gender on entrepreneurs' blended value creation goals. *Small Business Economics, 48*(1), 225-257.Hockerts, 2015

https://www.environmentandsociety.org/mml/un-world-commission-environment-and-development-ed-report-world-commission-environment-and (Accessed on 26-07-2020)

Kirzner, I.M., 1973. Competition and Entrepreneurship. University of Chicago Press, Chicago, IL

Koe, W. L., Omar, R., & Majid, I. A. (2014). Factors associated with propensity for sustainable entrepreneurship. *Procedia-Social and Behavioral Sciences, 130*, 65-74

Kuckertz, A., & Wagner, M. (2010). The influence of sustainability orientation on entrepreneurial intentions—Investigating the role of business experience. *Journal of business venturing, 25*(5), 524-539.

Levie, J., & Autio, E. (2008). A theoretical grounding and test of the GEM model. *Small business economics, 31*(3), 235-263.

Majid, I. A., & Koe, W. L. (2012). Sustainable entrepreneurship (SE): A revised model based on triple bottom line (TBL). *International Journal of Academic Research in Business and Social Sciences, 2*(6), 293.

Nuringsih, K., Nuryasman, M. N., & IwanPrasodjo, R. A. (2019). Sustainable entrepreneurial intention: The perceived of triple bottom line among female students. *Jurnal Manajemen, 23*(2), 168-190.

Pacheco, D. F., Dean, T. J., & Payne, D. S. (2010). Escaping the green prison: Entrepreneurship and the creation of opportunities for sustainable development. *Journal of Business Venturing, 25*(5), 464-480.

Peng, H., Li, B., Zhou, C., & Sadowski, B. M. (2021). How does the appeal of environmental values influence sustainable entrepreneurial intention? *International journal of environmental research and public health, 18*(3), 1070.

Polas, M. R. H., Raju, V., Muhibbullah, M., & Tabash, M. I. (2021). Rural women characteristics and sustainable entrepreneurial intention: a road to economic growth in Bangladesh. *Journal of Enterprising Communities: People and Places in the Global Economy*, (ahead-of-print).

Romero-Colmenares, L. M., & Reyes-Rodríguez, J. F. (2022). Sustainable entrepreneurial intentions: Exploration of a model based on the theory of planned behaviour among university students in north-east Colombia. *The International Journal of Management Education, 20*(2), 100627.

Shane, Scott, and Sankaran Venkataraman (2000). "The promise of entrepreneurship as a field of research." *Academy of management review* **25.1 217-226.**

Shepherd, D. A., & Patzelt, H. (2011). The New Field of Sustainable Entrepreneurship: Studying Entrepreneurial Action Linking "What Is to Be Sustained" With "What Is to Be Developed." *Entrepreneurship: Theory and Practice, 35*(1), 137–163.

Sung, C. S., & Park, J. Y. (2018). Sustainability orientation and entrepreneurship orientation: is there a tradeoff relationship between them? *Sustainability, 10*(2), 379.

Vuorio, A. M., Puumalainen, K., & Fellnhofer, K. (2017). Drivers of entrepreneurial intentions in sustainable entrepreneurship. *International Journal of Entrepreneurial Behavior & Research, 24*(2), 359-381.

Wagner, M.; Maximilians (2012). Ventures for the public good and entrepreneurial intentions: An empirical analysis of sustainability orientation as a determining factor, Journal of Small Business Enterprises., 25, 519531

Yasir, N., Mahmood, N., Mehmood, H. S., Babar, M., Irfan, M., & Liren, A. (2021). Impact of environmental, social values and the consideration of future consequences for the development of a sustainable entrepreneurial intention. *Sustainability, 13*(5), 2648.Agu, 2021

Author Details

Chapter 1. Contemporary Issues in Human Resource Management

1.1 Women At Work- A Boon to Society

Rashi Kulkarni
Student, Bachelors in Management Studies,
R.A. Podar College of Commerce and Economics (Autonomous), Mumbai
15.rashik@gmail.com

1.2 Impact of Leadership Styles of School Heads/Principals on Outcomes of leadership in Public Schools using Full Range Leadership Model (FRLM): Evidence from Select Educational Institutions of the Kashmir Division of J & K State

Zubair Ahmad Khan
Research Scholar, Department of Humanities, Social Sciences and Management,
National Institute of Technology Srinagar, J&K, India
zubair.scholar_hss@nitsri.net

Dr. Mohd Rafiq Teli
Assistant Professor, Department of Humanities, Social Sciences and Management
National Institute of Technology Srinagar, J&K, India
m.rafiq@nitsri.net

| 1.3 | Exploring The Relationship Between Women Empowerment and Higher Education: A Review |

Nadiya Nazeer
Research Scholar, Department of Management Studies,
University of Kashmir
nadiyanazeer9@gmail.com

Dr. Farzana Gulzar
Sr. Assistant Professor, Department of Management Studies, University of Kashmir
farzanashahrukh@uok.edu.in

Chapter 2. Contemporary Issues in Financial Management

| 2.1 | Professionalization And Managerialization of Family Firms: Influence of induction of the next-generation |

Tulsi Jayakumar
Professor, Economics and Executive Director,
Centre for Family Business & Entrepreneurship, SPJIMR, Mumbai
tulsi.jayakumar@spjimr.org

| 2.2 | Self Help Groups and Youth Empowerment: A Study of Union Territory of Jammu and Kashmir. |

Syed Javed Iqbal Kamili
Principal, Vishwa Bharti Women's College,
Rainawari, Srinagar, J&K, India
javedkamili@gmail.com

Prof. (Dr.) Mohi Ud Din Sangmi
Head, Department of Commerce,
University of Kashmir, Srinagar, J&K, India
sangmi2k@gmail.com

2.3   Assessment Of Financial Literacy Across Various Demographic Groups in India

Ms. Sana Bala
Assistant Professor, Department of Management Studies,
Government College for Women, Nawakadal, Srinagar, J&K
sanabala103@gmail.com

Prof. Farooq Ahmad Shah
Dean, School of Business Studies,
Central University of Kashmir, J&K
farooq_dms@cukashmir.ac.in

Chapter 3. Contemporary Issues in Technology Management

3.1   Blockchain Technology in The Financial Sector: A Bibliometric Analysis of the Dimensions Ai Database

Rachana Jaiswal
Assistant Professor, Department of Business Management,
HNB Garhwal (A Central) University, Uttarakhand
rachanajaiswal.ibmr@gmail.com

3.2   Cryptocurrency Market in Pandemic Exhibited Unusual Behavior

Anil Vaidya
Professor, Information Management,
S. P. Jain Institute of Management & Research, Mumbai
anil.vaidya@spjimr.org

3.3   Role Of ICT in Promoting Financial Inclusion Among Rural Households: An Empirical Evidence from Kashmir Valley, India - A Case Study

Mohd Iqbal Dar
Research Scholar, Department of Commerce,
Punjabi University, Patiala, Punjab
dariqbal2010@gmail.com

Irfan Ahmad Sheikh
Assistant Professor, Department of Management Studies,
SSM College of Engineering & Technology, Kashmir
sirsheikhs@gmail.com

Dr. Sugandha Chhibber
Assistant Professor, Department of Commerce
Goswami Ganesh Dutta Sanatan Dharma College, Kheri Gurna-Banur, Punjab
sugandha.chhibber@gmail.com

3.4	Mental Health Apps: Using Technology to Accelerate The Curve On Acceptability Amongst College Students.

Ms. Karishma Khadiwala
Assistant Professor, Department of Commerce and Business Management, R.A. Podar College of Commerce & Economics (Autonomous), Matunga, Mumbai
karishma.khadiwala@gmail.com

Chapter 4. Challenges brought up by COVID-19 pandemic

4.1	Effect of Lockdown on Consumer Behavior with Reference to Usage of Fitness Apps in Mumbai District.

Ms. Sunita A. Panja
Assistant Professor, Department of Accountancy
R.A.Podar College of Commerce and Economics (Autonomous)
rai.sunita84@gmail.com

Ms. Nikita M. Tanksali
Assistant Professor, Department of Accountancy
R.A.Podar College of Commerce and Economics (Autonomous)
nikitatanksali@gmail.com

4.2 Mask: A Protective Measure or A Potential Hazard?

Pallavi Anant Gurav
Student (UG), Department of Biochemistry,
Ramnarain Ruia Autonomous College, Mumbai
guravp137@gmail.com

Shreya Ravi Agrawal
Student (UG), Department of Biochemistry,
Ramnarain Ruia Autonomous College, Mumbai
agrawalshreyausgs@gmail.com

Priyanka Dinanath Koli
Assistant Professor, Department of Biochemistry,
Ramnarain Ruia Autonomous College, Mumbai
priyankakoli@ruiacollege.edu

Aditi Umesh Patwardhan
Assistant Professor, Department of Biochemistry,
Ramnarain Ruia Autonomous College, Mumbai
aditipatwardhan@ruiacollege.edu

4.3 Maintaining Corporate Culture with Special Reference to Remote Working in Covid-19 Crisis: Issues and Challenges.

Ishrat Shaheen
Scholar, School of Business Studies,
Islamic University of Science and Technology, Awantipora- Pulwama (J&K)
mirishrat@yahoo.com

4.4 Leading Through the Crisis of 2020

Dr Rahul Mirchandani
Chairman & Managing Director, Aries Agro Limited
ariesagro@ariesagro.com

4.5	Re-Engineering of Hybrid Workplace System for Management Education: An Empirical Analysis

Dr. Mehraj Ud Din Shah
Associate Professor, Department of Commerce,
Central University of Kashmir, J&K
drshahmehraj@cukashmir.ac.in

Chapter 5. Entrepreneurship and Sustainability

5.1	New Indian Food Plate and Its Implications on Agriculture And Human Health

Dr. Amruta Krishna Patil
Assistant Professor, Department of Accountancy,
R.A. Podar college of Commerce and Economics (Autonomous), Mumbai
dramrutapatil19@gmail.com

5.2	Entrepreneurs In Jammu and Kashmir—A Case Study of Women Entrepreneurs

Dr. Shabana Ali
Associate Professor, Department of Management Studies,
Govt. College for Women, Nawakadal, Srinagar, J&K, India
shabana_mba1@rediffmail.com

5.3	Does gender play a role in Sustainability orientations? A study on Sustainable entrepreneurship.

Saba Nazir Reshi
Research Scholar, Department of Humanities, Social Sciences and Management, National Institute of Technology Srinagar, J&K, India
saba.reshi_hss@nitsri.net

Dr. Mohd Rafiq Teli
Assistant Professor, Department of Humanities, Social Sciences and Management
National Institute of Technology Srinagar, J&K, India
m.rafiq@nitsri.net

Editor Information

Dr. Tahir Ahmad Wani is an Assistant Professor at the Department of Humanities, Social Sciences & Management, NIT Srinagar wherein he teaches various Management related subjects to Management & Engineering students. Before joining NIT Srinagar, Dr. Tahir was working at the Business School, University of Kashmir. He has an MBA from the same institute and holds a PhD in Technology Marketing from the esteemed Jamia Millia Islamia University. He was also selected for the prestigious Post-Doctoral Fellowship at the Indian Institute of Management Calcutta. Dr. Tahir has a rich research background and has written extensively on various management issues. He has also conducted workshops on quantitative analysis and participated in numerous workshops and conferences in reputed institutions thoughtful India. He is also actively participating in various research projects.

Dr. Sumaira Jan is an assistant professor in the area of entrepreneurship at the department of HSS&M at NIT Srinagar with a background in strategic entrepreneurship, women entrepreneurship and small and medium enterprises. She has been teaching courses such as Innovation, New Venture Planning, Entrepreneurial Behavior and Learning, Business Planning for more than two years at universities such as G D Goenka University, IILM Institute for Higher Education, and Kashmir University. Prior to taking up the current role in 2021, Sumaira Jan served at G D Goenka University, Gurugram where she was Assistant Professor of Entrepreneurship. She has published more than 20 research papers in journals and with publishers of national and international repute Like Sage, Wiley, NI-MSME, Entrepreneurship Development Institute of India, Ahmedabad etc. She has also presented papers in various national and international conferences and seminars and attended numerous workshops. Sumaira Jan holds PhD from Jamia Millia Islamia University; MBA (Marketing) from Jamia Millia Islamia University; and BBA (Management) from the Islamic University of Science and Technology. She is also a gold medalist in her graduation programme.

Dr. Nufazil Altaf Ahangar is a faculty in the area of Finance and Accounting at Department of Humanities, Social Sciences and Management, National Institute of Technology Srinagar. Before joining National Institute of Technology Srinagar he served Department of Management Studies, Central University of Kashmir as Assistant Professor. His research interests include Corporate Finance, Emerging Market Finance, Emerging Industries, Constrained Optimization, Financial Economics and Applied Econometrics. His research work has been published in international journals of repute such as International Journal of Managerial Finance, Managerial and Decision Economics. He has also published a book titled "Capital Structure Dynamics in Indian MSMEs" with Palgarve Macmillan. Besides publishing he is actively presenting his research work in different international and national conferences and seminars. Dr. Ahangar has been awarded Highly Commended Paper Award 2020 by Emerald Publishing.

Dr. Mohd. Rafiq Teli is an Assistant Professor in the Department of Humanities, Social Sciences & Management, NIT Srinagar. He has a teaching experience of more than 4 years. He has a PhD in Human Resource Development from the University of Kashmir and his areas of specialization are Human Resource Development, Human Resource Management and Organizational Behavior. Dr. Mohd. Rafiq Teli has published research papers in various National and International journals and has attended several Conferences, Seminars and Workshops conducted by various institutions.

Dr Rahul Mirchandani has 23 years of experience as Director of Aries Agro Limited. Ranked amongst the 30 Most Innovative CEOs in India in 2014, he has pioneered several unique marketing processes and brand management tactics at Aries. He holds a Doctorate in Management

Studies from NMIMS University, Mumbai and is also a Chartered Financial Analyst (CFA) and holds an MBA from the University of Canberra, Australia. Rahul has delivered sessions on Innovation and Entrepreneurship at the Oxford University, UK and has lectured at over 50 B-Schools in India. A Past National Chairman of the Confederation of Indian Industry's Young Indians (CII-Yi), he is the architect of Yi's Farmers Net program and has served on the CII Agriculture, Innovation, International Policy and India@75 National Councils. He has been the Chairman for the Yi's Next Practices platform and has also chaired Yi's International Relations and Partnerships and is the Founder of the Commonwealth Alliance of Young Entrepreneurs- Asia (CAYE-Asia). He is the recipient of the Bharat Ratna Rajiv Gandhi Yuva Shakti Award 2010 in recognition of outstanding achievements towards Youth Empowerment and Inclusive Growth.

 **Theatre Of The Self**

Syngrity conducted a Theatre of the Self workshop with participants of the ICCBT in Srinagar on May 21st 2022. Theatre of the Self is an interactive and inclusive play shop that uses the art of IMPROV THEATRE to offer engaging insights about the self. Improvisation, Impro or Improv, is a form of live theatre in which the plot, characters and dialogue of a game, scene or story are made up in the moment. The workshop sets up a safe and fun environment for a person to undergo experiential self-directed learning through a creative release.

Through the interactive exercises and activities of the workshop, participants experienced learning and reflection around unconscious bias, leadership, agility, collaboration and the need for gender equality on an intellectual, physical and emotional level. The workshop allowed participants to share anecdotes connecting these concepts with their personal lives and they spoke about the need for an ecosystem of allyship that they can rely on and draw support from in today's fast-changing world. The workshop constituted a space for their self-discovery and personal growth.

FACILITATED BY: Vikram Badhwar and Blessin Varkey

Innovation & Entrepreneurship Foundation

ThinkPod innovation and entrepreneurship foundation in an attempt to foster and accelerate innovative learning focuses to engage, educate, and empower youth in Jammu and Kashmir.

Created to incubate and nurture innovation, our aim is to create a diverse, inclusive, and thriving community of students, innovators, entrepreneurs, and change makers that help boost the economy of Jammu and Kashmir. The facility, designed and built as a collaborative Lab space, brings together Incubation Model and an Innovation Lab alongside a premium co-working space at Srinagar. The Lab is equipped with tools, resources, computers, 3D printers, where prototypes can be developed.

The Innovation Lab focuses on generating ideas, experiment, learn, develop and conceptualize different ideas and creativity to help drive greater efficiencies and deliver the best possible outcomes. We believe in embracing new makers and sparking curiosity that can lead to incubating a new culture of innovation.

www.thinkpodcowork.com | thinkpodcowork@gmail.com | 0194-2312038, +91- 9596 400411

GoodMoneyMan is a wealth product distributing firm primarily for a select group of very successful business owners and professionals, who among other things aspire to a work-optional lifestyle. The team has developed and refined a process to put all pieces of the financial puzzle together and they call it the D-3 Investment process. . Led from the front by **Gopi Kishan Agarwal**.

DISCOVERY | DESIGN | DEPLOY

The primary focus is to help clients create wealth by offering customized solutions. They are centered on facilitating financial independence for their clients and steering them towards a work-optional lifestyle. Along the way, ultimately they help them slow life down, restore liberation & order & ensure they are enjoying the fruits of their work ethic and sense of purpose.

WHAT DO WE OFFER?

MUTUAL FUNDS	PORTFOLIO MANAGEMENT SERVICES
HEALTH & TERM INSURANCE	RISK MANAGEMENT
BEHAVIOUR MANAGEMENT	PASSIVE INCOME GENERATION

Mohan Kr Agarwal is an ambitious second-generation entrepreneur. He has been actively involved with GoodMoneyMan as a Director, a family-run personal finance company since 2017. He is a keen learner who is always on the lookout for opportunities to interact with and learn from leaders in diverse fields. He aims to expand the business to different cities to enable people to manage their finances better. He has a deep interest in analyzing and studying the stock market. He also loves to cycle, play golf.
Active involvement with Young Indians (YI) and Junior Chamber international (JCI) comes naturally to him. **He is Pursing PGPFMB from S P Jain Institute of Management and Research (SPJIMR).**

Registered Corporate office: 82 Sarat Bose Road "samarpan" Kolkata 700026
Contact No. +91 8981706365 | Email: Mohan@goodmoneyman.com

www.ingramcontent.com/pod-product-compliance
Lightning Source LLC
Chambersburg PA
CBHW020725180526
45163CB00001B/113